PERFORMANCE APPRAISALS
THAT WORK

Features **150** Samples for Every Situation

Corey Sandler
and Janice Keefe

Adams Media
Avon, Massachusetts

Published by
Adams Media, an F+W Publications Company
57 Littlefield Street, Avon, MA 02322. U.S.A.
www.adamsmedia.com

ISBN: 1-59337-405-4

Printed in the United States of America.

J   I   H   G   F   E   D   C   B   A

Library of Congress Cataloging-in-Publication Data
Sandler, Corey, 1950-
Performance appraisals that work / Corey Sandler and Janice Keefe.
p.   cm.
ISBN 1-59337-405-4
1. Employees--Rating of. 2. Performance standards. I. Keefe, Janice. II. Title.

HF5549.5.R3S262 2005
658.3'125--dc22
2005016012

This publication is designed to provide accurate and authoritative information with regard to the subject matter covered. It is sold with the understanding that the publisher is not engaged in rendering legal, accounting, or other professional advice. If legal advice or other expert assistance is required, the services of a competent professional person should be sought.

—From a *Declaration of Principles* jointly adopted by a Committee of the American Bar Association and a Committee of Publishers and Associations

Many of the designations used by manufacturers and sellers to distinguish their products are claimed as trademarks. Where those designations appear in this book and Adams Media was aware of a trademark claim, the designations have been printed with initial capital letters.

This book is available at quantity discounts for bulk purchases.
For information, please call 1-800-872-5627.

Contents

Dedication

*To our families, who have shown us both
the true measure of a life's work.*

Acknowledgments

A book is a piece of business that also begins with an idea, followed by months of hard work. Though this finished book bears just our two names on the cover, there were dozens of capable and creative people involved in its conceptualization, design, production, and distribution.

We'd like to thank the capable editors and production staff at Adams Media, including Danielle Chiotti, Larry Shea, and Eugenia L. Orlandi, in conjunction with trusted agent Gene Brissie.

And thanks to you, reader, for buying this book. We wish you great success in managing your staff and in your own rise up the corporate, institutional, or government ladder.

Corey Sandler and Janice Keefe

NAILING JELL-O TO THE WALL

WHAT MAKES A GOOD SECRETARY? How do you evaluate the performance of a corporate trainer? What information do you need in order to decide if a bureaucrat is worthy of a promotion?

Alas, what kind of a case do you need to build to begin the dismissal process for an underperforming employee or to deny a raise or promotion?

In most situations, writing a performance appraisal is like nailing Jell-O to the wall. It's more art than science, and you've got to be very careful with your work lest you end up with a sticky mess.

A job where performance can be judged by counting the number of widgets assembled or miles driven may seem to be simple and completely objective. But how well put together were the widgets? Was there an unusually high rate of failure for the devices? Was there an unacceptable level of waste involved? Although the number of miles driven is a finite and easily measurable amount, was the employee a safe and law-abiding driver?

What about jobs that demand creativity or positions that are supervisory in nature? How can they be measured fairly and meaningfully?

In *Performance Appraisals That Work* you'll find a collection of employee evaluations that you can use as building blocks to craft employee appraisals or evaluations in businesses, institutions, organizations, and government agencies.

Unlike many other books, we'll deal with real-world situations where not everything is perfectly satisfactory: workers who **meet or exceed** expectations, those who **need improvement** on job skills, and staffers who deliver **unsatisfactory** performance.

This book includes a wide range of job categories, including secretarial and clerical, sales and marketing, managerial, and professional. The sample evaluations can be adapted for use at businesses big and small, nonprofit organizations, colleges and other educational institutions, government agencies, and military organizations.

You'll learn how to prepare for and set the stage for an employee evaluation. You'll also find tips on how to document performance, how to write the appraisal, and how to present it to the employee. The heart of the book includes paragraphs and sections that give examples of actual language that could be used in an employee evaluation.

The purpose of the evaluations in this book is to help fill in the appraisal section of standard forms or to help complete a free-form written appraisal, if that is the style used at your organization. You are free to pick and choose sections from various job evaluations as appropriate or to mix and match good, bad, and ordinary appraisals within the same job.

The appraisals are presented in a formal, third-person voice for use in written appraisals: "Ms. Goodenough needs to substantially improve her skills in updating computer databases." This is the most professional approach in general, especially when dealing with volatile or sensitive personalities and egos. In writing it looks (and is) a lot less confrontational than: "You have failed to do what you were asked."

When you make an oral presentation of your findings, you'll most likely have to switch to the first person. Do so with care. "In looking at your performance during the past year, it is apparent that you have not taken full advantage of training and education offered here, and it has affected your ability to represent the company properly on sales calls."

Each of the evaluations begins with a job title and a list of the most important skills or types of work associated with that or a similar job. After that we present three types of evaluation:

Meets or Exceeds Expectations. Our hero is Mr. Paragon, a man of excellence. The commendations in his evaluation are often aimed at documenting his eligibility for advancement or an increase in salary.

Needs Improvement. Ms. Goodenough is just good enough for the job. She may be poised to climb the corporate or organizational ladder, or she may be perfectly happy to continue in her current position. Comments in the evaluation are intended to assist her in improving her skills or keeping pace with change in the organization.

Unsatisfactory. Mr. Belowpar's job performance is way beneath expectations. Tread carefully here: remember that you are evaluating performance and not personality, politics, beliefs, or other personal traits. In this sort of evaluation, there are generally two paths to follow: The first is intended to lead to redemption through specific directions and demands for change, and the second prepares the road to dismissal.

Directions for improvement can include requirements for additional training or for alterations in behavior and performance that are already within the abilities of the staffer.

The employee can also be instructed to accomplish specific goals within a specific period of time. The goals must be reasonable and defensible in the case of a challenge in the form of a lawsuit or discrimination claim. When in doubt, consult with your human resources department or an attorney or both; a small amount of preparation could save you and your organization from a huge deal of trouble and expense.

Take the Time to Think

The evaluator is making judgments that can have a profound impact on the lives of others: promotions, raises, transfers, new assignments, or dismissal. Take your time and act with care:

- Because it is the right thing to do;
- Because valued and accomplished employees are looking forward to the opportunity for guidance and the uninterrupted attention of their supervisor; and
- Because there are state and federal laws, collective bargaining agreements, and organizational guidelines that must be followed. Make sure you understand the legal ramifications of the process; seek training and advice from your human resources department or legal counsel if you have any questions about the process.

The most important rule to follow is this: Match the description to the employee, not the other way around. Spend the time to think about the qualities—good, bad, or indifferent—of employees you supervise or are otherwise asked to evaluate.

Consider whether the problems you see are the result of improper behavior, a bad match between an employee's skills and background and the job, or a lack of training.

The sample evaluations in this book can also be used to set the general process that leads to dismissal at most companies or institutions. The evaluations do not include action plans for termination of workers demonstrating unsatisfactory performance, which differ widely from company to company. Evaluators should work with their human resources department to follow policies.

You might also want to consult the *Performance Appraisal Phrase Book*, also by Corey Sandler and Janice Keefe and published by Adams Media, which presents phrases that are organized by qualitative, quantitative, managerial, and professional attributes.

CHAPTER 1

AN EVALUATION
WITH PURPOSE

WE BEGIN WITH THE PREMISE that employee evaluations serve important *purposes*. Set up and performed properly, they are a key element of the way a company, organization, or institution accomplishes its goals.

We are, after all, dealing with *people* and not machines.

We can look at a tool and say that it is effective and worth the money spent on it for purchase, maintenance, and upkeep because it produces a specific number of widgets of a measurable quality in a certain period of time. The tool can be monitored—by a human or by a computer—on a minute-by-minute basis to assure that its performance stays at an expected, acceptable level.

When the point comes that the tool is no longer performing adequately—because of old age, technological obsolescence, or a change in the organization's needs or goals—it can be dispassionately removed from service. There are no laws, union grievance processes, or human rights that attach to a machine. Sell it, scrap it, or push it to the side.

Not so with the people on your staff. There is a significant cost in hiring, training, supervising, and evaluating human beings. But people also have legal protections against discrimination in hiring, their treatment in the workplace, and safeguards against unjustified dismissal. They may be a member of a union or other bargaining unit and have special contract provisions. And they have *feelings*.

As an employer or a supervisor, all of these factors are important. The bottom line is that as an employer or supervisor you simply must treat people fairly and with respect. It is also the right thing to do. It is that responsibility that underlies the various purposes for making an employee evaluation:

Making an appraisal of performance for a satisfactory employee—The appraisal may be scheduled to assess an employee's eligibility for promotion, for an increase in pay grade, or the appropriateness of a transfer to a new department or assignment. As part of this appraisal, it may be determined that the worker needs new training or education or other support to help him or her continue to climb the corporate, institutional, or agency ladder.

Setting the path for an employee seeking upward mobility in the workplace—Workers may welcome clear guidance from a supervisor on how to position themselves for higher-paying and/or more responsible jobs in the organization. The employee evaluation can help them set goals and understand pathways to those goals. It is also important to understand that not all workers have their eye on the ladder; some are perfectly happy with delivering satisfactory or exemplary performance at the job level they currently hold. As a supervisor, you may need to recognize this sort of person; some organizations may be perfectly happy with someone with that sort of attitude, while others may not. In any case, as a supervisor you may know more than the employee does about the future of a particular job classification; it may fall to you to inform the employee that it may be necessary for them to prepare for a change in responsibilities as the organization itself changes.

Performing an assessment of performance for a worker delivering a less-than-adequate level of performance—The goal here is to set reasonable and specific goals and objectives for improvement, evaluate the need for additional training and education, or set the path for demotion or reassignment to a less-demanding job.

Measuring the progress toward goals set in a previous review—The employee may have been asked to seek additional training or education or may have been specifically directed to make changes in behavior or techniques used on the job. The worker may have been directed to accomplish specific goals, for example, an increase in productivity, an improvement in cooperation with other departments or individuals, or better service to customers or clients. The evaluation should be able to review progress or the lack of progress against specific elements of the previous review.

Initiating a consistent, fair, defensible, and legal process that leads to the dismissal of an employee delivering an unacceptable level of performance—In a properly run organization, this is the action of last resort. It comes after the worker has received one or more unsatisfactory evaluations and has been offered education, training, and other options intended to help him or her get back on track. In most organizations, the dismissal process may require the involvement of the human resources department, in-house or outside legal counsel, and other services. The organization may choose (or be required) to offer outplacement assistance or referrals. Be sure you understand your organization's policies and follow them exactly.

An important note: The process discussed here for using an employee evaluation to dismiss or suspend an underperforming worker, or one who does not adhere to clearly stated and enforced rules of conduct, assumes that the staffer has not broken any laws or been credibly accused of such violation.

If you find yourself involved with an employee accused of discrimination, sexual harassment, theft, abuse of controlled substances, or any other such possible criminal or civil violations, you should immediately contact your organization's human resources and legal departments and follow their guidance.

It is not your job to attempt to rehabilitate someone who has been accused or convicted of violating the law, no matter what your personal opinion of the staffer or the law may be. Seek guidance from the responsible department.

The Enterprise: Private, Public, Educational, Governmental

The authors of this book have, in their own careers, worked for small, privately held companies, several major corporations, a multibillion dollar privately held international company, a law firm, a lobbying organization, state agencies, state authorities, a large business cooperative, a prestigious university, and a privately funded research center, among other jobs.

In this book we may use the terms company, organization, institution, or enterprise in the various evaluations. In doing so we are intending to refer to private companies, corporations, educational institutions, government agencies, and any other type of workplace. Although there are differences in specific processes for employee evaluations, they are more alike than they are different.

In any case, no one book about employee evaluations can claim to offer all of the possible variations among private enterprise; corporations; educational institutions; and local, state, and federal government. Union contracts, collective bargaining agreements, state laws, and company policies also vary considerably.

However, all of these organizations must operate within the boundaries of laws against workplace discrimination, harassment, and employment regulations. Any of the sample employee evaluations in this book can be adapted to fit the particular needs of your organization.

Similarly, we cannot predict all of the possible types of employees and particular situations with which you will have to deal. But the samples in this book are intended to give you a model that can be used for a wide range of human interactions.

Think of this book as a collection of recipes that can be easily modified to meet a wide range of needs. Depending on your situation, you can mix and match, adapt and change, and use bits and pieces of language from the evaluations here as you need.

We should also note that some organizations use a numerical rating system together with a written report and occasionally even use a numerical system as a complete substitute for words and phrases. In theory, this is supposed to help standardize the evaluation process. However, it's still a subjective matter: How do you decide whether a customer service representative's support of the company's mission statement is worth an 87 or an 88 or a 5 or a 6 on a scale of 7?

Even in an enterprise that exclusively uses numerical ratings, the sample appraisals in this book can be used to help you explain your ratings in an oral presentation to the employee or in any written report you may attach to the ratings or later file.

Possible Outcomes for Evaluations

For a successful employee, the evaluation process can and should be a very positive experience. We all like to hear praise about our accomplishments and positive evaluations of our prospects for advancement in responsibilities and pay.

The successful worker may also welcome the opportunity for an uninterrupted face-to-face meeting with a supervisor to be able to make suggestions for greater productivity or new programs. It is also the chance to make clear—and put on the record—interest in advancement and new challenges.

Your goal as a supervisor is to make sure a successful employee clearly understands the organization's appreciation and to listen carefully to the hopes and needs of a valuable staff member.

For a struggling employee, an evaluation can also be an opportunity for positive change. The supervisor can offer a lifeline to success in the form of training, education, and mentoring.

The employee can use the evaluation as a forum to explain past difficulties and to make clear the desire to improve. It is the goal of the supervisor to engage the staffer in a respectful discussion of shortcomings.

Among the possible results of a meeting with a struggling employee are:

- Development of a program to help him or her succeed with measurable goals that can be assessed at a future evaluation;
- Recognition of a problem with the resources offered this particular employee or an entire department and a plan to rectify that situation; or
- Acknowledgment that the employee has been given a job or a responsibility that is not appropriate.

Once again, each of these outcomes can be cast as a constructive and valuable process intended to retain a staff member. At the same time, any goals set should be specific and measurable; it is not helpful to the employee or the organization to merely demand an improvement in performance.

For a failed employee—someone who has not responded to previous evaluations that sought to improve skills and performance—eventually the situation will arrive at a final appraisal.

This is not a happy ending for the worker or for the company, which has invested a considerable amount of time and money in the employee. The end of the road is involuntary reassignment or dismissal; at most organizations, this requires the involvement of the human resources department and sometimes in-house or outside legal counsel.

From the organization's side of the table, regardless of the circumstances, the final appraisal requires a firm, precise, and consistent approach. The employee should still be treated with respect—for moral and compassionate reasons—and as a matter of legal protection for you and the organization.

Some institutions offer outplacement services, counseling, and other assistance to any laid-off employee; others do so on a case-by-case basis. Again, consult with your human resources department to determine the policy.

The Difference Between Goals and Standards

It is very important to draw the distinction between goals and standards. A goal is a target, while a standard is a rule; an employee can be disciplined or dismissed for serious violations of either.

Some goals are quite specific and can be judged objectively—sales targets are either met or not met, for example. Other goals—such as quality of service—are judged more subjectively.

Standards can also be specific—violation of criminal or civil law is not acceptable behavior—or can require subjective judgments: Is an employee properly representing the company?

Goals are targets the organization hopes to attain: a particular amount of sales, a certain level of service, or an expansion or change to the scope of the enterprise. The employee may have a set of personal goals: to receive a promotion or increase in salary, to change career paths, or to improve training and education.

There needs to be agreement between the employee and employer about what are reasonable goals. If the worker does not subscribe to the goal, this is setting the path to an unsatisfactory employee evaluation. If the supervisor or employer does not support the employee's goals, this should be communicated to the staffer: "Your goal is not realistic," or "Your goal is not one that the organization is prepared to endorse."

Standards are the ways the organization goes about meeting its mission statement. They may include ethical values and levels of quality. Nearly every organization must operate within a set of local, state, and federal regulations and laws.

At most organizations, standards are set in the employee handbook or in other publications prepared by the human resources department. The standards often include codes of conduct, a formal declaration of adherence to legalities, and a mission statement that lays out a corporate culture.

There is no excuse for an employee not to read and understand the organization's standards; similarly an enterprise has the responsibility to make every effort to ensure that workers are familiar with all standards and expectations.

Serious Business

As a supervisor, you will find that there are a number of ways that you can set the tone for an employee evaluation:

1. "I don't like this any more than you do, but my boss tells me I've got to do this."
2. "This is going to hurt me a lot more than it will hurt you."
3. "Let's take advantage of this required process to assess how you're doing in your job and look for ways to help you move up the ladder in responsibilities, challenges, and salary."
4. "We've got a problem. You are not meeting our expectations, and I'm afraid that unless certain very specific goals are achieved, we may be forced to let you go. Let's talk about how we can keep that from happening."

Nowhere in those four descriptions will you see the words: "Isn't this a lot of fun?" That's mostly because employee evaluations aren't intended as entertainment. Evaluations (or appraisals, as they are sometimes called) exist for four very important reasons:

- A reasonable search for a fair and objective way to gauge the performance of an employee and deliver appropriate salary increases and promotions;
- A constructive means to identify shortcomings in training or experience and offer assistance;
- An impartial method to set the pathway to dismissal for someone who has proven to be unable to perform at expected levels or who has violated company policies; and
- A documented procedure for employee management that can withstand legal or union contract challenges.

Every Institution Is Different

Just as no two people are the same, you are also not likely to find that any two businesses, institutions, or government entities will have exactly the same formal process for employee evaluation.

The differences may be the result of a particular corporate or agency culture, or they may be due to varying interpretations of federal or state laws or specific components of collective bargaining or union contracts.

When it comes down to it, all relationships between a supervisor and an employee, between staffers and customers or clients, or between coworkers are human affairs. As we all know, when humans interact just about anything can happen—rational or irrational.

The key to employee evaluations is to find a way to regularize the appraisal of on-the-job performance. The first goal is to remove obvious biases including race, sex, religion, ethnicity, political beliefs, and other irrelevant attributes from the equation. The second goal is to objectively judge performance through the use of words and phrases that can be equally applied to all members of the staff.

Some organizations go beyond the use of words and phrases and build in numerical ratings. These allow computer analyses of appraisals to demonstrate compliance with company policies and government mandates. Organizations can appraise the work of various supervisors, once again in the search for fair and objective evaluations.

Be positive in any way you can, but don't undermine your authority—or the company or organization's ability to discipline or dismiss an employee—by saying things that are not true, just for the sake of being kind. The fact is that, just as the cops on television (and in real life) say: "Anything you say can and will be used against you."

The best policy in employee evaluation and most everything else is respectful and careful honesty.

Getting Ready for Meaningful Evaluation

In order to have a successful evaluation, you need to follow certain steps and guidelines such as the following, each of which is explained further later:

- Be prepared.
- Have a plan.

- Be transparent.
- Judge only behavior and accomplishments.
- Be clear and precise.
- Set reasonable goals.
- Establish realistic deadlines.
- Be open to the employee's side of the story.

BE PREPARED

Nothing you say at an employee evaluation should come as a total surprise to the worker receiving the appraisal. If a staffer has had great success, he or she should already know of the organization's appreciation through regular interaction with supervisors and recipients of services; if he or she has been struggling, the supervisor or department head should have been involved at the earliest signs of trouble. If the employee had previously been given a less-than-favorable evaluation, that appraisal should have been very specific in outlining future expectations.

You should take the time to be completely up to date on current assignments and accomplishments of the employee. If the staffer does not work directly for you, review the situation with his or her immediate supervisor.

If there are any specific complaints from supervisors, coworkers, clients, or customers, you should read them and conduct any necessary investigation to obtain full details; if any of the complaints appear to cross over to illegal behavior or to serious violations of the organization's policies, you should immediately involve the human resources or legal department.

If the complaints do not rise to that level, you should be prepared to carefully and respectfully discuss them with the staffer; use your judgment (and consult with human resources if needed) to decide how specific you should be in outlining the details of any particular complaint.

If your organization's policy calls for the employee to fill out a self-evaluation form before the formal appraisal is conducted, schedule a brief meeting to clearly explain the process and answer any procedural questions.

Underlying the entire performance appraisal process is the creation and maintenance of a set of standards: a job description, a mission statement, and a methodology for review. As a supervisor, you need to know all of these components well, and you have the reasonable right to expect that the employee you are evaluating has read and understands them well.

An important note: In most organizations, the job description is prepared and kept up to date by the human resources department in conjunction with a department head or supervisor.

It is not fair—and it also puts you in a weak legal position—to make critical comments on job performance about an employee who has not been given a clear and specific job description. Similarly, a judgment of inadequate performance on tasks that are not in the job description is generally not supportable.

Changes can and should be made to a job description as conditions and responsibilities evolve, but the human resources department and supervisors must discuss the new description with the employee and offer any appropriate assistance in meeting the new requirements.

HAVE A PLAN

Before you conduct the formal evaluation session, you should have reached some tentative conclusions about the employee's performance in the period being evaluated. Is this a tale of success, a problem to be addressed, a time to assess a specific set of previously enunciated goals, or a story heading for an unhappy ending?

Prepare your written evaluation as well as your talking points. It is your job to call the meeting and control its flow; although it is important to listen to anything and everything the employee has to say—within the bounds of propriety and legalities—you have to stick to the plan.

The employee should be given a reasonable amount of time to hear your evaluation and respond. A staffer who feels he or she has not been heard or has not been given sufficient time is not likely to be satisfied with the process.

Be sure you fully understand your organization's policies for evaluations. You may be able to take a training course or ask a member of the human resources team to sit in on an evaluation where you anticipate the possibility of a problem. Be prepared to firmly but politely steer the conversation away from confrontation and inappropriate areas or to end the session if it gets out of control.

BE TRANSPARENT

Employees should know in advance all of the details of the process, and if they are not asked to perform a self-assessment, they should see in advance the blank form you will use.

14

Workers should be given a week or more of advance notification, and the scheduling of the evaluation itself should take into account any pressing deadlines or assignments.

JUDGE ONLY BEHAVIOR AND ACCOMPLISHMENTS

Steer clear of anything outside of the job requirements. In this day and age it should be obvious that a person's race, sex, sexual orientation, religion, politics, and personal beliefs are areas that are generally off-limits when it comes to evaluating a person's job performance. (There are certain circumstances where some of these personal attributes, as well as health status or disability, may be taken into account in hiring; consult your in-house or outside counsel well before you approach these areas in an evaluation.)

An employee evaluation is not a matter of whether you like a person or object (or approve) of someone's personal attributes. Your task is to fairly and consistently judge whether the employee has done what has been asked of him or her and has met reasonable goals.

BE CLEAR AND PRECISE

Ambiguity is your enemy. An evaluation that says "Ms. Jones has not been doing such a great job lately" does not help the employee improve and does not establish a path toward dismissal or reassignment if that is eventually deemed necessary.

In the written evaluation and its oral presentation, you need to be as precise as possible: "You have fallen below sales goals for three consecutive quarters," or "You were directed to oversee the establishment of a computer-tagged inventory process to be effective on or before January 1, and this was not accomplished."

SET REASONABLE GOALS

Be fair. Your goal is to help the employee become successful or improve his or her level of productivity. Demanding an unreasonable accomplishment, not offering appropriate training or assistance, or setting an unreachable goal is a recipe for failure.

Companies want their employees to succeed; there is no good reason to hire someone, make the investment of time and money, and then go through the detailed process of employee evaluation without making an attempt to help workers make a productive contribution.

ESTABLISH REALISTIC DEADLINES

Fairness includes granting sufficient time to complete assignments. Once again, setting a goal that cannot be met is not going to lead to a positive result—and could put your organization at risk of a lawsuit for job discrimination or violation of other employment regulations.

BE OPEN TO THE EMPLOYEE'S SIDE OF THE STORY

You just might be wrong, or there might be an acceptable reason why an employee has not met expectations. Your employee might have some constructive ideas to improve his or her own job or general operations.

Does the employee make a credible case that he or she has not received sufficient training or support? Is there a conflict with another employee or department? Is it possible that company or organizational procedures make it difficult or impossible to accomplish goals, or does the employee have good suggestions to improve operations?

There is also the possibility that an employee's personal situation has interfered with productivity or otherwise affected behavior. It is generally not proper to inquire about personal life or health; if an employee offers information that is relevant to his or her job situation, it is appropriate to listen. Consult your human resources department or legal counsel to be sure you do not put yourself in the position of violating confidentiality or employee discrimination laws.

The Evaluation Process

As we have noted, there are probably as many different particular processes for an employee evaluation as there are variations in types of companies, organizations, and institutions.

One thing that is generally common is the use of a standardized evaluation form. The reasons for the use of a form are many, including:

- Assuring a consistent format and scoring method when evaluations are conducted by more than one person, and to allow for continuity across time;
- Helping to assure compliance with state and federal employment regulations and laws through the involvement of an employment attorney or human resources specialist in its drafting;
- Connecting the evaluation to the organization's mission statement;

- Creating and maintaining a record of praise, critiques, and direction given employees as part of the promotion and salary review process; and
- Maintaining a legally defensible paper (or electronic file) trail to support any disciplinary or dismissal process.

Most institutions perform evaluations on an annual basis, although some may go through the process more frequently. If an employee receives a less-than-satisfactory appraisal, another evaluation may be scheduled for as quickly as 30, 60, or 90 days.

It is not inappropriate to preface a request for an evaluation meeting by saying something positive such as: "Mary, you've had a good year, and I will say so in my evaluation. Let's also look for ways for you to expand your job responsibilities in the year to come," or "John, I know it's been a rough year for you, but I think we can find some good avenues to improvement for the future."

Those sorts of comments can serve to reduce the tension many employees may feel. However, if you are expecting to deliver a negative appraisal including the possibility of beginning a process that may lead to dismissal, be careful not to say something that may be held against you later. For example, let's say you tell an underperforming staffer, "Harry, you've been a great salesman this year; let's schedule your evaluation session for tomorrow at 9 A.M." But when you are behind closed doors, if you later try to build a case that Harry has been a failure as a salesman you may find your words thrown back at you—in an argument or perhaps in a lawsuit.

In any case, it is important that you as the evaluator maintain control of the process. You should set the schedule, control the amount of time involved, and firmly but politely keep the discussion within the bounds set by your company or institution's policies.

Here are some typical schedules and procedures for the conduct of employee evaluations:

SUPERVISOR REVIEW

The evaluator fills out a detailed appraisal of the employee's performance since the last completed report, noting accomplishments, improvements to skills, and specific shortcomings on tasks, training, and adherence to company policies.

At the evaluation meeting, the supervisor reviews the form with the employee and invites comments and responses; the employee can file a written response or merely sign off on the report prepared by the supervisor.

SELF-ASSESSMENT PLUS SUPERVISOR REVIEW

The employee is asked to fill out a self-assessment of his or her performance during the period since the most recent appraisal and provide a copy to the evaluator.

The employee is usually asked to compare accomplishment and performance to the job description for their position. He or she may be asked to make suggestions for training or other assistance to allow them to seek additional responsibilities or promotion.

Most workers have a pretty good sense of whether they are succeeding or falling behind expectations—if they don't, their supervisor has not been doing a good job of communicating with them.

At the same time, the evaluator fills out a full Supervisor Review.

When the evaluation is conducted, the employee and the supervisor review both forms together. The supervisor's evaluation represents the organization's official document, although it may be amended on the basis of the self-assessment or the discussion that follows.

In some organizations, the employee's self-assessment is automatically filed along with the supervisor's report; at other institutions, it is attached only at the request of the employee.

In the best of situations, this format can be a very productive method for evaluation since it asks the employee to consider his or her own accomplishments and then facilitates a cooperative discussion between the supervisor and employee.

In a situation where there are significant differences between the supervisor and the employee or if the worker is uncooperative, this format may be less than ideal: The give-and-take may generate much more heat than light.

JOINT ASSESSMENT

In this method, the evaluator and the employee fill out the form together.

Although this format does allow for a great deal of give and take between the evaluator and the employee, the process can become strained if there are significant differences. The evaluator has to maintain control of the process and must be willing and able to enter a comment that is at variance from the employee's opinion.

The staffer is generally given the right to enter a dissent to a finding or to file a full response to the evaluation.

A Multiple-Step Process

Whatever the method used to develop the evaluation document, the purpose remains to further the company's objectives and the employee's goals.

At some companies, the evaluator may give the employee a written copy of the preliminary assessment; other institutions may keep the initial session to an informal oral discussion.

In most situations, institutions will plan about a week's gap between the initial session and the follow-up meeting.

CREATING A DIALOGUE

In the best situation, the meeting will be a dialogue and not a one-sided presentation. In the worst case, the initial meeting or subsequent sessions could devolve into an argument.

As an evaluator, you should already have a good sense of the personality and the working history of the employee with whom you will be meeting. If you anticipate sullen silence or an unresponsive session, you can prepare yourself to deliver a soliloquy. If past experience, notes in the personnel file, or events in the workplace lead you to expect a confrontation, you can prepare yourself for that; some companies might offer to have a representative of the human resources department accompany you to any evaluation where problems may be expected.

In evaluating a seasoned employee, the basic question is: Have the objectives set last year been met?

As a supervisor, you should also ask yourself: "What should I be doing to help this employee succeed? Have I been specific in my direction and clear in my offers of assistance?"

FOLLOW-UP MEETINGS

The goal of the second meeting is to bring together the evaluator's comments and the employee's self-assessment and add to it goals and objectives for the coming year. Once again, the best situation calls for a discussion with contributions from both sides, but some employees will choose to sit quietly or object.

Ask the employee if he or she understands the comments you have made, and seek input on opportunities for advancement or solutions to problems. Answer any questions you can, staying within your area of expertise and responsibility; if you are asked about human resources or legal issues, refer the employee to the appropriate department.

At the next session, the evaluator presents a written report on the employee. The appraisal may follow a formal structure and include numerical ratings or may be a written report intended as a memo to be included in the employee's personnel file.

The report generally includes positive comments (where appropriate) that would support a raise in pay or promotion. Most evaluations also point out areas where an employee could improve skills and training or could seek advancement. Many evaluations also include significant and specific comments on areas where improvement is needed, where performance has fallen short of expectations, or where specific company policies have been violated or ignored.

Where there are less-than-satisfactory ratings, the appraiser should offer specific goals for improvement or direct the employee to seek specific training.

Depending on the company, institution, or agency, the human resources department and the legal department may require the evaluator to use specific language and set reasonable but firm deadlines for accomplishment of remedial training or improvements in performance.

Make certain you understand your company or organization's procedures. Seek training from the human resources or legal department if you have any questions about equal opportunity employment and other job-related issues.

Objectives you set should be realistic and impartial and should fit within the job description. Goals should be measurable. Telling a salesperson that sales should improve is not easily assessed; directing that sales increase by at least 10 percent gives a specific yardstick. Anything that steps beyond realistic and impartial bounds may open your company or organization to legal challenges.

The final step in the process of evaluation generally requires the employee to sign a copy of the written appraisal, including its recommendations and deadlines.

In most cases, the employee is merely acknowledging receipt of the evaluation and not necessarily that he or she agreed with its contents. Some institutions allow the employee to add written comments—including objections to some or all of the elements of the appraisal—as a separate memo that is also placed in the personnel file.

An important note: Not all underperforming employees can be rehabilitated, and it is important to follow a fair and consistent path—with legally defensible written records—to prepare for the dismissal or involuntary reassignment of a worker.

Because there are so many different policies, we will not attempt in this book to advise the specifics of a dismissal policy for your institution; consult the human resources department or in-house counsel for assistance. In general, the human resources department will use the paperwork of an employee evaluation and other information in a separate dismissal process if such action is warranted.

Salary and Promotion Review

Except at the smallest of organizations, it generally makes sense to completely separate the evaluation session from any salary review or promotion meeting. Despite the fact that the two are, in the end, inextricably linked at most organizations, the two are kept separate. Some organizations have different people or different departments handle the salary and promotion side of the process; at others, there is a mandated waiting period between the evaluation and any discussion of promotion or increases in salary.

Among the reasons are:

- Doing so allows the evaluator to listen to the responses of the employee and take them into account in the final report;
- Keeping the performance evaluation and a salary review separate can help reduce conflict when there are significant differences of opinion about the quality of work; and
- A two-part process keeps the evaluation session focused sharply on performance, which is the organization's primary interest.

In the chapters that follow, you will find more than 150 examples of written evaluations for employees in more than 50 different job types. In combination with the procedures described in this first chapter, you can adapt the language and ideas you'll find in them to create fair and precise evaluations for your own employees.

But first, here are three generic appraisals that will show you the structure we use for the appraisals in each job category. You may be able to use these evaluations—one positive, one calling for improvement, and one negative—as the base for all of your work, adding other elements from the specific jobs described in the rest of the book.

Generic Employee Appraisals

MEETS OR EXCEEDS

Mr. Paragon has met and exceeded all expectations set forth in his job description and subsequent assignments by his supervisor and other senior staff members.

He has consistently demonstrated a willing, "can-do" attitude. When asked to perform a new task, he researches the organization's available resources, works closely with human resources and training departments, and keeps his supervisors current on progress. He has never failed to meet a deadline and time after time has delivered work of superior quality.

Mr. Paragon has shown great dedication to the company's mission statement:

- A commitment to the highest levels of customer service, delivered with professionalism, pride, and company spirit;
- Allegiance to the enterprise's promise to provide employees with a caring and stable working environment with equal opportunity for personal growth and advancement;
- Respect for the dignity, individual, and shared needs of the staff;
- A devotion to tolerance of personal beliefs and backgrounds while maintaining the company's firm commitment to an environment that does not discriminate in any way on racial, religious, sexual, or political issues.

Reports from customers and clients uniformly depict Mr. Paragon as an exemplary representative of the company. He demonstrates a deep understanding of products and services and works very closely with sales and marketing departments to communicate possible business opportunities.

Mr. Paragon has consistently stayed within his departmental budget, seeking guidance and additional sources of funding from supervisors and other departments whenever an assignment goes beyond ordinary operations.

One of Mr. Paragon's strengths is his ability to communicate in written and verbal form; he has been called upon to author several company policy statements and has also been of service in editing the work of others.

In addition, he has proven to be a highly valued and respected member of committees that reach across the enterprise. He works well in group situations as well as in individual assignments.

Mr. Paragon has demonstrated exceptional leadership skills in supervising his own staff, including serving as a mentor to new employees and assisting others in their own career goals. He has regularly shown willingness to share his experiences and knowledge with others in his department and throughout the enterprise.

On a number of occasions, Mr. Paragon has taken the lead in responding to and managing emergency situations. When possible, he has closely followed the organization's predefined guidelines and protocols; he has also shown exceptional and appropriate innovation in dealing with unplanned-for exigencies.

At the time of his first employee appraisal, it was observed that Mr. Paragon had difficulty in managing conflicting demands on his time; it was noted that this may have been due to his great willingness to attempt to respond to all requests without setting priorities. He was asked to meet with the training department to seek assistance in this matter, and he did so almost immediately.

He has since shown great improvements in handling multiple critical assignments, prioritizing when necessary and seeking assistance to complete equally important urgent projects.

Mr. Paragon has maintained a perfect attendance record and on more than one occasion has been willing to alter personal plans when an urgent project arises. He has established a well-designed structure to cover for his absence when he is out of the office attending training and other needs and during scheduled vacation periods.

He has taken advantage of every opportunity to improve his skills and training in performing his core assignment and has shown great interest and ability in preparing himself for future advancement in the company. With this evaluation, it is recommended that human resources schedule an assessment of advanced career opportunities within the organization for Mr. Paragon and offer advice on necessary training and accreditation.

By copy of this evaluation, the director of human resources is asked to report to the executive committee within 90 days on a plan to create a fast-track advancement schedule for Mr. Paragon.

NEEDS IMPROVEMENT

Ms. Goodenough has not yet fully met the expectations set forth in her job description and subsequent assignments by her supervisor and other senior staff members.

Although she has accepted and generally adequately performed new assignments and tasks, she has not always demonstrated a gracious attitude in doing so. She is asked to devote the time to fully research the organization's available resources, working closely with human resources and training departments and keeping her supervisors current on progress.

In some instances, she has been unable to meet deadlines or to deliver work of acceptable quality.

Ms. Goodenough is directed to meet with the human resources department to review the company's mission statement, especially in regard to our commitment to the highest levels of customer service, delivered with professionalism, pride, and company spirit.

Supervisors have received mixed reviews from customers and clients about Ms. Goodenough's demeanor and abilities as a representative of the company. She needs to greatly expand her understanding of products and services and work very closely with sales and marketing departments to communicate possible business opportunities.

On several occasions Ms. Goodenough has spent considerably more than her departmental budget without authorization; she is directed to seek guidance on obtaining additional sources of funding from supervisors and other departments whenever an assignment goes beyond ordinary operations.

Ms. Goodenough's written and verbal communication skills are generally adequate but sometimes below expectations. Some of her supervised staff has observed that some instructions and assignments are ambiguous or difficult to interpret. With this evaluation, she is asked to meet with the training department to seek courses and personal mentoring on communications skills. She is authorized to attend courses or seek assistance from consultants, as approved by the training department.

As a member of various task forces and committees that reach across the enterprise, she has not demonstrated leadership or significant contributions. She is asked to seek guidance and training in this matter and will be re-evaluated on communications skills within 90 days.

Ms. Goodenough has not demonstrated adequate leadership skills in supervising her own staff. She should be willing and able to serve as a mentor to new employees and assist others in their own career goals. Department heads should also share experiences and knowledge with others in their departments and throughout the enterprise.

Key to the accomplishment of her job is the ability to respond to and manage emergency situations and unexpected and sometimes conflicting crises. In the past 12 months, Ms. Goodenough has not shown the ability to independently follow the organization's predefined guidelines and protocols for emergencies or unexpected problems.

At the time of her first employee appraisal, it was observed that Ms. Goodenough seemed to have difficulty in managing conflicting demands on her time; it was noted that this may have been due to an attempt to respond to all requests without setting priorities. She was asked to meet with the training department to seek assistance in this matter.

As of this date, there is no evidence that Ms. Goodenough has sought to deal with this apparent problem, and she continues to experience problems in handling multiple critical assignments. She lacks the skills to prioritize when necessary and to seek assistance to complete equally important and urgent projects.

Although she has maintained an adequate attendance record, within company guidelines for allowable absences and vacations, on several occasions she has been unavailable to assist in emergency situations because of personal plans. She has also failed to establish a well-designed structure to cover for her absence when she is out of the office attending training and other needs and during scheduled vacation periods.

Although the organization believes she has the ability to improve her skills and training in performing her core assignment and to prepare herself for future advancement, she has not taken advantage of available training.

With this evaluation, it is recommended that human resources schedule an assessment of advanced career opportunities within the organization for Ms. Goodenough and offer advice on necessary training and accreditation.

UNSATISFACTORY

Mr. Belowpar has failed to meet the expectations set forth in his job description and subsequent assignments by his supervisor and other senior staff members. Despite repeated direction to improve the quality of his work and to seek training, he has not done so within the specified time period.

He has on occasion objected to additional responsibilities and tasks, and when he has accepted new assignments, he has from time to time made inappropriate verbal and written comments about his workload and supervisors. He has regularly missed deadlines or delivered work of unacceptable quality.

Mr. Belowpar is directed to make it his highest priority over the next two weeks to fully review the company's mission statement, especially in regard to our commitment to the highest levels of customer service, delivered with professionalism, pride, and company spirit. He is further asked to meet with the department of human resources to learn about the organization's available resources. He will be reappraised on these matters within 21 days.

Customer comments and clients have been almost uniformly negative when they have rated Mr. Belowpar's demeanor and abilities as a representative of the company. He is directed to greatly expand his understanding of products and services and work very closely with sales and marketing departments to communicate possible business opportunities. With this appraisal, he is notified that he will be reviewed on progress in these areas within 30 days.

Mr. Belowpar has overspent his departmental budget without authorization for each of the past four quarters; he is instructed to seek guidance on monitoring budget lines and obtaining additional sources of funding from supervisors and other departments whenever an assignment goes beyond ordinary operations. The accounting office and training departments will be notified and asked to be available to Mr. Belowpar; he will be re-evaluated on this matter in 45 days.

Mr. Belowpar's written and verbal communication skills are inadequate for the job. Instructions to staff have been ambiguous or difficult to interpret, according to interviews with employees under his supervision. With this evaluation, he is directed to meet with the training department to seek courses and personal mentoring on communications skills. He is authorized to attend courses or seek assistance from consultants, as approved by the training department. It is expected that Mr. Belowpar will be able to demonstrate significant improvement in this area between now and his next scheduled appraisal.

As a member of various task forces and committees that reach across the enterprise, Mr. Belowpar has not represented his department well, offering little in the way of leadership or input. He is asked to seek guidance and training in this matter and will be re-evaluated on this matter within 90 days.

Based on employee surveys and exit interviews, Mr. Belowpar has not demonstrated an acceptable level of leadership in supervising his own staff. He has been unwilling or unable to serve as a mentor to new employees and shown no capacity to assist others in their own career goals. He is directed to meet with the training department within 10 days to set up a schedule of courses and consultations on this matter and will be re-evaluated on supervisory skills at the time of his next scheduled appraisal.

Mr. Belowpar has not been of significant assistance to the company in responding to and managing emergency situations and unexpected and sometimes conflicting crises. He has not shown himself to be able to follow established written guidelines and protocols for emergencies or unexpected problems and has not sought assistance when appropriate.

In his most recent appraisal prior to this one, his supervisor observed that Mr. Belowpar demonstrated significant difficulty in managing conflicting demands on his time. Mr. Belowpar acknowledged at the time that this was the case. He told the evaluator that this was due to difficulty in setting priorities.

He was directed to meet with the training department to seek assistance in this matter. This has not occurred, and the problem continues. He is assigned to make this a high priority for training; he is asked to report to the executive committee within 30 days on progress in this area and will be formally re-evaluated on this matter in 90 days.

Mr. Belowpar has exceeded company guidelines for allowable absences, and on several occasions, he has been unavailable to assist in emergency situations because of personal plans and vacations inappropriately scheduled for times when demand for his services could be anticipated to be at a high level.

He has also failed to establish acceptable coverage for his absence when he is out of the office attending training and other needs and during scheduled vacation periods. He is directed to produce such a plan and have it approved by his supervisor within 30 days.

Although the organization believes he has the ability to improve his skills and training in performing his core assignment and to prepare himself for future advancement, he has not taken advantage of available training.

If the various goals and directives outlined in this appraisal are not accomplished on the dates specified, it is the recommendation of this evaluator that the human resources department consider initiating a dismissal process for Mr. Belowpar.

CHAPTER 2

FINANCIAL AND ACCOUNTING

Accountant

Payroll Specialist

Tax Specialist

Internal Auditor

Risk Analyst

Accountant

Accounting principles
Accounting reports
Attention to detail
Budgets
Electronic payment vouchers
Federal regulations
GAAP (Generally Accepted Accounting Principles)
MIS department
Purchasing department
State regulations
Supervision of staff
Training and certification
Unanticipated expenses

MEETS OR EXCEEDS

Mr. Paragon demonstrates a superior knowledge of accounting principles and attention to detail in the processing of reports and reconciliation of departmental transactions.

He works very well with junior staff, supervising their work and assuring they receive necessary advanced training and certification.

Under his direction, the department smoothly transitioned from a manual check writing and banking process to acceptance and processing of electronic payment vouchers, integrating the accompanying information into standard accounting records and producing reports that can be read on a real-time basis by appropriate supervisors and executive management.

Mr. Paragon has demonstrated consistency and accuracy in the creation of all standard and special-purpose accounting reports as directed or requested for particular needs.

As directed in his job description, Mr. Paragon meets regularly with representatives of other departments to review the status of their accounts and to respond to any inquiries about entries. On his own initiative, he has arranged for advanced training courses and company-approved software to allow other staffers to better understand accounting procedures.

Mr. Paragon has demonstrated exemplary performance in setting up protocols to assure compliance with generally accepted accounting principles as well as state and federal regulations and laws.

He has worked closely with the purchasing department to assure that accounting records can be readily used to track compliance with company guidelines on purchasing and other expenditures. Mr. Paragon has also assured that appropriate internal controls are in place and maintained to assure that the company follows all applicable laws and regulations and that its records meet the requirements of outside independent auditors.

Mr. Paragon has demonstrated an excellent commitment to crafting the format and content of reports to allow senior management and department heads to quickly compare financial performance and records to the company's business plans, budgets, and long-term objectives. Working with the MIS department, he initiated a system to automatically flag any unanticipated expenses, underperforming income streams, and other anomalies.

NEEDS IMPROVEMENT

Ms. Goodenough needs to improve her understanding of accounting principles and must pay more attention to the details involved in the processing of reports and reconciliation of departmental transactions.

Members of the junior staff have reported difficulty in obtaining guidance and access to advanced training and certification necessary to complete their work; Ms. Goodenough is directed, as part of this evaluation, to work to improve relations with supervised staff and to take advantage of available management courses offered by the company's training department.

The transition to widespread acceptance and processing of electronic payment vouchers and the integrating of the accompanying information into standard accounting records has lagged behind the expectations of the executive committee; Ms. Goodenough is directed to make this process a high priority in the next 60 days.

Ms. Goodenough has proved to be inconsistent and sometimes inflexible in her ability to create special-purpose accounting reports as directed or requested for particular needs. She has not demonstrated an acceptable level of commitment to crafting the format and content of reports to allow senior management and department heads to quickly compare financial performance and records to the company's business plans, budgets, and long-term objectives.

She needs to meet regularly with representatives of other departments to review the status of their accounts and to respond to any inquiries about entries. Her present office policy calls for written requests for all reviews, and this has resulted in unacceptable backlogs.

Ms. Goodenough needs to open a dialogue with the purchasing department to assure that accounting records can be readily used to track compliance with company guidelines on purchasing and other expenditures.

UNSATISFACTORY

Mr. Belowpar has failed to demonstrate an acceptable level of understanding of accounting principles; as part of this evaluation, he is directed to seek available training and certification.

Mr. Belowpar has failed to create a trustworthy system of protocols to assure compliance with generally accepted accounting principles as well as state and federal regulations and laws. He has also not shown that appropriate internal controls are in place and maintained to assure that the company follows all applicable laws and regulations and that its records meet the requirements of outside independent auditors.

He must devote himself to paying more attention to the details involved in the processing of reports and reconciliation of departmental transactions.

It is apparent from evaluations conducted with members of the junior staff that Mr. Belowpar has not been an effective and proactive manager. There has been an unusually high level of turnover in the accounting department, and the human resources department has asked Mr. Belowpar to take advantage of available management courses offered by the company's training department. He is directed to do so as part of this evaluation.

Mr. Belowpar has been unable to deliver special-purpose accounting reports as requested for particular needs. He has not demonstrated an acceptable level of commitment to crafting the format and content of reports to allow senior management and department heads to quickly compare financial performance and records to the company's business plans, budgets, and long-term objectives.

Another area of underperformance lies in the request of the purchasing department for the creation of a system to assure that accounting records can be readily used to track compliance with company guidelines on purchasing and other expenditures. Mr. Belowpar has not responded to three memos requesting he meet with the purchasing department head for this purpose; with this evaluation, he is directed to hold such a meeting within 15 days and produce a reasonable timeline for accomplishment of this mission critical assignment within 30 days.

Payroll Specialist

Accounting
Check printing
Confidentiality of employee records
Cost centers
Credit unions
Debit cards
Employee stock ownership programs
FICA contributions
Health insurance
Payroll specialist
Pension plans
State and federal employment laws
Tax withholding
Temporary workers
Time cards
Union dues
United Way
Work schedules

MEETS OR EXCEEDS

Ms. Paragon has ably managed the payroll functions of the accounting department. She has made significant improvements in the accuracy and timeliness of payroll checks and has worked closely with human resources and other departments to add other valuable services.

Working in conjunction with the MIS department and the staff of the accounting department, Ms. Paragon led the way in bringing payroll functions back in-house. This is expected to save the company more than $50,000 per year, amortizing the cost of new software and check printing equipment over an 18-month period.

Ms. Paragon has demonstrated excellent attention to detail in analyzing work schedules and time cards for hourly workers, assuring that staff and departments follow company policies as set out in the employee handbook. She also meets regularly with the human resources and legal departments to review compliance with state and federal employment laws.

Ms. Paragon has demonstrated superior attention to detail in the verification of time cards and assignment of hours to cost centers. She has also shown excellent skills in managing deductions for health insurance, pension plans, employee stock ownership programs, and other voluntary programs including credit union payments, United Way contributions, and union dues.

During periods when the manufacturing and shipping departments add temporary part-time workers, Ms. Paragon has demonstrated exceptional ability in managing relations with temporary employment agencies.

Ms. Paragon has expanded services offered through the payroll department to include availability of employee debit cards for use in the company cafeteria and options for deductions from payroll checks for in-house child care services.

Ms. Paragon works closely with the software consultant that installed the payroll program, serving as liaison with the company's in-house tax specialist to assure proper withholding of tax from paychecks, deposit of employee and company tax payments, and processing of employee and company FICA contributions. Working with a task force of representatives of every major department, Ms. Paragon successfully implemented monthly distribution of customized database records about employment and payroll trends.

Her successful overhaul of the recordkeeping system of the payroll department has resulted in immediate access to information requests from federal, state, and local agencies as necessary. At the same time, Ms. Paragon has demonstrated an excellent understanding of the privacy rights of employees and has maintained the confidentiality of worker records.

NEEDS IMPROVEMENT

Ms. Goodenough has shown some areas of inadequate management in overseeing the payroll functions of the accounting department. She has not adequately dealt with recurring problems with the accuracy of payroll and timely delivery of checks to out-of-town employees.

In January of this past year, the accounting department moved payroll functions back in-house, ending outsourcing to a private data processing company. Although this has saved the company the cost of the outside service, problems in performing the work under Ms. Goodenough's supervision have resulted in significant unanticipated expenses. With this evaluation, Ms. Goodenough is directed to meet with the MIS director and the software consultant who provided the payroll program; she is directed to produce a plan within 15 days to address the problems.

Ms. Goodenough needs to greatly improve her attention to detail in analyzing work schedules and time cards for hourly workers, assuring that staff and departments follow company policies as set out in the employee handbook. The human resources department has noted more than a dozen instances where workers exceeded allowable hours. She must also meet regularly with the human resources and legal departments to review compliance with state and federal employment laws.

In a related matter, Ms. Goodenough has not adequately verified time cards and assignment of hours to cost centers. This has resulted in significant errors in applying the cost of wages to appropriate departmental budgets.

Another area of concern involves accounting for payment to temporary employment agencies for manufacturing and shipping staff brought in for seasonal or other special needs. The company auditor reports incomplete or inaccurate time records for temporary workers over the past nine months. Ms. Goodenough is directed to meet with the auditor and the human resources director within 30 days to establish new procedures to track such workers.

Ms. Goodenough needs to improve the management of deductions for health insurance, pension plans, employee stock ownership programs, and other voluntary programs including credit union payments, United Way contributions, and union dues.

At her previous evaluation, Ms. Goodenough was asked to expand services offered through the payroll department to include availability of employee debit cards for use in the company cafeteria and options for deductions from payroll checks for in-house child care services. This has not been accomplished, and with this evaluation, she is directed to make this a high priority for implementation within 60 days.

The report of a task force of representatives of every major department asking for monthly distribution of customized database records about employment and payroll trends was delivered to Ms. Goodenough nearly a year ago; with this evaluation, she is directed to begin production of these reports within 30 days.

An outside auditor from a federal agency reported to the executive committee several violations of confidentiality requirements for personnel records. The executive committee has not heard back from Ms. Goodenough as to whether this potentially serious problem has been rectified; she is directed to respond to the committee within 10 days to apprise them of proper safeguards for the privacy of employee records.

UNSATISFACTORY

Mr. Belowpar has failed to adequately manage the payroll functions of the accounting department. Among particular areas of concern are recurring problems with the accuracy of payroll and timely delivery of checks to out-of-town employees.

In January of this past year, the accounting department moved payroll functions back in-house, ending outsourcing to a private data processing company. Because of serious errors committed under Mr. Belowpar's management, the company has incurred significant unanticipated expenses that have more than equaled the cost savings expected.

Mr. Belowpar is directed to meet with the MIS director and the software consultant who provided the payroll program; he is directed to produce a plan within 15 days to address the problems.

The legal department has expressed concerns about inadequate record-keeping in the payroll department. Mr. Belowpar is directed to meet with the human resources and legal departments within 10 days to review compliance with state and federal employment laws and to come up with a plan to rectify problems within 21 days.

Mr. Belowpar has not shown that he understands proper procedures and safeguards for the management of deductions for health insurance, pension plans, employee stock ownership programs, and other voluntary programs including credit union payments, United Way contributions, and union dues.

A task force of representatives of every major department asked for monthly distribution of customized database records about employment and payroll trends six months ago; Mr. Belowpar's efforts in response were unacceptable as to form and substance. With this evaluation, he is directed to meet with the MIS director within 10 days to develop a plan that will result in the production of these reports within 30 days and monthly thereafter.

Tax Specialist

Branch offices
Payroll records
Payroll specialist
Sales and use taxes
Tax codes
Tax compliance
Tax laws and regulations
Tax-exempt entities
Travel and entertainment expenses
W-2 forms
Withholding

MEETS OR EXCEEDS

Mr. Paragon has demonstrated exceptional skills in managing the technical side of tax compliance as well as offering research and counsel to the legal and sales departments and the executive committee.

He has shown a high degree of cooperation with the payroll specialist in assuring that proper tax withholding and recordkeeping is accomplished. The company has operations in thirty-two states and three foreign countries, and Mr. Paragon has shown great proficiency in applying differing tax codes to employees working at headquarters and in branch offices.

Mr. Paragon exhibits a strong attention to detail in verifying computer analyses of payroll and tax payments; he backs up the effort with regular manual inspections of accounts and individual payroll records including spot checks to reconcile W-2s to paychecks and hand calculation of gross and net payments.

He possesses exceptional written and verbal skills and is able to participate as an in-house expert in committee meetings discussing the impact of changes to tax laws and regulations and to advise the legal department and the executive committee on strategies to reduce corporate tax obligations.

Mr. Paragon works closely with the MIS department to assure the proper maintenance of tax records and reports and oversees production of a tax calendar used by the accounting, sales, payroll, and legal departments in preparing reports, returns, and payments.

In conjunction with the company's outside tax lawyer, he serves as the liaison between the enterprise and local, state, and federal tax agencies.

Mr. Paragon has assisted the sales department in automating the application of sales and use taxes in those states where these levies are collected. He has also provided excellent guidance to the sales department in managing dealings with tax-exempt entities, which in various states may include schools, religious institutions, resellers, and certain types of businesses.

With the head of the legal department, Mr. Paragon cochaired an inhouse seminar about current tax codes regarding travel and entertainment expenses, charitable contributions, payroll, and fringe benefit issues.

He has done a superb job of keeping up to date on the changing federal, state, and local tax codes. He regularly attends trade shows and conventions and has received several advanced certifications from professional organizations. He works closely with the training department to create and keep current courses for employees in the payroll and accounting departments and assists the human resources department in updating the employee handbook and policies regarding travel and other activities.

NEEDS IMPROVEMENT

Although Mr. Goodenough has demonstrated adequate skills in managing certain aspects of the technical side of tax compliance, he has not proved capable of offering research and counsel to the legal and sales departments and the executive committee.

He needs to improve his cooperation with the payroll specialist to assure that proper tax withholding and recordkeeping is accomplished. The company has operations in thirty-two states and three foreign countries, and Mr. Goodenough has required outside assistance from consultants in applying differing tax codes to employees working at headquarters and in branch offices. It is the expectation of the accounting department that such consulting contracts will not be continued beyond this fiscal year; with this evaluation, he is directed to seek training and professional certification to enable him to oversee all tax requirements in every jurisdiction in which the company operates.

Mr. Goodenough has not shown sufficient attention to detail in verifying computer analyses of payroll and tax payments; he is asked to conduct monthly manual inspections of accounts and individual payroll records including spot checks to reconcile W-2s to paychecks and hand calculation of gross and net payments.

Mr. Goodenough's skills in written and verbal communication are below expectations for an in-house expert. He has been ineffective at committee meetings in discussions of the impact of changes to tax laws and regulations and advising the legal department and the executive committee on strategies to reduce corporate tax obligations. He is directed to seek assistance from the training department, including available coaching on communication skills.

Mr. Goodenough must improve his cooperation with the MIS department to assure the proper maintenance of tax records and reports. At his previous evaluation, he was asked to oversee production of a tax calendar for use by the accounting, sales, payroll, and legal departments in preparing reports, returns, and payments. As of this date, the project has not been implemented; he is directed to meet with the MIS department within 15 days to set a schedule for introduction of the calendar within 45 days.

The sales department has asked Mr. Goodenough for assistance in automating the application of sales and use taxes in those states where these levies are collected. With this evaluation, he is directed to make this a high priority for accomplishment within 90 days and to report to the head of the sales department on progress every 15 days.

In January, Mr. Goodenough was not an effective participant in an in-house seminar discussing current tax codes regarding travel and entertainment expenses, charitable contributions, payroll, and fringe benefit issues. He is asked to improve his understanding of these matters within 30 days; he will be re-evaluated on this core competency at that time.

He needs to greatly improve his up-to-date knowledge about changing federal, state, and local tax codes. He is advised to attend trade shows and conventions and seek advanced certifications from professional organizations.

Mr. Goodenough should work closely with the training department to create and keep current courses for employees in the payroll and accounting departments and assist the human resources department in updating the employee handbook and policies regarding travel and other activities.

UNSATISFACTORY

Ms. Belowpar has failed to demonstrate an acceptable level of skill in managing the technical side of tax compliance and has not proved capable of offering research and counsel to the legal and sales departments and the executive committee.

The company has been forced to incur significant unanticipated expenses for consultants and the payment of penalties for missed deadlines for certain tax filings.

It is essential that Ms. Belowpar improve her cooperation with the payroll specialist to assure that proper tax withholding and recordkeeping is accomplished. It is the expectation of the accounting department that consulting contracts to assist Ms. Belowpar in dealing with out-of-state and foreign tax issues will not be continued beyond this fiscal year; with this evaluation, she is directed to seek training and professional certification to enable her to oversee all tax requirements in every jurisdiction in which the company operates. She is directed to report to the head of the accounting department within 30 days to discuss her progress in these areas.

Ms. Belowpar has failed to show a minimal level of attention to detail in verifying computer analyses of payroll and tax payments. With this evaluation, she is directed to conduct monthly manual inspections of accounts and individual payroll records including spot checks to reconcile W-2s to paychecks and hand calculation of gross and net payments. She is to provide a written report to the legal department head on the first business day of each month until further notice.

Ms. Belowpar's skills in written and verbal communication are below an acceptable level for an in-house expert. She is directed to seek assistance from the training department within 30 days, including available coaching on communication skills.

At her most recent evaluation, Ms. Belowpar was asked to oversee production of a tax calendar for use by the accounting, sales, payroll, and legal departments in preparing reports, returns, and payments. This project has not been implemented; she is directed to produce such a calendar within 30 days and update it on a monthly basis.

Ms. Belowpar has not responded to several requests from the sales department seeking assistance in automating the application of sales and use taxes in those states where these levies are collected. With this evaluation, she is directed to report on her progress in this matter to the head of the sales department within 15 days.

Ms. Belowpar must significantly improve her knowledge of changing federal, state, and local tax codes. She is advised to attend trade shows and conventions and seek advanced certifications from professional organizations.

Ms. Belowpar is directed to work with the training department to create and keep current courses for employees in the payroll and accounting departments and assist the human resources department in updating the employee handbook and policies regarding travel and other activities. With this evaluation, she is directed to make this a high priority for accomplishment within the next 30 days.

Internal Auditor

Accounts payable
Accounts receivable
Auditor
External auditor
Fraud
GAAP (Generally Accepted Accounting Principles)
Internal auditor
Investor fraud
Journal entries
Ledger entries
Loss
Manufacturing ratios
Statistical analysis tools
Warehouse management

MEETS OR EXCEEDS

Mr. Paragon has demonstrated superb skills and dedication to accuracy in the conduct of his job as internal auditor. He fully recognizes the nature of his assignment as a critical safeguard against errors and omissions and improper activities and procedures in accounting, inventory, and other fiscal areas.

He has shown exceptional skill in examining and analyzing accounting records to determine the financial status of the enterprise. He monitors accounts receivable and accounts payable, producing independent reports for the executive committee. He has shown himself to be very flexible in assisting the executive committee and the board of directors in special research on fiscal matters.

When called upon to do so, he has delivered substantial and valuable recommendations for management on fiscal matters.

Mr. Paragon has done an excellent job of reviewing inventory reports and applying statistical analysis tools to stockroom orders and sales reports to assure that proper manufacturing ratios are applied. In doing so, he also worked with consultants and the MIS department to build in automated warnings to guard against waste and to flag possible errors, fraud, or loss.

He has shown proper diligence in the conduct of unannounced inspections of the warehouse and stockroom to check on inventory levels.

When requested and as appropriate, Mr. Paragon has shown himself to be of valuable assistance to the company's outside auditor to help reconcile discrepancies or support the external auditing function.

Mr. Paragon displays excellent skills in checking books to verify journal and ledger entries and brings any significant discrepancies to the attention of the executive committee. He also demonstrates a commitment to assuring that generally accepted accounting principles are followed in recording transactions.

He has done an excellent job of coordinating his efforts with other departments in assuring that the investor fraud protections of the Sarbanes-Oxley Act and other laws and regulations are followed.

NEEDS IMPROVEMENT

Ms. Goodenough has not demonstrated a sufficient level of skill and dedication to accuracy in the conduct of her job as internal auditor. She is advised to seek training and professional certification in support of her role as a critical safeguard against errors and omissions and improper activities and procedures in accounting, inventory, and other fiscal areas. With this evaluation, she is asked to meet with the training department within 30 days to seek further education.

She must improve her ability to examine and analyze accounting records to determine the financial status of the enterprise. The job description for internal auditor includes monitoring accounts receivable and accounts payable and producing independent reports for the executive committee; in doing so, Ms. Goodenough has not consistently delivered reports of professional quality.

Ms. Goodenough also needs to be able to deliver substantial and valuable recommendations for management on fiscal matters. Her efforts in these areas have been inadequate.

Ms. Goodenough has not adequately fulfilled her assignment to review inventory reports and apply statistical analysis tools to stockroom orders and sales reports to assure that proper manufacturing ratios are applied. She is directed to meet with the training department within 30 days to seek assistance on these tasks and others; she will be re-evaluated on the quality of her inventory reports in 90 days.

When requested and as appropriate, Ms. Goodenough needs to make herself of assistance to the company's outside auditor to help reconcile discrepancies or support the external auditing function. She is asked to meet with the in-house legal department within 30 days to review appropriate interaction between the internal auditor and the outside auditor.

Ms. Goodenough must improve her background and skills in checking books to verify journal and ledger entries and bring any significant discrepancies to the attention of the executive committee. She has not shown a commitment to assuring that generally accepted accounting principles are followed in recording transactions. She will be re-evaluated on these matters in 30 days.

With this evaluation, Ms. Goodenough is asked to improve her efforts with other departments in assuring that the investor fraud protections of the Sarbanes-Oxley Act and other laws and regulations are followed.

UNSATISFACTORY

Mr. Belowpar has failed to demonstrate an acceptable level of skill and dedication to accuracy in the conduct of his job as internal auditor. With this evaluation, he is directed to seek training and professional certification in support of his role as a critical safeguard against errors and omissions and improper activities and procedures in accounting, inventory, and other fiscal areas. He is instructed to meet with the training department within 15 days to seek further education and will be re-evaluated on his performance in 45 days.

Mr. Belowpar must take immediate steps to improve his ability to examine and analyze accounting records to determine the financial status of the enterprise. The job description for internal auditor includes producing independent reports for the executive committee; Mr. Belowpar has consistently delivered reports that are beneath professional quality. The executive committee directs that he be re-evaluated on progress in this area within 30 days.

Mr. Belowpar has failed to fulfill his assignment to review inventory reports and apply statistical analysis tools to stockroom orders and sales reports to assure that proper manufacturing ratios are applied. The quality of his work in this area is well below expectations and professional quality. He is directed to meet with the training department within 10 days to set a program of education on these tasks and others; he will be re-evaluated on the quality of his inventory reports in 60 days.

In a memo sent to the executive committee by the company's outside auditor, Mr. Belowpar is said to have been uncooperative when asked to help reconcile discrepancies. He is directed to meet with the in-house legal department within 10 days to review appropriate interaction between the internal auditor and the outside auditor.

Risk Analyst

Backups of electronic data
Bonding of employees
Claims database
Employee handbook
Liability
Occupational safety
Outsourcing
Risk analysis
Statistical analysis
Workers' compensation
Workplace safety

MEETS OR EXCEEDS

Ms. Paragon has performed admirably in her assignment as risk analyst. She has assisted the company in reducing hazards to employees, customers, and visitors by instituting safety programs, analyzing potential areas of danger and liability, and working with the insurance, legal, and office services departments in their own efforts.

She has demonstrated a high degree of initiative and skill in working with insurance carriers and occupational safety consultants to survey the workplace and suggest changes. She has worked with the in-house insurance department to obtain credits or higher ratings for the company from insurance carriers in recognition of improvements to the workplace.

Ms. Paragon initiated a number of programs that resulted in significant savings to the company, including:

- A program to bond warehouse and shipping department workers;
- An enterprisewide task force that examined the advantages and disadvantages of outsourcing high-risk tasks; and
- Consultation with the MIS department to assure off-site backups of critical electronic data.

Ms. Paragon has shown excellent cooperation with the human resources department in dealing with workers' compensation claims. She delivers detailed and accurate research on all accidents.

At the time of her hiring, she was asked to establish and maintain a database of claims within six months; she accomplished that task in less than half that time. Working closely with the MIS department, Ms. Paragon went on to develop a sophisticated statistical risk analysis report that prioritizes activities and assets by correlation to actual losses and claims over time.

In cooperation with the human resources department, Ms. Paragon keeps sections on health, safety, and risk avoidance in the employee handbook up to date. After consultation with the in-house legal department, she does an excellent job of adapting and applying new guidelines from federal, state, and local government agencies.

Ms. Paragon has demonstrated a deep commitment to ongoing training in her specialty. She has taken advantage of advanced certification from professional organizations and has received approval to pursue postgraduate studies under the company's tuition reimbursement program.

NEEDS IMPROVEMENT

Mr. Goodenough has not distinguished himself in his assignment as risk analyst. He needs to better assist the company in reducing hazards to employees, customers, and visitors by instituting safety programs, analyzing potential areas of danger and liability, and working with the insurance, legal, and office services departments in their own efforts.

He is asked to initiate greater contact with insurance carriers and occupational safety consultants to survey the workplace and suggest changes.

Three months ago, Mr. Goodenough was asked by the executive committee to study three programs that could yield significant savings to the company:

- A program to bond warehouse and shipping department workers;
- An enterprisewide task force to examine the advantages and disadvantages of outsourcing high-risk tasks; and
- Consultation with the MIS department to assure off-site backups of critical electronic data.

As of the date of this evaluation, Mr. Goodenough has not reported back to the executive committee on these matters. He is directed to meet with the committee within 45 days to report on his findings and make suggestions for changes to operations.

With this evaluation, Mr. Goodenough is asked to establish a database of claims within six months; once it is in place, he is directed to work closely with the MIS department to develop a statistical risk analysis report that prioritizes activities and assets by correlation to actual losses and claims over time.

Mr. Goodenough needs to improve his cooperation with the human resources department in order to keep sections on health, safety, and risk avoidance in the employee handbook up to date.

He has not demonstrated a sufficient commitment to ongoing training in his specialty. Mr. Goodenough is asked to take advantage of advanced certification from professional organizations.

UNSATISFACTORY

Mr. Belowpar has failed to demonstrate adequate skills as a risk analyst. He is directed to seek additional training to better assist the company in reducing hazards to employees, customers, and visitors by instituting safety programs, analyzing potential areas of danger and liability, and working with the insurance, legal, and office services departments in their own efforts.

At the time of his hiring, Mr. Belowpar was asked to establish a database of claims within six months; the project has not been completed. With this evaluation, he is directed to make creation and maintenance of this database his highest priority; he will be re-evaluated on this matter after 45 days.

Mr. Belowpar has not given assistance to the human resources department in keeping sections on health, safety, and risk avoidance in the employee handbook up to date. He is directed to meet with that department within 15 days; he will be re-evaluated on this matter after 45 days.

CHAPTER 3

SALES
AND
MARKETING

Sales Representative

Customer Service Representative

Customer Support Engineer

Advertising Coordinator

Promotions Manager

Marketing Coordinator

Market Researcher

Public Relations Coordinator

Sales Representative

Advocate for the customer
Community involvement
Integration of data
Leads and referrals
Paperwork
Product positioning
Sales channels
Sales database
Sales targets

MEETS OR EXCEEDS

Mr. Paragon was the company's most productive salesperson over the past 12 months. He exceeded every sales target and helped the company expand its products and services into new areas that will set the stage for future growth.

He has demonstrated an excellent understanding of products and services and represents the company well in meetings with customers and in his participation in industry trade shows and events.

On his own initiative, Mr. Paragon has passed along to the marketing and research and development departments suggestions and requests from customers that have resulted in significant improvements to products. He has also consistently offered valuable guidance to the marketing department in positioning products and opening new sales channels.

Mr. Paragon has served ably as chair of a task force with the MIS and marketing departments to seek improvements to the company's sales database. As a result of that committee's work, there has been a marked improvement in integration of data among departments. For example, a customer support representative will receive a full report on purchases and other past history with a customer before beginning a telephone conversation. The shipping department is able to access full details of past orders before arranging for deliveries of new orders.

In keeping with the company's mission statement, Mr. Paragon has demonstrated superior abilities as an advocate for the customer. He has sought and received product modifications, special financing, and special support for preferred customers.

He has been extremely responsive to follow up on new leads and referrals received from various sources including marketing partners, industry sources, and promotions. Analysis of sales records indicates an extremely high percentage of conversion of leads to actual sales.

Surveys and polls of customers give Mr. Paragon the highest possible marks for his attention to their needs, follow-through on orders, and post-delivery support.

He devotes a great deal of time to keeping current on the company's products and services through the in-house training department and has also sought and received advanced certification from several professional organizations.

He has represented the company well in the community by maintaining a high profile and being active in causes that reflect favorably on the organization.

He has shown a great attention to detail in handling the reports and paperwork that are a necessary component of the job.

NEEDS IMPROVEMENT

Mr. Goodenough needs to greatly improve his productivity as a salesperson. Over the past 12 months, he has not met most sales targets and has not shown an ability to help the company expand its products and services into new areas that will set the stage for future growth.

He needs to demonstrate a markedly improved understanding of products and services and further needs to better represent the company in meetings with customers and in his participation in industry trade shows and events.

An initiative by the director of sales, issued 12 months ago, called upon sales representatives to pass along suggestions and requests from customers to the marketing and research and development departments. Mr. Goodenough has not offered guidance to the marketing department in positioning products and opening new sales channels; with this evaluation, he is directed to meet with the head of the sales department to review this assignment.

Mr. Goodenough has not made any useful contributions to the sales and marketing task force that sought improvements to the company's sales database. The goal of that group was to improve the integration of data among departments.

Mr. Goodenough has not shown himself to be an effective advocate for the customer, a key element of the company's mission statement. He has not sought product modifications, special financing, and special support for preferred customers.

Mr. Goodenough has also not adequately followed up on new leads and referrals received from various sources including marketing partners, industry sources, and promotions. Analysis of sales records indicates an extremely low percentage of conversion of leads to actual sales.

Surveys and polls of customers give Mr. Goodenough very low marks for attention to their needs, follow-through on orders, and postdelivery support.

Mr. Goodenough has not devoted a sufficient amount of time to keeping current on the company's products and services through the in-house training department; he has also not taken advantage of available advanced certification from professional organizations. With this evaluation, he is directed to meet with the training department to seek opportunities to enhance his understanding of job responsibilities and opportunities.

He has not shown great attention to detail in handling the reports and paperwork that are a necessary component of the job. He is instructed to meet with the senior sales secretary to review forms and procedures.

UNSATISFACTORY

Ms. Belowpar has not demonstrated an adequate level of productivity as a salesperson. Over the past 12 months, she has failed to meet a single sales target. She has also not shown an adequate ability to help the company expand its products and services into new areas that will set the stage for future growth.

She has not shown an acceptable level of understanding of products and services and has not done well as a representative of the company in meetings with customers and in her participation in industry trade shows and events.

An initiative by the director of sales, issued 12 months ago, called upon sales representatives to pass along suggestions and requests from customers to the marketing and research and development departments. Ms. Belowpar has not participated in this program in any form; with this evaluation, she is directed to meet with the head of the sales department within 10 days to review this assignment. She will be re-evaluated on this matter in 45 days.

Ms. Belowpar has not followed up on new leads and referrals received from various sources including marketing partners, industry sources, and promotions. Analysis of sales records shows that her list of regular customers has declined in number over the past 12 months.

Surveys and polls of customers give Ms. Belowpar unacceptable marks for attention to their needs, follow-through on orders, and postdelivery support.

Ms. Belowpar has not kept current on the company's products and services through the in-house training department; she has also not taken advantage of available advanced certification from professional organizations. With this evaluation, she is directed to meet with the training department within 15 days to develop a curriculum of courses to enhance her understanding of job responsibilities and opportunities.

She has not shown great attention to detail in handling the reports and paperwork that are a necessary component of the job. She is instructed to meet with the senior sales secretary within 15 days to review forms and procedures; she will be re-evaluated on this matter in 45 days.

Customer Service Representative

Authorization for return
Caller ID
Client surveys
Customer service
Escalation of customer concerns
Online chat
Order taking
Resolution of problems
Tracking orders
Troubleshooting
Unnecessary repairs

MEETS OR EXCEEDS

Mr. Paragon has excelled as a senior customer service representative. According to customer surveys and evaluations of recorded telephone sessions, he represents the enterprise with great skill and knowledge and delivers courteous and effective service to customers.

Although the bulk of the company's orders are taken by the sales force, the customer service department is also capable of accepting and processing orders, and Mr. Paragon has capably assisted the sales department when asked to do so.

The job description for customer service employees, as outlined in the company handbook, calls for them to be advocates on behalf of the customer. Mr. Paragon has demonstrated a strong commitment to learning about all of the company's products and services and delivers excellent assistance to customers in seeking the resolution of problems or any special requests. When necessary, he courteously escalates customer concerns to a supervisor or a departmental manager.

He has superb telephone skills and makes excellent use of computer programs to check inventory, place orders, and track shipments. He works well with the customer support department, helping customers get the most out of troubleshooting expertise before issuing a return authorization; in doing so, he saves the customer the inconvenience of returning a product and reduces the company's costs in making unnecessary repairs.

Mr. Paragon demonstrates great flexibility in his ability to adjust to changing product lines and procedures. He served as the department's representative on a task force with the MIS department that redesigned the appearance and functions of the customer service database.

He has taken advantage of courses offered through the training department and has received advanced certification from professional associations.

Mr. Paragon has led the department in development of measurement of dealings with customers, including surveys of clients and postdelivery calls from the department to follow up on customer satisfaction. He produces reports for the department and supervisors that provide input on trends among customers and help to update procedures.

Mr. Paragon has taken an active role in investigating new technologies for the department, including connecting the sales database to incoming caller ID to allow instant recognition of customers. He has also participated in a pilot program to add live online chat features to the company Web site, allowing customers and potential clients to communicate with customer service over the Internet.

NEEDS IMPROVEMENT

Ms. Goodenough needs to greatly improve her skills as a senior customer service representative. According to customer surveys and evaluations of recorded telephone sessions, she has on occasion delivered misleading or inaccurate information and has not consistently been courteous and effective to customers.

Although the bulk of the company's orders are taken by the sales force, the job description for the customer service department also calls on representatives to be capable of accepting and processing orders; Ms. Goodenough has regularly passed along orders to other staffers or has otherwise been unwilling to assist the sales department when asked to do so.

Ms. Goodenough has not demonstrated a strong commitment to learning about all of the company's products and services. With this evaluation, she is directed to seek additional in-house training and to meet with the head of the customer service department within 30 days for a re-evaluation of her capabilities in this area.

She has not consistently demonstrated proficiency with telephone systems and computer programs to check inventory, place orders, and track shipments. She has not shown an ability to work effectively with the customer support department, helping customers get the most out of trouble-shooting expertise before issuing a return authorization. As a result, she has on occasion inconvenienced customers with avoidable returns and incurred costs to the company in making unnecessary repairs.

Ms. Goodenough has not demonstrated sufficient flexibility in adjusting to changing product lines and procedures. She has not taken advantage of courses offered through the training department or received advanced certification from professional associations. With this evaluation, she is instructed to meet with the training department within 15 days to seek further instruction.

UNSATISFACTORY

Mr. Belowpar has failed to demonstrate adequate skills as a senior customer service representative. According to customer surveys and evaluations of recorded telephone sessions, he regularly delivers misleading or inaccurate information and has not consistently been courteous and effective to customers. With this evaluation, he is directed to seek counseling and education from the training department on proper dealings with customers; he will be re-evaluated on these skills within 45 days.

Mr. Belowpar has consistently declined to accept orders from customers, referring them to the sales department. This is not in keeping with the job description for a customer service representative. With this evaluation, he is directed to seek the necessary sales training within 30 days.

Mr. Belowpar does not show a necessary understanding of the company's products and services. He must seek additional in-house training and meet with the head of the customer service department within 30 days for a re-evaluation of his capabilities in this area.

He has not mastered the use of telephone systems and computer programs to check inventory, place orders, and track shipments; these are all key components of his job. In addition, he has regularly failed to work effectively with the customer support department, seeking troubleshooting expertise before issuing a return authorization. As a result, he has on numerous occasions inconvenienced customers with avoidable returns and incurred costs to the company in making unnecessary repairs.

Customer Support Engineer

Comment cards
Communications skills
Customer support
Customer surveys
Database
Documentation
Instruction manual
Telephone presence
Research and development

MEETS OR EXCEEDS

Ms. Paragon delivers exemplary work as a customer support engineer; based on customer surveys and comment cards, she represents the company very well and solves problems at an above-average rate.

She demonstrates excellent oral and written communications skills and has shown an ability to respond professionally and courteously to customers who may be calling at times of stress.

Among her strengths are a strong understanding of the company's products and the needs of its customers. She has made the effort to educate herself on products and has participated in every available training session.

Ms. Paragon has demonstrated her ability to work closely with research, development, and engineering departments to test unreleased products in search of points of failure and to offer input on usability issues.

As a senior customer support engineer, Ms. Paragon regularly consults with in-house and outside documentation and instruction manual authors to assure the accuracy and utility of written materials provided to customers.

She has worked closely and effectively with the sales department to permit herself to fully understand the reasons for the development of new products and the marketing objectives behind them.

Ms. Paragon has led the way to develop a database of customer problems and has documented troubleshooting steps and successful solutions. The database is available to other support engineers for their dealings with customers, and Ms. Paragon meets regularly with research and development teams to deliver feedback based on frequently occurring problems and failures.

She also initiated a program to collect requests for changes and enhancements to products suggested by customers.

NEEDS IMPROVEMENT

Ms. Goodenough needs to improve her telephone presence and her knowledge of company products; customer surveys and comment cards indicate a barely adequate level of satisfaction with her responses to calls for support.

She needs to improve her oral and written communications skills in dealing with customers, working especially to improve her courtesy with customers who may be calling at times of stress.

Ms. Goodenough has not demonstrated a strong understanding of the company's products and the needs of its customers. With this evaluation, she is directed to educate herself on products and participate in available training sessions.

In order to enhance her skills as a customer support engineer, she needs to work closely and effectively with the sales department; this will permit her to fully understand the reasons for the development of new products and the marketing objectives behind them.

Ms. Goodenough needs to master the use of the database of customer problems and troubleshooting steps taken that have resulted in successful solutions. As part of that process, she needs to meet regularly with research and development teams to deliver feedback based on frequently occurring problems and failures.

UNSATISFACTORY

Based on surveys and comment cards, Mr. Belowpar has exhibited an unacceptable attitude and effectiveness in some of his dealings with customers. He is directed to take training courses to deal with his telephone presence.

His oral and written communications skills are barely acceptable in the best of cases, and some customers have complained to supervisors about rudeness or ineffectiveness in dealing with clients with especially demanding requests.

Mr. Belowpar is not current on the company's products and has not made the effort to educate himself about customer needs; with this evaluation, he is directed to consult with the training and sales departments to seek assistance.

Mr. Belowpar has not demonstrated a satisfactory level of competency in the use of the database of customer problems and troubleshooting steps that have resulted in successful solutions. He is directed to seek training on computer skills as a high priority in the next 30 days.

Advertising Coordinator

Advertising agencies
Catalogs
Charitable events
Company handbook
Conventions
Cost per sales lead
Internet advertising
Not-for-profit organizations
Review selection of advertising agency
Sales and marketing materials
Sales literature
Tracking advertising results
Tracking expenses
Trade shows

MEETS OR EXCEEDS

Mr. Paragon has delivered excellent work as advertising coordinator for the company, overseeing in-house production of sales and marketing materials and working closely with outside advertising and promotion companies. Department heads report sales that can be tracked directly to advertising campaigns have increased to record levels over the past year.

He was instrumental in organizing and running a review of the company's previous advertising and promotion efforts, working closely and effectively with marketing, sales, and promotion departments. After determining the needs for future campaigns, he demonstrated exceptional leadership as chairman of the review committee for the selection of a new advertising agency for the company.

Mr. Paragon initiated an in-house tracking system to determine the effectiveness of ads and promotional efforts, producing highly accurate estimations of the true cost per sales lead generated. For his work in this project, Mr. Paragon was highlighted in several industry publications.

He does an excellent job of keeping up to date on industry trends, technologies, and suppliers and is an active member of several national professional organizations.

Mr. Paragon has also become involved with a number of not-for-profit organizations in the community, garnering goodwill through promotional and charitable events the company has sponsored.

As advertising coordinator, he has demonstrated exceptional skills in monitoring the placement and results of Internet advertising on our own Web site and in cooperative endeavors with suppliers and resellers.

Mr. Paragon has fulfilled all of his assignments for design and production of in-house sales literature and catalogs, working closely with department heads including creative services, sales, marketing, and promotion.

In conjunction with the meeting planner, Mr. Paragon has shown superb management skills in developing displays, booths, and exhibits for trade shows and conventions. Under his initiative, the company purchased a reusable modular booth system that has already saved the company more than $20,000 in temporary construction costs in its first year of use.

Mr. Paragon has worked to improve his computer skills and knowledge, volunteering for several training courses offered within the company and enrolling in an advanced certification program offered by a professional organization.

He helped rewrite the section of the company handbook that details policies and procedures that must be followed by departments before they commission any print or electronic advertising or promotional materials. He has effectively advised the executive committee on ways to keep advertising costs within budgetary goals while continuing to increase awareness of the company and its products and services.

Mr. Paragon has worked closely with the MIS department to computerize the tracking of advertising and promotional expenditures and developed a system to notify department heads when costs exceed planned levels. He has directed a member of his staff to review all invoices for advertising and promotional services and materials to verify accuracy and assure proper assignment of costs to departmental budgets.

NEEDS IMPROVEMENT

Ms. Goodenough needs to improve her ability to oversee in-house production of sales and marketing materials and work more closely with outside advertising and promotion companies. Department heads report they have not received sufficient tracking information to help them assess the value of recent advertising campaigns.

She was directed six months ago by the executive committee to conduct a review of the company's previous advertising and promotion efforts; the results of that study have not been presented to the marketing manager or the executive committee as of the date of this evaluation.

Following completion of that review—which the executive committee now asks to be delivered within 60 days—Ms. Goodenough is directed to meet with the marketing, sales, and promotion departments to determine needs for future campaigns and consider the selection of a new advertising agency for the company.

Progress on an in-house tracking system to determine the effectiveness of ads and promotional efforts, a current assignment for the advertising coordinator, has fallen well behind the scheduled date of completion.

Ms. Goodenough has not demonstrated a commitment to keeping up to date on industry trends, technologies, and suppliers. She is advised to seek certification and training available through national professional organizations.

The company's involvement with not-for-profit organizations in the community has dropped off significantly in recent years, squandering opportunities to generate goodwill through participation in promotional and charitable events. She is requested to meet with the human resources and marketing departments to review lists of favored charities and organizations.

As advertising coordinator, Ms. Goodenough needs to improve her computer skills and knowledge and become more involved in monitoring the placement and results of Internet advertising on our own Web site and in cooperative endeavors with suppliers and resellers.

An area of concern to the executive committee is the rising cost of in-house sales literature and catalogs. As advertising coordinator, Ms. Goodenough needs to work more closely with department heads including creative services, sales, marketing, and promotion and to seek cost savings through the use of in-house and outside facilities.

Costs for displays, booths, and exhibits at trade shows and conventions have risen well above expectations. Ms. Goodenough is directed to meet with the meeting planner to explore ways to control these expenditures.

She needs to devote time to complete the revision to the section of the company handbook detailing policies and procedures that must be followed by departments before they commission any print or electronic advertising or promotional materials.

While Ms. Goodenough has worked with the MIS department as part of an ongoing effort to computerize the tracking of advertising and promotional expenditures, the task has not yet been completed. The executive committee has asked that the full system also be able to notify department heads when costs exceed planned levels.

UNSATISFACTORY

Mr. Belowpar has failed to display adequate skills in overseeing in-house production of sales and marketing materials. He has also not demonstrated the aptitude to closely monitor the work of outside advertising and promotion companies.

Department heads complain of an absence of tracking information to help them assess the value of recent advertising campaigns.

Based on comments from other department heads, Mr. Belowpar has not kept up to date on industry trends, technologies, and suppliers. He has not taken advantage of available certification and training offered by national professional organizations, and with this evaluation, he is instructed to do so.

Mr. Belowpar has also failed to demonstrate working knowledge of computer skills necessary for tracking and budgetary purposes and must also become more involved in monitoring the placement and results of Internet advertising on our own Web site and in cooperative endeavors with suppliers and resellers.

The cost of in-house sales literature and catalogs has risen well above budget expectations, and Mr. Belowpar must be more direct in communicating with department heads about excessive spending that will be charged to their accounts. At the same time, he is directed to work closely with department heads including creative services, sales, marketing, and promotion and to seek cost savings through the use of in-house and outside facilities.

Promotions Manager

Discounts to customers
Marketing partners
Polls of customers and clients
Product launches
Promotional efforts
Resellers
Sales contests
Spifs (sales promotion incentive funds)
Trade shows

MEETS OR EXCEEDS

The company's promotional efforts for its products and services have been conducted in a highly effective and professional manner under the guidance of Ms. Paragon. She has worked very closely and effectively with the sales and marketing department to raise awareness of the company in every sector in which it participates.

Ms. Paragon has demonstrated superior skills in targeting resellers, marketing partners, and end-user customers through promotional efforts including discounts, special bundles of products or services, contests, spifs (sales promotion incentive funds), and coordination with advertising, marketing, and public relations departments.

Successful company promotions initiated by Ms. Paragon have included events at trade shows, exhibitions, product placement in television shows and motion pictures, and experimental efforts using the Internet.

Ms. Paragon has demonstrated exceptional commitment to cooperating as a member of product launch and sales task forces. She has shown herself to be fully up to date on all company products and services and has effectively coordinated promotional efforts with the ongoing campaigns of the advertising and marketing staffs. She led the way in the commissioning of a poll of customers and would-be clients which resulted in significant enhancements to products, sales efforts, and promotion.

She has shown excellent skills in overseeing the design and production of promotional materials. Working closely with the marketing department, she has developed a reasonable budget for her department's efforts and has stayed within her allowable expenditures.

Ms. Paragon keeps current on trends in the industry and attends appropriate trade shows and conventions. She has received certification from several professional associations. In cooperation with the training department, she has helped create courses for members of her staff; she has also sought opportunities for advanced training through area colleges and associations.

Ms. Paragon has shown excellent written and verbal communications skills and has been asked to be a member of teams making presentations about the company to major clients.

NEEDS IMPROVEMENT

The company's promotional efforts for its products and services have fallen significantly below expectations under the guidance of Mr. Goodenough. He has not exhibited a high degree of effectiveness and cooperation with the sales and marketing department in efforts to raise awareness of the company in every sector in which it participates.

Mr. Goodenough has not followed through on requests from the marketing department to target resellers, marketing partners, and end-user customers through promotional efforts including discounts, special bundles of products or services, contests, and spifs (sales promotion incentive funds). He has shown less than adequate coordination with the advertising, marketing, and public relations departments.

Other areas where promotional efforts have fallen short include events at trade shows, exhibitions, product placement in television shows and motion pictures, and experimental efforts using the Internet.

Mr. Goodenough has shown inadequate commitment to participation as a member of product launch and sales task forces. He has not demonstrated a full understanding of company products and services and has been unable to effectively coordinate promotional efforts with the ongoing campaigns of the advertising and marketing staffs. With this evaluation, he is directed to meet with the marketing department head within 15 days to establish a 60-day plan that will result in an acceptable level of knowledge about the company and its goals.

He has not shown sufficient skills in the oversight of design and production of promotional materials. He must develop safeguards to prevent overspending his budget unless he receives advanced written approval from the director of the marketing department.

Mr. Goodenough has failed to keep current on trends in the industry. He is asked to meet with the director of the training department within 30 days to develop a plan to improve his knowledge in this area. He is advised to seek courses and certification from professional associations. At the same time, he should seek courses for members of his staff and opportunities for advanced training through area colleges and associations.

UNSATISFACTORY

The company's promotional efforts for its products and services have not met satisfactory levels under Ms. Belowpar's management. The quality of promotions has been below expectations, response to campaigns has been unacceptably weak, and expenditures have regularly exceeded budget lines without preauthorization from the marketing department.

Overall, Ms. Belowpar has failed to demonstrate effectiveness and cooperation with the sales and marketing department in efforts to raise awareness of the company in every sector in which it participates.

As outlined in her most recent evaluation, Ms. Belowpar was requested by the marketing department to target resellers, marketing partners, and end-user customers through promotional efforts including discounts, special bundles of products or services, contests, and spifs (sales promotion incentive funds). What little efforts made were undertaken without the proper coordination with the advertising, marketing, and public relations departments.

Ms. Belowpar has also neglected promotional efforts at trade shows and exhibitions; the sales department has reported a significant drop-off in sales at conventions despite a strong effort on their part to place the company's products and services in a favorable competitive position.

For unexplained reasons, Ms. Belowpar has failed to participate as a member of task forces on product launches and sales efforts. She has also failed to demonstrate a full understanding of company products and services and has been unable to effectively coordinate promotional efforts with the ongoing campaigns of the advertising and marketing staffs. With this evaluation, she is directed to make this her highest priority. She is instructed to meet with the marketing department head within 10 days and to establish a plan that will result in an acceptable level of knowledge about the company and its goals. She will be re-evaluated on accomplishment of this specific task within 60 days.

Ms. Belowpar has also shown herself to be unsuccessful in the oversight of the design and production of promotional materials. With this evaluation, she is directed to produce, within 15 days, a set of safeguards to prevent overspending her budget without receiving advanced written approval from the director of the marketing department.

Ms. Belowpar has failed to keep current on trends in the industry. She is instructed to meet with the director of the training department within 30 days to develop a plan to improve her knowledge in this area. She is advised to seek courses and certification from professional associations. At the same time, she is asked to seek courses for members of her staff and opportunities for advanced training through area colleges and associations. She will be re-evaluated on her accomplishments in this area within 60 days.

Marketing Coordinator

Advertising
Advertising agencies
Advertising tracking programs
Cooperative advertising
Digital photo and illustration software
Internet marketing
Press conferences
Press kits
Product introductions
Sales collateral materials
Web development tools

MEETS OR EXCEEDS

In his first year as marketing coordinator, Mr. Paragon has developed and implemented a number of effective and innovative strategies to expand the company's advertising presence. He greatly expanded the use of the Internet for marketing, promotion, and sales. Under his initiatives, the company made excellent use of cooperative advertising with some of its manufacturing, sales, and marketing partners.

He has demonstrated great understanding of the team effort required for marketing, working extremely well with other related departments including public relations, sales, and investor relations. His introduction of advanced computer-based tracking programs has allowed the company to better understand the effectiveness of campaigns and to assign a realistic estimate of advertising expenses as a component of the overall cost of a product.

Mr. Paragon was asked by the executive committee to organize and run a task force to make much more effective use of the Internet in advertising products and services and to provide support to our customers. The resulting campaign has been a great success and will be expanded in coming years.

He has shown a high degree of skill in working with the sales department to develop sales collateral materials; he effectively and professionally coordinates the writing and design of brochures in-house or supervises the work of outside agencies.

Mr. Paragon has devoted himself to learning all of the details of the company and its products, as well as meeting with the sales and product support departments to become acquainted with customers. He has made excellent use of available instruction through the training department, has sought specialized certification from professional associations, and has enrolled in postgraduate college courses. The training department has approved all of his requests for tuition reimbursement, and he has received very high grades from instructors.

Mr. Paragon has demonstrated competency in the use of computer databases, Web development tools, and digital photo and illustration editing software. On his own initiative, he has worked with the MIS department to fully automate and keep current information about mailings and distribution and has made excellent use of tracking codes to gauge the effectiveness of marketing campaigns and expenditures.

He has exhibited excellent cooperation with the public relations department in the preparation of press kits and in companywide coordination of publicity events including major product introductions, press conferences, and community events. Mr. Paragon is also an active and effective contributor to planning committees for company participation at trade shows and conventions.

Working with the sales and marketing departments, he assists in the setting of advertising budgets and the selection of outside agencies when required. He has demonstrated great skills as the company's principal liaison to its outside advertising agency, supervising production of presentations to the sales and marketing departments and tracking and managing the costs of campaigns.

NEEDS IMPROVEMENT

In her first year as marketing coordinator, Ms. Goodenough has not yet demonstrated a sufficient level of competency in the development and implementation of effective and innovative strategies to expand the company's advertising presence.

At the time of her hiring, she was asked to greatly expand the use of the Internet for marketing, promotion, and sales. Although there have been a number of committee meetings and some tentative efforts in this area, the net result has been well below companywide expectations. With this evaluation, she is directed to make this a high priority for accomplishment in the next 90 days; she will be re-evaluated on this matter after that period of time.

Ms. Goodenough has not made good use of available cooperative advertising money and campaigns with some of the company's manufacturing, sales, and marketing partners.

She has not demonstrated great understanding of the team effort required for marketing and has had difficulty working with other related departments including public relations, sales, and investor relations.

Ms. Goodenough was asked by the head of marketing to investigate and implement advanced computer-based tracking programs to allow the company to better understand the effectiveness of campaigns and to assign a realistic estimate of advertising expenses as a component of the overall cost of a product. This has not been accomplished. With this evaluation, she is asked to prepare a report on tracking programs and make proposals for their introduction. The report is to be presented to her direct supervisor within 30 days, and once her proposal has been approved by the executive committee, it is expected that new software will be put into place no later than 60 days afterward. The MIS department has been asked to offer all available assistance to Ms. Goodenough in her efforts on this matter.

Ms. Goodenough needs to improve her ability to work with the sales department to develop sales collateral materials; she must be more effective and professional in the coordination of writing and design of brochures in-house and supervising the work of outside agencies.

Ms. Goodenough has not demonstrated sufficient attention to learning all of the details of the company and its products, as well as meeting with the sales and product support departments to become acquainted with customers. Ms. Goodenough has also exhibited less-than-adequate competency in the use of computer databases, Web development tools, and digital photo and illustration editing software. She is directed to make use of available instruction through the training department and to seek specialized certification from professional associations and appropriate college courses where available. She will be re-evaluated on these matters in 90 days.

She needs to show a higher degree of cooperation with the public relations department in the preparation of press kits and in companywide coordination of publicity events including major product introductions, press conferences, and community events. Ms. Goodenough must also become an active and effective contributor to planning committees for company participation at trade shows and conventions.

Ms. Goodenough is asked to review the job description for marketing coordinator and to improve her efforts to work with the sales and marketing departments to assist in the setting of advertising budgets and the selection of outside agencies when required.

She must greatly improve her skills as the company's principal liaison to its outside advertising agency, supervising production of presentations to the sales and marketing departments and tracking and managing the costs of campaigns.

UNSATISFACTORY

In his first year as marketing coordinator, Mr. Belowpar has failed to demonstrate competency in fulfilling his assignment to enhance and expand the company's advertising and marketing.

At the time of his promotion to his current post, he was asked to greatly expand the use of the Internet for marketing, promotion, and sales. This has not been accomplished in any meaningful way. With this evaluation, Mr. Belowpar is directed to make this a high priority for accomplishment in the next 90 days; he will be re-evaluated on this matter after that period of time.

Mr. Belowpar has not made use of available cooperative advertising money and campaigns with some of the company's manufacturing, sales, and marketing partners. He is directed to meet with the sales coordinator to make plans for use of these available programs.

He has not worked well with other related departments including public relations, sales, and investor relations in team efforts for the launch and ongoing promotion of products and services.

Mr. Belowpar has also failed to improve his skills in developing sales collateral materials in cooperation with the sales deparment; he must be more effective and professional in the coordination of writing and design of brochures in-house and supervising the work of outside agencies.

Mr. Belowpar has not devoted an adequate amount of attention to the details of the company and its products. He has also neglected his assignment to meet regularly with the sales and product support departments to become acquainted with customers.

Mr. Belowpar has also not shown a professional level of proficiency in the use of computer databases, Web development tools, and digital photo and illustration editing software. He is directed to make use of available instruction through the training department and to seek specialized certification from professional associations and appropriate college courses where available. He will be re-evaluated on these matters in 90 days.

Mr. Belowpar has not properly assisted the public relations department in the preparation of press kits and in companywide coordination of publicity events including major product introductions, press conferences, and activities in the community. Mr. Belowpar must also become an active and effective contributor to planning committees for company participation at trade shows and conventions. With this evaluation, he is directed to meet with the human resources department within 10 days to review the elements of the job description for the marketing coordinator. He will be re-evaluated on this matter in 90 days.

Market Researcher

Competitive analysis
E-mail surveys
Focus groups
Internet surveys
Market research
Qualitative research
Quantitative research
Surveys
Telephone surveys

MEETS OR EXCEEDS

Ms. Paragon has delivered excellent work as a market researcher, assisting the company in assessing the need for new products and services and the sales of existing offerings. Her research has also been of great value to the marketing department in examining the offerings of competitors.

Over the course of the past year, Ms. Paragon has introduced state-of-the-art systems for the gathering and analysis of quantitative and qualitative research. She expanded the company's quantitative research methods to include e-mail and Internet surveys as well as more traditional telephone and mail assessments; she has applied sophisticated statistical analysis to the results and worked closely with the MIS department to prepare easily accessible reports.

Ms. Paragon introduced the company's first systematic qualitative product research center, working with a consultant to conduct focus groups of current and potential customers. She demonstrated a high degree of cooperation with the marketing and sales departments in constructing the focus group scripts.

She displayed great attention to detail in researching information about competitors in the market, delivering details on products, prices, and sales and distribution channels.

As asked by the executive committee, Ms. Paragon convened a task force to study the company's research needs and to assist departments in developing strategies to make effective use of research reports. She also worked closely with the training department to develop relevant courses and to identify opportunities for advanced learning through professional associations and area institutions of higher education.

Ms. Paragon has worked closely with departments throughout the company to develop tools to allow accurate estimates of the cost of research projects.

NEEDS IMPROVEMENT

Ms. Goodenough must greatly improve her performance as a market researcher to better assist the company in assessing the need for new products and services and the sales of existing offerings. She also must provide better research on the offerings of competitors.

The marketing department has expressed concerns about the value of quantitative and qualitative research conducted under Ms. Goodenough's management. With this evaluation, she is asked to meet with the training department to seek advanced courses and certification from professional associations. Further, she is asked to make a presentation to the marketing and sales departments within 60 days laying out possible expansions to the research efforts, including e-mail and Internet surveys as well as improved efforts for more traditional telephone and mail assessments.

Ms. Goodenough is also asked to report to the executive committee within 90 days about options to improve qualitative product research, including the conduct of focus groups of current and potential customers.

The quality of analysis of competitors in the market, including data on products, prices, and sales and distribution channels, has been less than adequate. With this evaluation, she is asked to consult with the training department about available courses and professional certification.

Ms. Goodenough is also directed to meet with the training department within 30 days to develop relevant courses to assist departments in developing strategies to make effective use of research reports.

UNSATISFACTORY

Mr. Belowpar has failed to deliver an adequate level of performance as a market researcher to assist the company in assessing the need for new products and services and the sales of existing offerings. He has also not improved the quality of research on the offerings of competitors.

At the time of his previous evaluation, Mr. Belowpar was asked to meet with the training department to seek advanced courses and certification from professional associations to advance his job skills. According to the training department, Mr. Belowpar has not availed himself of any further education arranged through their office. With this evaluation, he is directed to meet with the head of the training department within 30 days to discuss this matter.

The quality of analysis of competitors in the market, including data on products, prices, and sales and distribution channels, has been inadequate. With this evaluation, Mr. Belowpar is directed to schedule a meeting with the department heads in marketing, sales, and manufacturing to seek their input on necessary improvements to competitive analysis reports.

Public Relations Coordinator

Advertising agencies
Broadcast interviews
Charitable functions
Crisis management
Deals with the media
Foundations
In-house advertising departments
Investor relations
Media inquiries
Outside public relations counsel
Personnel matters
Press releases
Public appearances
Public relations
Relations with the media
Represents the company
Requests for interviews
Web design
Webmaster

MEETS OR EXCEEDS

Mr. Paragon enhances the company's efforts with great skill, dealing effectively with inquiries from the media and the general public and working proactively with the company's outside public relations firm and advertising agency. He possesses excellent communications skills for written releases, articulates positions adeptly, and works well with other departments in planning public relations needs.

Working under the guidelines set by the director of public relations and the executive committee, Mr. Paragon serves as the company's principal point of contact for all incoming requests for information and interviews from the media. He has shown great success in creating a database of local media outlets and personnel and has cultivated excellent relations with reporters.

Mr. Paragon represents the company very well in public appearances including charitable functions, foundations, and community events. He has delivered a positive message in broadcast and print interviews and has ably assisted executives in preparing for interviews of their own.

Mr. Paragon regularly meets with department heads and staff to discuss ongoing public relations efforts and to inform them of company policy about how to deal with reporters who contact them directly. Staff is given pointers on how to politely redirect all such inquiries to the public relations department.

Similarly, Mr. Paragon understands proper procedure in dealing with inquiries from shareholders and financial institutions, referring inquiries to the CFO and the investor relations department.

He has demonstrated exemplary skills in working with the marketing, sales, and promotion departments to create, establish, and maintain campaigns in support of company goals. Mr. Paragon has demonstrated a high degree of professionalism in coordinating company initiatives with the work of in-house and outside advertising agencies.

Mr. Paragon has embraced the opportunity to work with the company's Web design consultant and our in-house webmaster to add press releases, press contact information, and an archive of news clippings to the Web site. Response to these additions from staff, customers, and the media has been very positive. The entire campaign was accomplished at minimal cost, adding existing material to the company's new Internet presence.

In times of crisis, including the unfortunate events surrounding the November fire at our Madaket warehouse, Mr. Paragon demonstrated an excellent ability to work well under pressure. He managed the crisis in an admirable fashion, keeping the media, our staff, and our customers up to date about the circumstances and delivering reassurances from executive management that there would be no significant impact on the company's ability to serve its customers.

One of the requirements of this job is to be very well organized and demonstrate great attention to detail; on both of these accounts, Mr. Paragon has shown himself to be a consummate professional. He spends a great deal of time getting to know key executives and management of the company and is well acquainted with the company's products, services, and mission statement; this background is reflected in his dealings with the press.

Reports from other department heads and supervisors indicate a high level of satisfaction with Mr. Paragon's performance.

He has demonstrated the ability to be discreet and to follow state and federal regulations regarding private personnel matters. He works well with the directors of the legal and human resources departments, seeking their guidance and participation on sensitive matters.

NEEDS IMPROVEMENT

Mr. Goodenough needs to improve his ability to communicate more effectively in dealing with inquiries from the media and the general public. His writing and verbal skills are not always strong enough in press releases and responding to inquiries from the media.

He needs to improve his ability to work with other departments and with outside public relations counsel in planning publicity and community relations needs.

Mr. Goodenough has not yet advanced his skills and experience to the point where he can represent the company as the principal point of contact for all incoming requests for information and interviews from the media. He has been directed to enroll in several available training courses offered by professional associations.

He has not made sufficient progress in creating a database of local media outlets and personnel and cultivating good relations with reporters. This is a key component of the job description, and Mr. Goodenough has been directed to make it a high priority within the next 60 days.

Mr. Goodenough has made a reasonably good effort as a representative of the company in public appearances including charitable functions, foundations, and community events. He would benefit from additional training on public speaking, speech writing, and event planning.

In order for him to fulfill the element of the job description that calls on the public relations coordinator to assist executives in preparing for interviews of their own, he will need additional training and supervision and has been directed to work on these skills.

Mr. Goodenough should meet more regularly with department heads and staff to discuss ongoing public relations efforts and to inform them of company policy about how to deal with reporters who contact them directly.

Similarly, Mr. Goodenough needs to better understand the legal and financial regulations that apply to inquiries from shareholders and financial institutions, referring such callers or correspondents to the CFO and the investor relations department.

Mr. Goodenough needs to improve his skills in working with the marketing, sales, and promotion departments to create, establish, and maintain campaigns in support of company goals. At the same time, he needs to sharpen his abilities in coordinating company initiatives with the work of in-house and outside advertising agencies.

Despite prompting from the director of public relations to do so, Mr. Goodenough has not taken advantage of the company's Web design consultant and our in-house webmaster to add press releases, press contact information, and an archive of news clippings to the Web site. With this evaluation, he is directed to begin sharing releases and information with the Web site staff within 30 days.

Mr. Goodenough has not yet demonstrated adequate crisis management skills. As an example, in the aftermath of the November fire at our Madaket warehouse, the director of public relations was forced to step in to manage the flow of information to the media, our staff, and our customers to deliver reassurances from executive management that there would be no significant impact on the company's ability to serve its customers.

One of the requirements of this job is to be very well organized and demonstrate great attention to detail; on both of these accounts, Mr. Goodenough needs improvement and would benefit from available training and professional courses. He needs to spend more time getting to know key executives and management of the company and become better acquainted with the company's products, services, and mission statement.

Mr. Goodenough also needs to improve his understanding of state and federal regulations regarding private personnel matters and to work better with the directors of the legal and human resources departments, seeking their guidance and participation on sensitive matters.

UNSATISFACTORY

Ms. Belowpar has not been effective in dealing with inquiries from the media and the general public, resulting in several incorrect or misleading news reports that required further clarification by senior executives.

Her writing skills are adequate, but she has not demonstrated an ability to communicate verbally with clarity and accuracy in responding to inquiries from the media. She has been directed to seek additional training from consultants and professional organizations and to meet regularly with the director of public relations to review her progress.

Ms. Belowpar has failed to show an ability to work with other departments and with outside public relations counsel in planning publicity and community relations needs.

She has not produced a database of local media outlets and personnel, despite specific instructions from the director to do so. This is a key component of the job description, and Ms. Belowpar has been directed to make it her highest priority and to report on her progress to the director of public relations within 30 days.

As of the date of this evaluation, Ms. Belowpar has not demonstrated the ability to represent the company well in public appearances including charitable functions, foundations, and community events. She has been directed to seek additional training on public speaking, speech writing, and event planning.

Ms. Belowpar must meet regularly with department heads and staff to discuss ongoing public relations efforts and to inform them of company policy about how to deal with reporters who contact them directly.

Similarly, Ms. Belowpar needs to understand when it is not appropriate for her to make comments or respond to inquiries in certain areas. These include inquiries from shareholders and financial institutions which must be referred to the CFO and the investor relations department.

She also has not demonstrated a full understanding of state and federal regulations regarding private personnel matters; as part of this evaluation, she is asked to meet with the directors of the legal and human resources departments, seeking their guidance and participation on sensitive matters.

Ms. Belowpar must be prepared to work with the marketing, sales, and promotion departments to create, establish, and maintain campaigns in support of company goals. Some of these initiatives require working with in-house and outside advertising agencies, and she must better manage these relationships.

In the aftermath of the November fire at our Madaket warehouse, Ms. Belowpar was unable to manage the flow of information to the media, our staff, and our customers. As a result, there was an impact on the company's ability to serve its customers. She has been directed to seek additional training on crisis management.

Ms. Belowpar has failed to demonstrate strong organizational skills and the ability to pay attention to detail; she also needs to spend more time getting to know key executives and management of the company and become better acquainted with the company's products, services, and mission statement. The training and human resources departments have been asked to assist Ms. Belowpar in obtaining training in these areas from consultants and professional organizations.

CHAPTER 4

MANUFACTURING

Manufacturing Supervisor

Quality Assurance Specialist

Field Service Representative

Manufacturing Supervisor

Computer-assisted drafting
Cost of manufacturing
Downtime
Hazardous chemicals
Job fairs
Maintenance schedules
Manufacturing processes
Mean time before failure
Occupational safety
Outsourcing
Quality assurance
Recruitment
Research

MEETS OR EXCEEDS

Mr. Paragon has performed ably as supervisor of manufacturing systems for the company. Under his stewardship, the plant has operated at a high level of efficiency and productivity with lower-than-anticipated downtime over the past 12 months.

Among his principal accomplishments has been his close cooperation with the quality assurance department, supporting efforts to build in quality and improve mean time before failure of all products.

Mr. Paragon has demonstrated superior abilities in working closely with the research and development department; he chaired a task force which included the purchasing and engineering departments that offered substantial recommendations to save costs in manufacturing processes and in design and materials.

He has shown a commitment to keeping current on all of the company's products and services and has taken advantage of in-house training as well as advanced certification offered by professional associations. He maintains access to specialized online research Web sites as well as reference materials for the entire department and encourages workers to make use of the library. Mr. Paragon has shown a high degree of cooperation with the training department to offer in-house courses and coordinate with area professional associations and colleges for specialized training.

He has shown exceptional commitment to the company's mission statement in his work with the human resources department to assist in the recruitment and hiring of skilled workers through job fairs and advertising.

On several occasions in the past year, Mr. Paragon has made recommendations to the department head for outsourcing of manufacturing or assembly tasks where it made economic sense to do so.

He has done an excellent job of integrating the manufacturing department's efforts with the purchasing and warehouse department to assure the timely arrival of materials and supplies.

The heads of the sales and marketing departments have commended Mr. Paragon's efforts in assisting them in accurately measuring the true cost of manufacturing and support, a key component of pricing. Working with the MIS department, he also significantly improved the collection and analysis of manufacturing production data, yielding up-to-the-minute reports that allow sales and marketing to predict availability of product. The same reports advise when inventories may run short or when production levels exceed sales by a significant margin.

Mr. Paragon demonstrates strong understanding of computer-assisted drafting, manufacturing control, and testing equipment. At the request of the vice president for manufacturing, Mr. Paragon ably represented the department on a task force investigating redesign of the plant and installation of new equipment.

He has shown a high degree of attention to detail in establishing and keeping current a maintenance schedule for manufacturing equipment and overseeing repair and replacement of parts as necessary. He has done an excellent job of informing the sales and marketing departments of scheduled and unanticipated shutdowns.

Mr. Paragon has also worked closely with the health and safety department to identify possible occupational safety hazards and to assure that the company complies with state and federal regulations regarding the storage and disposal of hazardous chemicals.

NEEDS IMPROVEMENT

Ms. Goodenough must improve her capabilities as supervisor of manufacturing systems for the company. Under her supervision, the plant's overall level of efficiency and productivity has declined by 15 percent over the past

12 months. In addition, the manufacturing line has suffered much higher-than-anticipated downtime in the same period.

She needs to greatly boost her level of cooperation with the quality assurance department, supporting efforts to build in quality and improve mean time before failure of all products.

Ms. Goodenough must also demonstrate a greater ability to work closely with the research and development department. At the time of her most recent evaluation, she was asked to establish and chair a task force that would bring together the manufacturing, purchasing, and engineering departments to offer recommendations to save costs in manufacturing processes and in design and materials. That task force was not convened until one month ago; with this evaluation, she is directed to make this group a high priority. She will be re-evaluated on this matter in 90 days.

Ms. Goodenough needs to show a better commitment to keeping current on all of the company's products and services. She is also asked to take advantage of in-house training as well as advanced certification offered by professional associations. She must enhance access to specialized online research Web sites and reference materials for any appropriate staff member. She is directed to cooperate with the training department in their efforts to offer in-house courses and coordinate with area professional associations and colleges for specialized training.

Ms. Goodenough has not made effective contributions to integrating the manufacturing department's efforts with the purchasing and warehouse department to assure the timely arrival of materials and supplies.

The heads of the sales and marketing departments have asked for Ms. Goodenough's assistance in accurately measuring the true cost of manufacturing and support, a key component of pricing. With this evaluation, she is directed to work with the MIS department to significantly improve the collection and analysis of manufacturing production data to yield up-to-the-minute reports that allow sales and marketing to predict availability of product.

Ms. Goodenough needs to improve her understanding of computer-assisted drafting, manufacturing control, and testing equipment. She is directed to meet with the training department within 30 days to plan for advanced education in these areas.

To help prevent unanticipated shutdowns of the manufacturing line, Ms. Goodenough must show a significantly higher degree of attention to detail in establishing and keeping current a maintenance schedule for manufacturing equipment and overseeing repair and replacement of parts as necessary.

Ms. Goodenough must open better lines of communication with the health and safety department to identify possible occupational safety hazards and to assure that the company complies with state and federal regulations regarding the storage and disposal of hazardous chemicals.

UNSATISFACTORY

Mr. Belowpar has not adequately performed his assigned duties as supervisor of manufacturing systems for the company. Under his supervision, the plant's overall level of efficiency and productivity has sharply declined over the past 12 months, resulting in significant losses to the company. The manufacturing line has suffered much higher-than-anticipated downtime in the same period.

Mr. Belowpar has failed to offer sufficient cooperation with the efforts of the quality assurance department to build in quality and improve mean time before failure of all products. With this evaluation, he is directed to meet with the head of that department within 15 days; he will be re-evaluated on this matter 90 days after the date of this appraisal.

Mr. Belowpar has also not demonstrated close collaboration with the research and development department. At the time of his most recent evaluation, he was asked to establish and chair a task force that would bring together the manufacturing, purchasing, and engineering departments to offer recommendations to save costs in manufacturing processes and in design and materials. That task force was never convened. With this evaluation, Mr. Belowpar is directed to establish this group within 15 days and present a report to the executive committee on short-term progress and long-term strategies within 60 days.

Mr. Belowpar has not kept current on all of the company's products and services. He is asked to take advantage of in-house training as well as advanced certification offered by professional associations. He will be re-evaluated on this matter within 60 days.

Further, Mr. Belowpar is directed to cooperate with the training department in their efforts to offer in-house courses and coordinate with area professional associations and colleges for specialized training.

The heads of the sales and marketing departments have asked for Mr. Belowpar's assistance in accurately measuring the true cost of manufacturing and support, a key component of pricing. It is noted that Mr. Belowpar responded to a memo from the marketing department saying that he had no time for such efforts; with this evaluation, Mr. Belowpar is advised that such assistance to sales and marketing is at the heart of the job description for the manufacturing supervisor. He is directed to work with the MIS department to significantly improve the collection and analysis of manufacturing production data to yield up-to-the-minute reports that allow sales and marketing to predict availability of product. He will be re-evaluated on this matter in 30 days and again in 90 days.

Mr. Belowpar has not demonstrated sufficient understanding of computer-assisted drafting, manufacturing control, and testing equipment. He is directed to meet with the training department within 30 days to plan for advanced education in these areas, including courses offered at area colleges. Such classes, with the approval of the training department, are eligible for tuition reimbursement.

Mr. Belowpar is directed to meet with the health and safety department head within 15 days to identify possible occupational safety hazards and to assure that the company complies with state and federal regulations regarding the storage and disposal of hazardous chemicals.

Quality Assurance Specialist

Destructive testing
Guarantees
ISO-9000
Manufacturing processes
Nondestructive testing
Quality assurance
Returns and repairs
Warranty repairs

MEETS OR EXCEEDS

Ms. Paragon has led a successful effort to improve the overall quality of all of the company's products. Under her guidance, the percentage of returned merchandise and on-site warranty repairs has declined by 17 percent over the course of the past year.

She also demonstrated great skills in seeking and obtaining ISO-9000 certification for the company's products, opening up several new markets for the sales department as a result.

Ms. Paragon has demonstrated exceptional skills in working with research and development, manufacturing, sales, and marketing to build in a high level of quality in all products. The added expense incurred in meeting these higher standards has been more than offset by reductions in the cost of returns and repairs, and the company has also been able to increase the price and profit for certain items because of ISO certification. In addition, the sales department has been able to extend warranty periods and guarantees without significant costs to the company.

She has kept current on quality assurance engineering through courses and certification offered by professional associations. Ms. Paragon regularly attends trade shows and conventions.

She has demonstrated a high level of cooperation with the manufacturing department in designing new inspection and testing processes. All products now undergo routine scheduled and random destructive and non-destructive testing.

Under her initiative, the manufacturing department produces detailed reports on the acceptability of product, and any unusual increase in failures can be quickly traced back to the quality of raw materials or problems with manufacturing procedures.

Ms. Paragon also works closely and effectively with the warehouse department to test and monitor inventory to guard against spoilage and deterioration over time.

She has demonstrated a high degree of commitment to the ongoing education and supervision of technicians in her department, working closely with the training department.

Ms. Paragon has been an effective leader of the quality assurance task force. Under her direction, the MIS department has instituted a series of statistical analysis programs that have shown exceptional abilities to predict and prevent manufacturing failures. She also works well with the research and development department to integrate quality control into engineering specifications and manufacturing processes.

NEEDS IMPROVEMENT

Mr. Goodenough has not shown adequate skills to improve the overall quality of all of the company's products. Over the course of the past year, the percentage of returned merchandise and on-site warranty repairs has increased by 12 percent, representing a significant and unanticipated cost to the company.

Despite requests from the sales and marketing departments that the company seek and receive ISO-9000 and other quality certifications for the company's products, Mr. Goodenough has been unable to assist the manufacturing department in meeting these standards. As a result, the sales department reports it has been unable to sell products in certain markets.

Mr. Goodenough has not shown sufficient expertise in working with the research and development, manufacturing, sales, and marketing departments to build in a high level of quality in all products. If done properly, any added expense incurred in meeting these higher standards will be more than offset by reductions in the cost of returns and repairs. It is also expected that with ISO certification that the company will also be able to increase the price and profit for certain items. Increased quality should also permit the sales department to extend warranty periods and guarantees without significant costs to the company.

With this evaluation, Mr. Goodenough is directed to make ISO-9000 certification and an overall improvement in the quality of the company's products his highest priority. He is asked to convene, within 15 days, a task force including all affected departments and to report to the executive committee on the committee's progress every 30 days.

He needs to improve his commitment to keeping current on quality assurance engineering through courses and certification offered by professional associations. Mr. Goodenough should regularly attend trade shows and conventions.

Mr. Goodenough has not demonstrated a high level of cooperation with the manufacturing department in designing new inspection and testing processes. All products should undergo routine scheduled and random destructive and nondestructive testing. As part of this process, the manufacturing department should produce detailed reports on the acceptability of product, and any unusual increase in failures should be easily traced back to the quality of raw materials or problems with manufacturing procedures.

Mr. Goodenough must work closely and effectively with the warehouse department to test and monitor inventory to guard against spoilage and deterioration over time. With this evaluation, he is directed to meet with the warehouse manager within 15 days to begin this process and is asked to report to the head of manufacturing within 30 days with a report on progress in this area.

He needs to demonstrate a higher degree of commitment to the ongoing education and supervision of technicians in his department, working closely with the training department.

UNSATISFACTORY

Mr. Belowpar has failed to improve the overall quality of the company's products. Over the course of the past year, the percentage of returned merchandise and on-site warranty repairs has increased by 23 percent, representing a significant and unanticipated cost to the company. According to the customer service department, product failures are traceable to sloppy assembly and substandard components.

Mr. Belowpar has failed to assist the manufacturing department in obtaining ISO-9000 and other quality certifications for the company's products. This was a specific directive in his previous evaluation, and Mr. Belowpar is now directed to prepare a plan to accomplish this mission-critical objective and present it to the executive committee within 15 days.

The lack of this certification and problems with the quality of manufacture has resulted in significant lost business opportunities for the company.

Mr. Belowpar needs to greatly improve his ability to work with the research and development, manufacturing, sales, and marketing departments to build in a high level of quality in all products. It is the expectation of the marketing department that any added expense incurred in meeting higher standards will be more than offset by reductions in the cost of returns and repairs. Increased quality should also permit the sales department to extend warranty periods and guarantees without significant costs to the company.

Mr. Belowpar needs to improve his commitment to keeping current on quality assurance engineering through courses and certification offered by professional associations. Mr. Belowpar should regularly attend trade shows and conventions.

Mr. Belowpar failed to demonstrate sufficient cooperation with the manufacturing department in designing new inspection and testing processes. All products should undergo routine scheduled and random destructive and nondestructive testing, and under Mr. Belowpar's guidance, the manufacturing department should produce detailed reports on the acceptability of product. Any unusual increase in failures should be easily traced back to the quality of raw materials or problems with manufacturing procedures.

Mr. Belowpar is directed to make it a high priority to work closely and effectively with the warehouse department to test and monitor inventory to guard against spoilage and deterioration over time. With this evaluation, he is directed to meet with the warehouse manager within 15 days to begin this process and report to the head of manufacturing within 30 days with a report on progress in this area.

Field Service Representative

Appointment schedule
Configuration of equipment
Customer surveys
Field service
Installation of equipment
On-call service
Remote diagnostics
Technical assistance to sales force
Telephone support

MEETS OR EXCEEDS

Mr. Paragon has done an exemplary job as a field service representative over the past 12 months; for many of our customers, he is the face of the company, working directly with our users on installation, configuration, maintenance, upgrade, and repair of equipment. He has consistently received the highest marks in surveys of customers.

He provides excellent feedback to the sales force and the manufacturing department on problems experienced by customers and requests for new features and modifications. Some of his reports have led to significant changes in the product line that have resulted in cost savings through reduced failures and helped boost the competitive position of the company.

Mr. Paragon shows a high degree of cooperation in providing technical assistance to the sales force in configuring orders. When the sales contract calls for his participation in the installation of new equipment, he consistently delivers excellent service.

Over the course of the past year, he has never failed to respond rapidly to emergency repair assignments when he has been on-call; he has also filled in as the secondary field service representative when the on-call staffer is unavailable or otherwise unable to respond in a timely manner.

Mr. Paragon has shown exceptional skills in managing his appointment calendar in order to provide maintenance on a scheduled basis. In meeting with customers, he recommends replacement of parts to help prevent breakdowns and suggests upgrades that will improve performance and reliability when it is appropriate to do so.

He has kept up to date on the latest tools available to service equipment sold by the company, including remote diagnostics that can be performed from the home office or on the road. Use of these diagnostics can sometimes allow the customer to make repairs or swap parts without the need for a visit from the field service representative or improve the delivery of service by allowing new parts to be shipped before an on-site visit is made.

Mr. Paragon has provided valuable assistance to the company's telephone support department by sharing information found in the field and by responding to calls or e-mails forwarded from customers.

He has done an excellent job of keeping current on the company's products and services and also devotes the time to meet with the sales staff to learn about clients. He exhibits excellent interpersonal and communications skills.

NEEDS IMPROVEMENT

Mr. Goodenough needs to greatly improve his performance as a field service representative. For many of our customers, he is the face of the company, working directly with our users on installation, configuration, maintenance, upgrade, and repair of equipment. Over the past 12 months, he has generally received barely acceptable to acceptable marks in surveys of customers.

He is asked to provide better feedback to the sales force and the manufacturing department on problems experienced by customers and requests for new features and modifications. The job description for a field service representative calls for such regular contact to help improve the quality of our products, reduce costs due to failures, and boost the competitive position of the company.

Over the course of the past 12 months, Mr. Goodenough has not shown a significant effort to provide technical assistance to the sales force in configuring orders. He also needs to improve his ability to assist customers in the installation of new equipment when a sales contract provides for such involvement. He is asked to meet with the training department within 15 days to seek assistance in these matters.

On several occasions in the past year when he has been on call, he has not responded within the amount of time set forth in company guidelines for emergency repair assignments. He is directed to review the employee handbook; he will be re-evaluated on this issue in 60 days.

Mr. Goodenough must improve the management of his appointment calendar in order to better provide maintenance on a scheduled basis. He is directed to meet with the training department to receive instruction on company guidelines to recommend replacement of parts to help prevent breakdowns and suggest upgrades that will improve performance and reliability when it is appropriate to do so.

He is instructed to spend more time to learn about the latest tools available to service equipment sold by the company, including remote diagnostics that can be performed from the home office or on the road. Company guidelines call for field service representatives to attempt to assist customers to make repairs or swap parts without the need for a visit when possible or to use remote diagnostics to improve the delivery of service by allowing new parts to be shipped before an on-site visit is made.

Mr. Goodenough also needs to be more diligent in providing assistance to the company's telephone support department, sharing information found in the field and responding to calls or e-mails forwarded from customers.

He needs to become better acquainted with the company's products and services and to also devote sufficient time to meet with the sales staff to learn about clients.

UNSATISFACTORY

Ms. Belowpar has delivered disappointing performance as a field service representative over the course of the past 12 months. For many of our customers, she is the face of the company, working directly with our users on installation, configuration, maintenance, upgrade, and repair of equipment. She has consistently received unacceptably low marks in surveys of customers.

She is directed to provide better feedback to the sales force and the manufacturing department on problems experienced by customers and requests for new features and modifications. The job description for a field service representative calls for such regular contact to help improve the quality of our products, reduce costs due to failures, and boost the competitive position of the company. She will be re-evaluated on this matter in 60 days.

Ms. Belowpar has failed to deliver sufficient technical assistance to the sales force in configuring orders. She also needs to improve her ability to assist customers in the installation of new equipment when a sales contract provides for such involvement. She is directed to meet with the training department within 15 days to design a course of instruction in these matters.

On several occasions in the past year, she has failed to respond to emergency repair assignments when she was on call. She is directed to review the employee handbook and meet with the head of the service department within 10 days; she will be re-evaluated on this issue in 60 days.

Ms. Belowpar must improve the management of her appointment calendar in order to better provide maintenance on a scheduled basis.

She is instructed to make it a high priority to learn more about the latest tools available to service equipment sold by the company, including remote diagnostics that can be performed from the home office or on the road. Company guidelines call for field service representatives to attempt to assist customers to make repairs or swap parts without the need for a visit when possible or to use remote diagnostics to improve the delivery of service by allowing new parts to be shipped before an on-site visit is made. She is directed to seek appropriate instruction through the training department and from professional associations.

Ms. Belowpar must be more diligent in providing assistance to the company's telephone support department, sharing information found in the field and responding to calls or e-mails forwarded from customers. She is directed to meet with the head of the telephone support department within 15 days to discuss their needs and develop a plan to respond to requests in a timely manner.

She needs to become better acquainted with the company's products and services and to also devote sufficient time to meet with the sales staff to learn about clients.

CHAPTER 5

PURCHASING, WAREHOUSING, AND SHIPPING

Purchasing Manager

Warehouse Manager

Stockroom Manager

Shipping Manager

Delivery Driver

Purchasing Manager

Bulk contracts for supplies and materials
Electronic tracking of purchases
Employee manual
Flexibility on purchasing decisions
Inventory levels
ISO-9000
Just-in-time inventory
Purchasing department
Quality standards
Renegotiate contracts and bids
Reorganizing purchasing department
Request for bids
Request for proposals
Spending levels
Unanticipated spending

MEETS OR EXCEEDS

Mr. Paragon has performed an exceptional job of reorganizing and modernizing the purchasing department. Under his leadership, average costs for nearly every material and service necessary for the functioning of the company have gone down or have risen at a level below the rate of inflation.

He has made an extraordinary effort in working closely with all department heads to help locate low-cost sources for commodities and supplies and to negotiate bulk contracts as appropriate.

The purchasing department, under Mr. Paragon's supervision, redesigned the company's purchasing procedures outlined in the employee manual to make the most efficient use of his department's expertise while offering department heads much-needed flexibility to make certain purchases at their own discretion. He was of particular help in assuring that the price level for items and services requiring the involvement of the purchasing department was made to match the needs of individual departments and the seniority of department heads.

Working with the legal and accounting departments, Mr. Paragon performed an exemplary service in updating the company's policies on seeking bids and proposals for services and products. The resulting forms were added to the company intranet so that they could be reviewed by various departments.

As directed by the executive committee, major purchases now require three competitive bids or an exemption approved by a senior vice president.

Mr. Paragon led the way in the process for electronic tracking of purchases, comparing expenditure levels to departmental budgets and issuing automated warnings to flag unanticipated or overly high spending in a particular period of time.

Mr. Paragon has initiated a highly effective program to review all contracts and bid prices on a regular basis; suppliers have been asked to renegotiate prices on products when competitive conditions have resulted in potential cost savings. The contract review committee has also extended its attention to elements of agreements beyond just the price; suppliers are asked to offer the lowest possible shipping costs and payment terms and offer the highest levels of customer support.

Working together with the warehouse manager, Mr. Paragon has implemented and regularly reviewed a just-in-time delivery scheme that reduces inventory and storage costs and cuts down on spoilage and waste.

Mr. Paragon has kept up to date on purchasing procedures and the products commonly bought by the company through his membership in professional associations, attendance at conventions, and online research.

Under his management, the purchasing department regularly meets with the manufacturing, engineering, and customer support departments to assure that products meet necessary levels of quality, including adherence to ISO-9000 standards as appropriate.

NEEDS IMPROVEMENT

Ms. Goodenough has lagged behind expectations in reorganizing and modernizing the purchasing department. Under her leadership, average costs for materials and services necessary for the functioning of the company have risen above budgetary plans.

She needs to redouble her efforts to work more closely with department heads to locate low-cost sources for commodities and supplies and to negotiate bulk contracts as appropriate.

The purchasing department, under Ms. Goodenough's supervision, was directed six months ago to redesign the company's purchasing procedures in the employee manual, but this task has not yet been accomplished.

Similarly, Ms. Goodenough was personally directed at her previous evaluation to work with the legal and accounting departments to update company policies on seeking bids and proposals for services and products. This needs to be a high priority for completion within the next 60 days.

The executive committee instructed Ms. Goodenough to lead a task force to develop a process to track by computer all major purchases and compare expenditure levels to departmental budgets. When implemented, the system is expected to issue automated warnings to flag unanticipated or overly high spending in a particular period of time.

Ms. Goodenough needs to improve her ability to review all contracts and bid prices on a regular basis; suppliers should be asked to renegotiate prices on products when competitive conditions have resulted in potential cost savings.

Another uncompleted assignment is the implementation of a just-in-time delivery scheme that reduces inventory and storage costs and cuts down on spoilage and waste.

Ms. Goodenough needs to improve her education on current purchasing procedures and the products commonly bought by the company; it is suggested that she join professional associations, attend conventions as appropriate, and pursue available training courses.

UNSATISFACTORY

Mr. Belowpar has not met expectations in reorganizing and modernizing the purchasing department. According to an analysis made by the accounting department, costs for materials and services necessary for the functioning of the company have risen significantly above industry averages.

Mr. Belowpar has been directed by the executive committee to convene a task force with department heads to seek an immediate and long-term reduction in costs, in line with the prices paid by similar companies and our direct competitors.

The executive committee instructed Mr. Belowpar to lead an initiative to develop a process to track by computer all major purchases and compare expenditure levels to departmental budgets. This system has not been implemented and should be considered an immediate high priority assignment; the committee has asked for a progress report within 15 days and expects completion within 60 days.

Mr. Belowpar has failed to set up a process to review all contracts and bid prices on a regular basis in search of cost savings.

Mr. Belowpar has not demonstrated a commitment to keeping up to date on current purchasing procedures and the products commonly bought by the company. He is directed to meet with the training department to explore available courses and professional associations.

Warehouse Manager

Bar codes
Facilities management
Inventory reports
Occupational safety
OSHA
Pilferage
Real-time inventory tracking
RF tagging
Warehouse facilities

MEETS OR EXCEEDS

Ms. Paragon has performed well above expectations as manager of the warehouse facility. She has demonstrated excellent cooperation with sales and manufacturing departments and has effectively dealt with previous problems of environmental controls and security.

Her principal contribution over the past three years has been the migration from manual accounting of finished product held in the warehouse to the institution of bar codes and other machine-readable ID tags. She is currently making a major contribution to the company as chairperson of the task force preparing for the conversion to RF tagging of all manufactured equipment.

Once implemented, RF tagging will permit real-time tracking of all types of equipment in the warehouse and such details as date of manufacture, serial number, mix of components, and location. Under Ms. Paragon's leadership, the company will, for the first time, be able to compute the exact cost of manufacture and storage for each individual item in the warehouse.

She has demonstrated a high degree of cooperation with the MIS department in the development of customized inventory reports and their availability to sales, marketing, manufacturing, and accounting departments.

Ms. Paragon has shown keen understanding of her role in the sales process, keeping in regular communication with sales and manufacturing departments to assure that the warehouse has sufficient product to meet expected orders and to advise when particular product lines are in overstock.

Ms. Paragon has effectively dealt with previous problems with the warehouse by working closely with the facilities management department to assure that the warehouse is maintained at acceptable levels of temperature and humidity. She has also shown great skill in working with the security department to reduce pilferage, a process that will be accelerated through the use of RF tags.

Ms. Paragon has worked well with the training department to insure availability of training on the use of forklifts and other equipment used in the warehouse; she has coordinated all efforts with the legal and government affairs departments for compliance with occupational safety regulations.

NEEDS IMPROVEMENT

Ms. Goodenough needs to improve her skills and training in order to better manage the warehouse facility. She must improve the level of cooperation with the sales and manufacturing departments.

She has struggled to adapt to recent changes in tracking procedures at the warehouse as the company has migrated from manual accounting of finished product to the institution of bar codes and other machine-readable ID tags. She needs to improve her understanding of RF tagging technology in order to make a meaningful contribution to the company as a member of the task force studying implementation of this technology.

Ms. Goodenough has fallen behind on requests from the sales, marketing, manufacturing, and accounting departments to develop and distribute customized inventory reports. With this evaluation, Ms. Goodenough is instructed to meet with the affected departments within 15 days and produce a reasonable schedule for delivery of the requested reports.

A key assignment for the warehouse manager is an understanding of her role in the sales process. Ms. Goodenough has not demonstrated a commitment to regular communication with the sales and manufacturing departments to assure that the warehouse has sufficient product to meet expected orders and to advise when particular product lines are in overstock.

When Ms. Goodenough assumed responsibility for management of the warehouse, she was advised of previous problems with leaks due to melting snow. In the ensuing six months, she has not made adequate progress in arranging for repair of the roof; with this evaluation, she is directed to meet with the facilities management department within 10 days to arrange for temporary and permanent solutions to this situation.

The warehouse continues to experience instances of pilferage and unaccounted for product; Ms. Goodenough is directed to meet with the security department within 10 days to develop a plan for improvements to locks, alarm systems, and watchkeeping.

Ms. Goodenough has cooperated with the training department to insure availability of training on the use of forklifts and other equipment used in the warehouse; however, a recent minor accident in the warehouse resulted in a finding by the Occupational Safety and Health Administration of several technical violations. With this evaluation, Ms. Goodenough is instructed to meet with the government relations department to assure full compliance with state and federal regulations.

UNSATISFACTORY

Mr. Belowpar has not shown himself to be an effective manager of the warehouse facility. He lacks current knowledge of the company's products, sales efforts, and warehouse procedures. He must also improve the level of cooperation with the sales and manufacturing departments.

According to the manufacturing department head—who is also a member with Mr. Belowpar of the task force set up by the executive committee for this purpose—he has resisted efforts to institute RF tagging of finished equipment stored in the warehouse.

Mr. Belowpar has failed to deliver customized inventory reports requested by the sales, marketing, manufacturing, and accounting departments at the time of his previous evaluation. He is directed to meet with the affected departments within 15 days and produce a reasonable schedule for delivery of the requested reports.

Several times in the past three months the warehouse has run out of stock ordered by major customers; in these instances, Mr. Belowpar failed to give advance warning to the sales and manufacturing departments to assure that the warehouse did not have sufficient product to meet orders. With this evaluation, Mr. Belowpar is directed to meet with the sales and manufacturing department heads to review procedures and reports.

The recent loss of $25,000 in inventory due to water damage in the warehouse could have been prevented by proper attention to maintenance issues. Mr. Belowpar was advised of the possibility of problems with the roof six months ago but failed to address the problem in a timely manner. Although that situation has been fixed, with this evaluation Mr. Belowpar is directed to meet with the facilities management department within 10 days to arrange for a survey of the condition of the entire facility.

Stockroom Manager

Bar coding
Bulk purchases
Computer tracking of inventory
Employee handbook
Facilities management
Pilferage and loss
Purchasing department
RF tagging
Stockroom

MEETS OR EXCEEDS

Mr. Paragon has demonstrated exceptional skills in managing stockroom operations. He has shown a high degree of organization and a commitment to company goals in serving our employees in overseeing the stockroom for office supplies and equipment and a separate facility that holds materials for the manufacturing line.

Working together with the MIS department, he has introduced bar coding and tracking software that allows instant location of items in the stockroom and permits the purchasing department to anticipate needs before shortages occur. Mr. Paragon has also shown a great deal of enthusiasm and understanding of the ongoing transition to RF tagging of items and products throughout the enterprise.

The use of the computer tracking and inventory system has substantially reduced excessive orders for certain items and permitted the implementation of a "just-in-time" delivery system that has saved the enterprise a significant amount of money. In doing so, Mr. Paragon has changed the role of the stockroom from a cost center to a division that can actively participate in holding down overall expenses of the company.

On his own initiative, Mr. Paragon has worked with facilities management to redesign the storage system in the stockrooms to make more efficient use of the space; this is an added benefit of the use of computer tracking of inventory.

Mr. Paragon has coordinated efforts with the shipping and receiving department, anticipating the arrival of large deliveries and making preparations for immediate acceptance and distribution of supplies ordered by departments.

He has worked very closely and effectively with the purchasing department to help negotiate contracts for bulk purchases of certain items and to otherwise seek low-cost sources for equipment and supplies on an as-needed basis.

He keeps current on trends and technologies in his field, attends trade shows and conventions dealing with office supplies and equipment, and coordinates his efforts with the buyer for the manufacturing department. Working with the training department, he has overseen the creation of a series of training courses for stockroom employees and has set up programs for advanced education through a nearby technical college.

Under his management the incidence of pilferage and loss has declined substantially. Employees are no longer permitted to "shop" the aisles of the stockroom and must instead requisition items through the online catalog or place orders for unusual items through the purchasing department. All orders above $200 in value require countersignature from a supervisor, and department heads are automatically notified of any unanticipated expenditures above budget lines.

He has done an excellent job in coordinating the operations of the stockroom with procedures instituted by the security department. As part of this effort, one staffer of the stockroom is on call 24 hours a day to respond to any emergency call for mission-critical supplies or raw materials.

Mr. Paragon has kept the human resources department apprised of changes in procedures so that they may be included in the employee handbook.

NEEDS IMPROVEMENT

Ms. Goodenough has not shown adequate skills in managing stockroom operations. Because materials and supplies are not organized well, there have been numerous instances of shortages of some important items and costly and wasteful oversupply of others.

Despite recommendations from the MIS department to introduce bar coding and tracking software to allow instant location of items in the stockroom, Ms. Goodenough has not done so. With this evaluation, she is directed to meet with the head of the MIS department within 30 days to begin planning such a system and to prepare for the companywide integration of RF tagging for all items and products.

Once a computerized inventory system is in place, Ms. Goodenough is directed to work with the purchasing department to institute a just-in-time delivery system for supplies and equipment, as appropriate. It is anticipated that this system will help the stockroom actively participate in holding down overall expenses of the company.

Ms. Goodenough has asked for additional storage rooms to hold supplies; before the company undertakes this expensive capital cost, she is asked to work with facilities management to seek ways to redesign the storage system in the stockrooms to make more efficient use of the current space. The addition of computerized inventory will assist in this reorganization effort.

Ms. Goodenough needs to coordinate her department's efforts with shipping and receiving to avoid instances where large deliveries arrived on the loading dock before space was made available in the stockrooms.

As part of the companywide effort to reduce costs, Ms. Goodenough is asked to work with the purchasing department to help negotiate contracts for bulk purchases of certain items and to otherwise seek low-cost sources for equipment and supplies on an as-needed basis.

Ms. Goodenough needs to keep current on trends and technologies in her field, attend trade shows and conventions dealing with office supplies and equipment, and coordinate her efforts with the buyer for the manufacturing department. Working with the training department, she is asked to assist in the creation of a series of training courses for stockroom employees and set up programs for advanced education through a nearby technical college.

The incidence of pilferage and loss has been unacceptably high over the course of the past year. With this evaluation, Ms. Goodenough is asked to meet with the security department within 15 days to develop a plan to better protect company assets. In addition, she is asked to meet with the purchasing department to institute new rules for the requisition of supplies including requiring countersignature from a supervisor and automatic notification to department heads of any unanticipated expenditures above budget lines. Once the new rules are promulgated, Ms. Goodenough is asked to inform the human resources department so that the changes in procedures may be included in the employee handbook.

UNSATISFACTORY

Mr. Belowpar has failed to manage the stockroom in an acceptable manner. Materials and supplies are highly disorganized, and there have been numerous instances of shortages of some important items and costly and wasteful oversupply of others.

In his most recent evaluation, Mr. Belowpar was instructed to work with the MIS department to introduce bar coding and tracking software to allow instant location of items in the stockroom. This has not been accomplished. He is now directed to meet with the head of the MIS department within 10 days to begin planning such a system. It is the expectation of the executive committee that computerized tracking of inventory be accomplished within 120 days.

Once a computerized inventory system is in place, Mr. Belowpar is directed to work with the purchasing department to institute a just-in-time delivery system for supplies and equipment, as appropriate. Mr. Belowpar is directed to meet with the purchasing department to develop plans for this change in ordering procedures within 90 days.

Mr. Belowpar has not followed through on recommendations to coordinate his department's efforts with shipping and receiving to avoid instances where large deliveries arrive on the loading dock before space is made available in the stockrooms. With this evaluation, Mr. Belowpar is directed to meet with the head of shipping and receiving within 30 days to immediately institute a system for regular communication between the departments.

As part of the companywide effort to reduce costs, Mr. Belowpar is directed to meet with a representative of the purchasing department to seek assistance in the negotiation of contracts for bulk purchases of certain items and to otherwise find low-cost sources for equipment and supplies on an as-needed basis.

Mr. Belowpar has not demonstrated a commitment to keeping current on trends and technologies in his field. He is asked to attend trade shows and conventions dealing with office supplies and equipment and coordinate his efforts with the buyer for the manufacturing department. Further, he is directed to work with the training department to assist in the creation of a series of training courses for stockroom employees and set up programs for advanced education through a nearby technical college.

With this evaluation, Mr. Belowpar is directed to meet with the security department within 15 days to develop a plan to better protect company assets from pilferage and loss. He is also directed to meet with the purchasing department within 30 days to institute new rules for the requisition of supplies including requiring countersignature from a supervisor and automatic notification to department heads of any unanticipated expenditures above budget lines. Once the new rules are promulgated, Mr. Belowpar is asked to inform the human resources department so that the changes in procedures may be included in the employee handbook.

Shipping Manager

Bills of lading
Common carriers
Courier services
Federal Express
Ground transportation
Occupational safety
OSHA
Overnight shippers
Packing materials
Service bureau
Tracking orders
Trucking companies
UPS

MEETS OR EXCEEDS

Ms. Paragon has exhibited a high degree of professionalism and attention to detail in her management of the shipping department. This sector of the company operates as a service bureau to the manufacturing and sales departments, and directors have reported great satisfaction with her abilities.

Over the course of the previous 12 months, Ms. Paragon has expanded the number of shipping options for all products, including low-cost ground transportation and highly reliable overnight delivery of rush orders. She has successfully negotiated bulk discount contracts with several major shippers including Federal Express and UPS.

Ms. Paragon has proven to be very flexible in dealing with special requests from customers including specific routing and the use of common carriers or particular trucking companies of their preference.

Working with two of the major overnight shipping companies, she has been able to improve the company's ability to send product to international destinations while removing the extra cost and time delay that had previously existed because of the use of a third-party customs expediter.

Under her management, the shipping department has begun short, weekly briefing sessions with the sales and manufacturing departments to learn about upcoming major shipments well in advance of their arrival in the shipping department. This has allowed the use of less-costly temporary help to handle unusually large volumes of shipments instead of adding full-time employees.

Ms. Paragon has worked closely with the training department to assure the availability of courses and special instruction to improve her staff's ability to prepare accurate bills of lading, compare them to invoices, and work with computer systems and forms required by shipping companies. The staff has also received appropriate training from vendors in the use of power equipment including forklifts, palletizers, and shrink-wrap devices. She has done an excellent job of informing the legal and human resources departments about the operations of this equipment in order to assure compliance with OSHA and other occupational safety agencies.

Under Ms. Paragon's management, the shipping department has greatly improved its ability to trace lost shipments and to deal with claims for damage received en route. Negotiated agreements with shippers allow the company to immediately resend orders without having to wait for the results of investigations.

On her own initiative, Ms. Paragon has convened a task force to investigate prepositioning products in warehouses maintained by several national shipping companies around the nation; this allows for rapid dispatch of equipment on short notice.

Ms. Paragon has demonstrated an outstanding commitment to understanding all of the company's products, working to assure that shipping equipment, packing material, and carriers are all capable of handling product properly. She has also kept up to date on current shipping trends and technologies, attending trade shows and conventions, and obtaining certification from professional organizations to support her in her work.

NEEDS IMPROVEMENT

Mr. Goodenough needs to improve his attention to detail in his management of the shipping department. This sector of the company operates as a service bureau to the manufacturing and sales departments, and directors have expressed concern about delays in delivering product to customers and several recent instances of damage en route.

Mr. Goodenough must expand the number of shipping options for all products, including low-cost ground transportation and overnight delivery of rush orders. In addition, he needs to work with the purchasing and legal departments to negotiate bulk discount contracts with major shippers including Federal Express and UPS. With this evaluation, he is directed to prepare a plan for new shipping options and present it to the head of the sales department within 15 days.

Mr. Goodenough also needs to become more flexible in dealing with special requests from customers including specific routing and the use of common carriers or particular trucking companies of their preference.

An area of particular concern to the sales department is a pattern of significant delays and unanticipated expenses for international shipments. In his last evaluation, Mr. Goodenough was asked to seek alternatives to the company's current international freight forwarder; as of this date, no such change has been made. With this evaluation, Mr. Goodenough is directed to prepare suggestions for changes in international shipping practices within 15 days and present them to the sales department at that time.

Under his management, the department has not adequately anticipated seasonal and other variations in shipping patterns, resulting in backlogs and delays or excessive staffing during slow periods. Mr. Goodenough is directed to meet with the sales and manufacturing departments once a week to learn about upcoming major shipments and to explore the use of less-costly temporary help to handle unusually large volumes of shipments instead of adding full-time employees.

Mr. Goodenough has not sought the assistance of the training department for courses and special instruction to improve his staff's ability to prepare accurate bills of lading, compare them to invoices, and work with computer systems and forms required by shipping companies. The staff should also be receiving appropriate training from vendors in the use of power equipment including forklifts, palletizers, and shrink-wrap devices; with this evaluation he is directed to meet with the legal and human resources departments to assure compliance with OSHA and other occupational safety agencies.

Under Mr. Goodenough's management, the shipping department has not taken advantage of available Internet tools to trace lost shipments and deal with claims for damage received en route. He is asked to make this a high priority for accomplishment within the next 30 days.

Mr. Goodenough has not shown a commitment to understanding all of the company's products and their specific needs for shipping equipment, packing material, and special carriers. He should make a better effort to keep up to date on current shipping trends and technologies, attend trade shows and conventions, and obtain certification from professional organizations to support his job performance.

UNSATISFACTORY

Ms. Belowpar has failed to devote adequate attention to detail in management of the shipping department. The sales department has expressed concern about significant delays in delivering product, damage en route, and improper packing of delicate items.

Despite specific requests for more options, Ms. Belowpar has failed to add other common carriers and specialized delivery services to the companies that have been used for the past decade. With this evaluation, she is directed to work with the purchasing and legal departments to negotiate bulk discount contracts with major shippers including Federal Express and UPS and alternative trucking companies; a plan for new shipping options is to be presented to the head of the sales department within 15 days.

Ms. Belowpar has failed to demonstrate flexibility in dealing with special requests from customers including specific routing and the use of common carriers or particular trucking companies of their preference.

The company has experienced significant unanticipated costs and lost business in dealing with overseas customers. Ms. Belowpar is directed to seek alternatives to the company's current international freight forwarder, including the use of services offered by major courier services including UPS and Federal Express. With this evaluation, Ms. Belowpar is directed to prepare a plan to completely overhaul international shipping practices within 30 days and present it to the sales department at that time.

Ms. Belowpar is directed to seek the assistance of the training department for courses and special instruction to improve the quality of her staff's work in preparing accurate bills of lading and working with computer systems and forms required by shipping companies.

The legal and human resources departments have expressed serious concern about the type and quality of training given employees in the use of power equipment including forklifts, palletizers, and shrink-wrap devices; with this evaluation, she is directed to meet with these departments to assure compliance with OSHA and other occupational safety agencies.

Ms. Belowpar does not have a clear understanding of all of the company's products and their specific needs for shipping equipment, packing material, and special carriers. With this evaluation, she is directed to make this a high priority for the next 60 days. Further, she is directed to meet with the training department to develop a plan to keep up to date on current shipping trends and technologies, attend trade shows and conventions, and obtain certification from professional organizations to support her in her work.

Delivery Driver

Alcohol testing
Automated external defibrillator
Commercial driver's license
Driving record
Drug testing
First aid
Moving violations
Pickups
Vehicle maintenance

MEETS OR EXCEEDS

Mr. Paragon has been an exemplary employee, representing the company very well as a driver making local pickups and deliveries and moving equipment and supplies between company facilities.

He has maintained a perfect driving record, well exceeding the minimum guidelines of no more than three moving violations in a three-year period set forth in the employee manual and as required by the company's insurance carrier. He has nevertheless sought out regular training through courses offered by professional driving schools and associations.

On his own initiative, Mr. Paragon has also received emergency first aid and first responder training, and the company has equipped his vehicle with an automated external defibrillator and advanced medical supplies, adding another level of protection for employees, clients, and visitors.

Mr. Paragon has demonstrated a high degree of responsibility in assuring that his company vehicle receives regular and preventive maintenance. He is also highly reliable in coordinating with the office services department to ensure the vehicle is properly registered and inspected and to demonstrate the driver's continued licensure as a commercial driver.

NEEDS IMPROVEMENT

Ms. Goodenough needs to improve her skills as a driver to better represent the company in making local pickups and deliveries and moving equipment and supplies between company facilities.

She has been involved in a minor accident and received two moving violations in the past year, which puts her at risk of dismissal or reassignment according to the guidelines set forth in the employee manual and as required by the company's insurance carrier. Working through the training department, she has been taking training courses offered by professional driving schools and associations.

Ms. Goodenough needs to work more closely with the office services department to assure that her company vehicle receives regular and preventive maintenance; the vehicle was cited for a nonfunctioning turn signal in a recent accident report.

UNSATISFACTORY

Mr. Belowpar has been temporarily reassigned to a clerical position while he is enrolled in remedial driving courses recommended by the training department. He needs to greatly improve his skills and receive insurance company certification as a driver before he will be permitted to resume duties making local pickups and deliveries and moving equipment and supplies between company facilities.

After two accidents and three moving violations in just under three years of service, Mr. Belowpar must fully cooperate with company policy and rules set by its insurance carrier, including unscheduled tests for drug and alcohol use.

Mr. Belowpar also needs to demonstrate his reliability in assuring that his company vehicle receives regular and preventive maintenance; the vehicle was cited for a nonfunctioning turn signal in a recent accident report.

He is also highly unreliable in coordinating with the office services department to ensure the vehicle is properly registered and inspected and to demonstrate the driver's continued licensure as a commercial driver.

CHAPTER 6

HUMAN RESOURCES

Human Resources Director

Benefits Manager

Training and Employee Development Director

Relocation Specialist

Human Resources Director

ADA (Americans with Disabilities Act)
Assisting department heads in hiring process
Boost performance levels
Discrimination
Downsizing
Employee evaluations
Employment
Identify and reward superior employees
Layoffs
Open-door policy
Outplacement
Promotion and advancement
Recruiting and screening job applicants
Revise employee handbook
Sexual harassment
Team player
Telecommuting program
Termination of employee
Training on equal opportunity hiring
Understanding company goals

MEETS OR EXCEEDS

Ms. Paragon does an excellent job of supporting company goals through recruiting and screening applicants for open positions as well as building a database of qualified candidates who have sent unsolicited inquiries about employment.

She has also shown a great depth of understanding of company goals, structure, and ongoing projects in assisting department heads in the hiring process.

Working with department heads and managers, she has helped set up a system to better identify and reward employees who have made significant contributions to the company or who have improved their skill sets and experiences.

Ms. Paragon shows herself to be an outstanding team player in working with department heads as they conduct annual employee evaluations.

Under her direction, the human resources department demonstrates exceptional skills in assisting managers to develop programs to boost the performance levels of staff in need of improvement or delivering unsatisfactory performance.

When necessary, she exhibits great professionalism and appropriate levels of compassion in dealing with employees who must be terminated.

When the company was forced to downsize its on-site maintenance department, Ms. Paragon led the effort to match as many employees as possible with open positions elsewhere in the company and coordinated the company's relations with an outplacement firm that successfully assisted most of the other affected workers.

She shows an exemplary commitment to the corporate mission statement in her work as chairperson of the committee to revise the employee handbook. The committee solicited input from executives, supervisors, and staff at all levels in the process of updating the handbook.

According to reports from our corporate legal department, Ms. Paragon has implemented an effective training program on state and federal equal opportunity hiring requirements.

She promises and delivers an open-door policy for all employees to discuss promotion and advancement opportunities.

Working with a task force set up with the MIS, payroll, and benefits manage_____ _____ ____ ___ ___ __ _____ __ _____ uccessful telecommuting prog_____ _____ _____ _____ _____ _____ rings for the company. At the sa_____ _____ _____ _____ _____ marks to measure the perform_____ _____ _____ _____ ___ the direct supervision of their _____

One _____ _____ _____ _____ _____ te on state and federal regulati_____ _____ _____ _____ ____ ment, discrimination, sexual h_____ _____ _____ _____ nericans with Disabilities Act) _____ _____ _____ gal staff in monitoring these ar_____ _____ _____ se mechanism to deal with any_____

NEEDS IMPRO

Ms. Goo_____ _____ _____ _____ mpany goals through recruiting _____ _____ _____ s. The department has yet to build a useable database of qualified candidates who have sent unsolicited inquiries about employment.

She needs to demonstrate a greater depth of understanding of company goals, structure, and ongoing projects in assisting department heads in the hiring process.

Department heads and managers have asked her to help set up a system to better identify and reward employees who have made significant contributions to the company or who have improved their skill sets and experiences. As of this date, this critical component of the mission statement has not yet been fulfilled.

Ms. Goodenough needs to sharpen her communications skills to be better able to work with department heads as they conduct annual employee evaluations. Throughout the company, managers seek assistance in developing programs to boost the performance levels of staff in need of improvement or delivering unsatisfactory performance.

When necessary, she exhibits appropriate levels of professionalism and compassion in dealing with employees who must be terminated.

When the company was forced to downsize its on-site maintenance department, Ms. Goodenough participated in creating a program to match as many employees as possible with open positions elsewhere in the company. If such a situation occurs again, department heads have asked the company to work with an outplacement firm to assist other affected workers.

As a participant in the committee to revise the employee handbook, Ms. Goodenough could have been more involved in soliciting input from executives, supervisors, and staff at all levels.

According to reports from our corporate legal department, Ms. Goodenough has begun to implement a training program on state and federal equal opportunity hiring requirements. This will be an area in which we will focus our attention in Ms. Goodenough's next review.

This employee should be more accommodating in dealing with employees seeking to discuss promotion and advancement opportunities.

Working with a task force set up with the MIS, payroll, and benefits managers, Ms. Goodenough offered only minimal assistance in creating a telecommuting program that holds the potential for significant cost savings for the company. She has been asked by the task force to help establish realistic benchmarks to measure the performance of telecommuters who are not under the direct supervision of their managers.

Ms. Goodenough needs to improve her coordination with in-house legal staff in monitoring state and federal regulations and court rulings in the areas of employment, discrimination, sexual harassment, and compliance with the ADA (Americans with Disabilities Act).

UNSATISFACTORY

Mr. Belowpar has failed to support company goals through recruiting and screening applicants for open positions. There is an unacceptable backlog of open positions, and department heads have complained of being asked to meet with applicants who have inadequate or inappropriate training and experience.

Despite requests for a database of qualified candidates who have sent unsolicited inquiries about employment, no such file has been created.

In general, Mr. Belowpar has not demonstrated a sufficient understanding of company goals, structure, and ongoing projects in assisting department heads in the hiring process.

Department heads and managers have reported to executive management the lack of a system to better identify and reward employees who have made significant contributions to the company or who have improved their skill sets and experiences. Mr. Belowpar was asked to address this during his most recent employee evaluation; as of this date, this critical component of the mission statement has not yet been fulfilled.

Mr. Belowpar does not exhibit adequate communications skills essential to working with department heads as they conduct annual employee evaluations. Throughout the company, managers seek assistance in developing programs to boost the performance levels of staff in need of improvement or delivering unsatisfactory performance.

Department heads have expressed concern about inappropriate comments and an unprofessional attitude in dealing with employees who must be terminated.

When the company was forced to downsize its on-site maintenance department, Mr. Belowpar was unable to create a program to match as many employees as possible with open positions elsewhere in the company, resulting in the loss of a number of valued staffers.

Mr. Belowpar was asked by the corporate legal department to implement a training program on state and federal equal opportunity hiring requirements. The resulting program is behind schedule and below expectations.

It has been brought to Mr. Belowpar's attention on numerous occasions that employees have concerns about approaching him to discuss promotion and advancement opportunities. With this evaluation, he is directed to meet with the executive committee to explore ways to better deal with this mission-critical issue.

Despite a written request from his supervisor, Mr. Belowpar did not participate in a task force set up with the MIS, payroll, and benefits managers seeking to create a telecommuting program that holds the potential for significant cost savings for the company.

Mr. Belowpar has demonstrated minimal coordination with in-house legal staff in monitoring state and federal regulations and court rulings in the areas of employment, discrimination, sexual harassment, and compliance with the ADA (Americans with Disabilities Act).

Benefits Manager

Attention to detail
Attention to the bottom line
Attracts high-quality applicants
Benefit packages
Bereavement leave
Cafeteria
Claims for insurance
College scholarship program
Cost control, benefits
Day care center
Discretion on personal issues
Employee discount program
Employee handbook
Family and Medical Leave Act
Health and fitness centers
Holidays
Insurance plans
Vacations
Workers' compensation

MEETS OR EXCEEDS

Mr. Paragon has been instrumental in designing and keeping current a set of benefits that enhances the lives of our employees, helps retain valuable workers, and attracts high-quality applicants for open positions in the company. At the same time, he has been diligent in working with benefits suppliers to keep costs in line with company goals.

A critical element of this job is keeping current on changing offerings from insurance and benefit providers. Mr. Paragon has demonstrated exceptional attention to the bottom line, while maintaining a high level of benefits for the employees.

Mr. Paragon demonstrates exemplary attention to detail in managing programs including health insurance, dental plans, disability insurance, and workers' compensation coverage. Employee surveys have indicated great satisfaction with information sessions about benefits, a program initiated by Mr. Paragon.

He successfully oversees implementation of company policies regarding bereavement leave, the Family and Medical Leave Act, and vacation and holiday time off.

Under his management, the benefits office has improved the delivery of 401(k), pension, and employee stock purchase programs.

Mr. Paragon worked closely with human resources and training departments to coordinate the tuition reimbursement benefit offered to employees; this initiative has resulted in improving the quality of work performed by staffers and opening new pathways to advancement.

Mr. Paragon responded quickly and effectively to management's request to develop a college scholarship program for dependents of full-time employees. He set up a committee of employees and department heads to establish criteria for scholarships and to review applications.

The benefits office, under Mr. Paragon's direction, has expanded ancillary benefits offered in cooperation with area businesses and associations and business partners of the company, including a vision discount program, group home and auto insurance discounts, and health and fitness center memberships. Working closely with the sales department, the benefits office has enhanced the employee discount program, allowing purchase of new and refurbished products.

At the request of employees, Mr. Paragon set up a task force to investigate establishing a subsidized on-site day care center, company cafeteria, and exercise room. The group's report will be reviewed by the executive committee when it is completed.

Mr. Paragon is consistently up to date on state and federal mandates for benefits for existing and former employees.

He exhibits appropriate discretion in discussing personal issues related to benefits. Based on survey reports, he works well on behalf of employees in pursuing payment of claims and in filing appeals for denial of service.

He maintains an excellent working relationship with the human resources department to keep current the employee handbook and conduct orientation sessions with new staffers to explain benefits.

NEEDS IMPROVEMENT

Mr. Goodenough needs to improve his ability to maintain a set of benefits that enhances the lives of our employees, helps retain valuable workers, and attracts high-quality applicants for open positions in the company. Some department heads have expressed concern about being at a competitive disadvantage to other area companies in a comparison of health and pension benefits.

Costs for the existing package of benefits have risen at a higher rate than expected, and executive management has directed Mr. Goodenough to seek ways to keep expenses in line with company goals.

A critical element of this job is keeping current on changing offerings from insurance and benefit providers. Mr. Goodenough has not yet demonstrated sufficient levels of attention to the bottom line, while maintaining a high level of benefits for the employees.

Based on employee surveys, Mr. Goodenough needs to better manage implementation of company policies regarding bereavement leave, the Family and Medical Leave Act, and vacation and holiday time off. With this evaluation, he has been asked to submit a plan to the executive committee that includes clarification of all personal leave policies.

Progress on the implementation of a tuition reimbursement benefit for current employees has not met the schedule put forth by the executive committee. Mr. Goodenough is directed to work more closely with the human resources and training departments to coordinate this benefit.

Mr. Goodenough has not responded in a timely manner to a management directive calling for the development of a college scholarship program for dependents of full-time employees. The program will require establishment of a committee of employees and department heads to set criteria for scholarships and review applications.

The benefits office, under Mr. Goodenough's direction, has been instructed to expand ancillary benefits offered in cooperation with area businesses and associations and business partners of the company, including a vision discount program, group home and auto insurance discounts, and health and fitness center memberships. As of this date, progress is below expectations.

Mr. Goodenough needs to spend more time bringing himself up to date on state and federal mandates for benefits for existing and former employees. The legal department has been asked to assist in development of a systematic effort in this area.

Although he exhibits appropriate discretion in discussing personal issues related to benefits, some employees have reported a lack of follow-through in pursuing payment of claims and in filing appeals for denial of service.

Mr. Goodenough needs to establish a better working relationship with the human resources department to keep current the employee handbook and conduct orientation sessions with new staffers to explain benefits.

UNSATISFACTORY

Ms. Belowpar has failed to maintain a set of benefits that enhances the lives of our employees, helps retain valuable workers, and attracts high-quality applicants for open positions in the company. As part of this evaluation, she is directed to produce a new plan within 30 days that meets company goals for benefits and cost.

Costs for the existing package of benefits have risen at an unacceptable rate, well above industry averages. Ms. Belowpar has been directed by the executive committee to work with an outside benefits consultant to seek new policies, suppliers, or coverage levels to bring expenses in line with budgetary goals.

Company policies regarding bereavement leave, the Family and Medical Leave Act, and vacation and holiday time off have not been adequately defined and managed. Ms. Belowpar is directed to work with the human resources department to correct this problem within 30 days.

Ms. Belowpar has neglected necessary updates to the tuition reimbursement benefit for current employees. Participation in the program is below expectations, and policies do not meet the needs of the company to improve productivity and enhance opportunities for advancement.

As of the date of this review, requested expansions to ancillary benefits offered in cooperation with area businesses and associations and business partners of the company have not been implemented.

Ms. Belowpar has failed to keep herself up to date on state and federal mandates for benefits for existing and former employees.

Based on employee reports, Ms. Belowpar has on occasion failed to demonstrate appropriate discretion in discussing personal issues related to benefits. She has been directed to meet with the legal and human resources department to discuss requirements in this area and to develop sufficient safeguards for private information.

She is directed to meet with the training department to explore available courses, seminars, and conventions to assist her in making recommendations for improved or alternative benefits. With this evaluation, Ms. Belowpar is instructed to prepare a report on progress in this area within 60 days.

Training and Employee Development Director

Certification
College courses
Compliance with state and federal regulations
Conflict resolution
Employee evaluations
Equipment suppliers
Interpersonal skills
Managerial skills
Personnel management
Professional organizations
Salary adjustments
Technical schools
Training and employee development

MEETS OR EXCEEDS

Under Mr. Paragon's direction the department of training and employee development has made major contributions to the company by enabling some of our best staff to enhance their skills and advance in the organization. He has created a catalog of courses, offered on a regular basis, that address technical and other job-specific needs, improve managerial skills, and open the doors to new opportunities.

Mr. Paragon has also provided effective training to support employees who are asked to address deficiencies identified in employee evaluations.

In addition, he has demonstrated a high degree of professionalism in creating and running courses that advance corporate goals, including compliance with state and federal regulations and laws.

Since taking over the department two years ago, Mr. Paragon has more than doubled the number of courses and training sessions offered in-house. He has effectively supported the core values and mission of the company with instruction on subjects including personnel management, interpersonal skills and conflict resolution, budgeting and accounting processes, engineering, and computer skills.

Under his initiative, the training department has created a monthly bulletin of course offerings that is posted throughout the company; working in conjunction with the MIS department, Mr. Paragon facilitated creation of an intranet Web site that lists courses and provides information about sign-up procedures.

Upon request from department heads and managers, he has shown himself to be quite willing to add special training on new products or processes and to customize existing offerings to support the efforts of sales, marketing, and promotion staff.

He has also created liaisons with area colleges and technical schools to permit employees to enroll in classes that support company goals. He has proactively worked with equipment suppliers offering training on machinery, tools, and software sold to the company.

On a case-by-case basis, the department has had great success in working with professional organizations, supporting employees seeking certification in specialized areas.

Mr. Paragon has maintained a close relationship with the department of human resources, ensuring that employee personnel records include information about employee accomplishments for use in salary adjustments and promotion.

As head of a service bureau to other departments within the company, Mr. Paragon has done an excellent job of keeping training costs within budgetary goals and working with departments to help them get the most for the money they spend on training.

NEEDS IMPROVEMENT

The department of training and employee development needs to greatly improve its ability to assist some of our best staff to enhance their skills and advance in the organization. Under Ms. Goodenough's direction, the catalog of courses has not kept pace with changes in the company's products and workforce.

The human resources department reports that the department of training has not been able to consistently provide effective training to support employees who are asked to address deficiencies identified in employee evaluations.

The legal and government relations departments have petitioned senior management for advanced training on compliance with state and federal regulations and laws. With this evaluation, Ms. Goodenough is directed to meet with affected departments within 30 days to set forth a plan to add remedial training and education on regulatory issues.

Ms. Goodenough is asked to invite department heads to participate in a quarterly meeting to review the types of courses and training sessions offered in-house, with special emphasis on those that directly support the core values and mission of the company. The group is asked to pay particular attention to subjects including personnel management, interpersonal skills and conflict resolution, budgeting and accounting processes, engineering, and computer skills.

She needs to demonstrate the flexibility to quickly add special training on new products or processes and to customize existing offerings to support the efforts of sales, marketing, and promotion staff.

Employees have asked to be able to be reimbursed for courses taken at area colleges and technical schools on subjects that support company goals. Ms. Goodenough is directed to meet with department heads to discuss these possibilities and adjust employee guidelines as appropriate. A similar effort needs to be mounted to address requests by employees to seek certification in specialized areas through professional organizations and at trade shows and conventions.

The training department should be more active in promoting course offerings through printed and electronic postings distributed throughout the company.

Ms. Goodenough needs to improve communication with the department of human resources, ensuring that employee personnel records include information about employee accomplishments for use in salary adjustments and promotion.

As head of a service bureau to other departments within the company, Ms. Goodenough needs to better inform departments of costs that will be billed to their budgets for training and to work with managers to help them get the most for the money they spend on training.

UNSATISFACTORY

The department of training and employee development has not been effective in supporting company goals to assist staff in enhancing their skills to enable them to advance in the organization. Under Mr. Belowpar's direction, the catalog of courses does not effectively support the company's changing products and workforce.

The human resources department reports that the department of training has failed to provide effective training to support employees who are asked to address deficiencies identified in employee evaluations.

The legal and government relations departments have begun their own programs of education on compliance with state and federal regulations and laws, a clear demonstration of the lack of such support from the training department. Mr. Belowpar is directed to meet with human resources and legal department heads within 15 days to set forth a plan to improve relations with the departments and to launch appropriate new educational offerings.

Beyond that, Mr. Belowpar is directed to invite department heads to join a task force to review the types of courses and training sessions offered in-house, with special emphasis on those that directly support the core values and mission of the company. The committee, which is to begin work within 45 days, is instructed to pay particular attention to subjects including personnel management, interpersonal skills and conflict resolution, budgeting and accounting processes, engineering, and computer skills.

Mr. Belowpar has failed to add special training on new products or processes in a timely fashion and to customize existing offerings to support the efforts of sales, marketing, and promotion staff. With this evaluation, he is asked to present a plan to the executive committee for this expansion of services within 30 days.

Mr. Belowpar has not kept the department of human resources informed of the progress of employees in training courses. As a result, employee personnel records do not include current information about employee accomplishments for use in salary adjustments and promotion.

As head of a service bureau to other departments within the company, Mr. Belowpar has not adequately informed departments of costs that will be billed to their budgets for training. This has resulted in a number of instances of unanticipated overspending.

Relocation Specialist

Branch offices
Bridge loans
Employee welcome kit
Housing assistance
Moving and storage assistance
Outplacement services
Real estate agents
Transferred employees

MEETS OR EXCEEDS

Ms. Paragon has ably fulfilled all of the elements of the job description for relocation specialist and has shown considerable initiative in expanding available services for new employees and staffers being transferred to other locations.

She has also been of considerable assistance to the human relations department in dealing with outplacement services, as appropriate, for employees who are dismissed or otherwise leave the organization.

She has established and maintained a close relationship with the human resources (HR) department to assist new hires in finding housing and dealing with other family related needs including schools, doctors, and services. HR reports a very high level of satisfaction with her assistance from new employees.

Ms. Paragon has developed a cooperative arrangement with a number of other area employers to assist spouses in finding new jobs in the area.

As requested, she prepared a comprehensive welcome kit for new employees with information on the area; available services; and cultural, religious, and educational facilities. On her own initiative, Ms. Paragon established an in-house welcome committee of employees and spouses willing to share recommendations on preschools, housing advice, and other local knowledge.

Ms. Paragon has done an excellent job of creating a database of real estate agents, rental agencies, and apartment complexes; she solicits feedback from new employees about their experiences to share information.

She has also been very successful in developing relations with area moving and storage companies and reviews and evaluates their performance; when appropriate, she works in conjunction with the human resources department to negotiate contracts for moving and relocation services for employees who are offered this sort of assistance as part of their employment contracts.

Similarly, as appropriate, Ms. Paragon has shown a high degree of competence in managing rental subsidies, assistance with real estate transactions, and bridge loans as appropriate for new hires or transferees within the organization.

Ms. Paragon has consistently demonstrated a strong understanding of the organization's mission and employee manual and works closely with the human resources department to offer a full range of services without going beyond reasonable and acceptable bounds.

She has ably assisted transferred employees, working with managers of branch offices and outside consultants to ease the transition to a new location.

Ms. Paragon has also delivered excellent service to the human resources department in providing assistance as a member of the outplacement team for staffers who leave the company for various reasons.

NEEDS IMPROVEMENT

Mr. Goodenough has not completely fulfilled all of the elements of the job description for relocation specialist. In addition, he needs to show more initiative in expanding available services for new employees and to be of assistance to the human relations department in dealing with outplacement services, as appropriate, for employees who are dismissed or otherwise leave the organization.

As part of his job description, he is expected to establish and maintain a close relationship with the human resources (HR) department to assist new hires in finding housing and dealing with other family related needs including schools, doctors, and services. This has not been accomplished; with this evaluation, Mr. Goodenough is directed to make this area a top priority. He will be re-evaluated on this matter in 120 days.

At the time of his hiring, Mr. Goodenough was asked to develop a cooperative arrangement with other area employers to assist spouses in finding new jobs in the area. We note only minimal progress in meeting this goal; this will be re-evaluated in a special assessment in 90 days.

Mr. Goodenough needs to do a better job of keeping current a database of real estate agents, rental agencies, and apartment complexes and to solicit feedback from new employees about their experiences to share information.

He has also not shown a great deal of success in developing relations with area moving and storage companies in order to be of assistance to the human resources department in the negotiation of contracts for moving and relocation services for employees who are offered this sort of assistance as part of their employment contracts.

Mr. Goodenough will be re-evaluated on his progress in updating the real estate and moving and storage company databases in 90 days.

Mr. Goodenough also needs to improve his oversight of management of rental subsidies, assistance with real estate transactions, and bridge loans as appropriate for new hires or transferees within the organization. The human resources department has had to become directly involved in these matters several times, an unnecessary duplication of effort.

Mr. Goodenough has demonstrated gaps in his understanding of the organization's products and services and needs to show a deeper under-standing of the organization's mission and employee manual.

As the organization expands operations in new areas, Mr. Goodenough needs to improve his ability to assist transferred employees, working with managers of branch offices and outside consultants to ease the transition to a new location.

UNSATISFACTORY

Mr. Belowpar has failed to fulfill the job description for relocation special-ist and has not shown any initiative in expanding available services for new employees and staffers being transferred to other locations.

He has also offered minimal assistance to human relations in dealing with outplacement services, as appropriate, for employees who are dis-missed or otherwise leave the organization.

As part of his job description—which was outlined to him at the time of his hiring—he was instructed to establish and maintain a close relationship with the human resources (HR) department to assist new hires in finding housing and dealing with other family related needs including schools, doc-tors, and services. HR reports a lack of cooperation from Mr. Belowpar, even after several specific requests from the director of human resources. With this evaluation, he is directed to immediately begin a dialogue with the HR department and to begin efforts to ensure compliance with this element of the job description. He will be re-evaluated on this matter within 90 days.

We have seen no evidence of success in establishing a cooperative arrangement with area employers to assist spouses in finding employment in the area.

The relocation specialist has not kept the previously established welcome kit for new employees up to date with information on the area; available services; and cultural, religious, and educational facilities. He has also allowed to lapse a successful in-house welcome committee of employees and spouses willing to share recommendations on preschools, housing advice, and other local knowledge.

Mr. Belowpar has also failed to maintain a database of real estate agents, rental agencies, and apartment complexes, and despite it being an element of the job description, he has not solicited feedback from new employees about their experiences to share information.

Similarly, he has neglected relations with area moving and storage companies and has thus been unable to be of assistance to the human resources department in negotiating contracts for moving and relocation services for employees who are offered this assistance as part of their employment contracts.

With this evaluation, Mr. Belowpar is directed to immediately develop a plan to improve his knowledge of area real estate and moving companies. He will be re-evaluated on progress in these areas in 90 days; accomplishment of this goal is to be considered a top priority assignment.

Mr. Belowpar has not shown an adequate understanding of the organization's mission and employee manual; on several occasions, he has given incorrect or misleading information to staffers about available services. He will be re-evaluated on his knowledge of policy within 30 days.

CHAPTER 7

OFFICE SUPPORT

Space and Facilities Planner

Telecommunications Manager

Research Librarian

Meeting Coordinator

Travel Coordinator

Security Manager

Mailroom Manager

Maintenance Foreman

Janitorial Foreman

Food Services Director

Space and Facilities Planner

Computer-aided design
Facilities planning
Internet
Intranet
Office design
Office furniture
Space planning
Storage space
Telecommunications facilities
(VOIP) Voice Over Internet Protocol

MEETS OR EXCEEDS

Mr. Paragon has performed admirably as a space and facilities planner, assisting the company in making the most of available office, storage, and production resources.

Working with outside architectural and office design consultants and vendors, Mr. Paragon supervised installation of state-of-the-art partitions and furniture that brought improved electrical and telecommunications facilities including intranet, Internet, and VOIP telephone cabling.

Mr. Paragon worked closely with facilities management to establish a budget for re-engineering and updating office spaces; the purchasing department commended his cooperation in the development of a master contract for furniture and fixtures. He has also been of counsel to the executive committee in all discussions involving major capital expenditures.

He has demonstrated a high degree of dedication to company values and the organization's mission statement and has shown a deep understanding of products, services, and goals.

Mr. Paragon has been an active and valued participant in planning sessions for future expansion and enhanced productivity for the enterprise. Several of his suggestions have resulted in significant cost savings and efficiencies.

He has done an excellent job of keeping up to date on new trends in facilities planning and management, taking courses and attending trade shows and conventions. He has created a library of catalogs and a directory of online resources available to all departments in preparing for changes to their workspaces.

Mr. Paragon implemented computer-based facilities planning software and has been proactive in offering access and training to department heads for use in blue-sky planning. Use of the computer-aided design software for preliminary planning has saved the company thousands of dollars in consultant's fees for each project.

NEEDS IMPROVEMENT

Ms. Goodenough needs to improve her abilities as a space and facilities planner in order to better assist the company in making the most of available office, storage, and production resources. She has not demonstrated a high degree of knowledge of available furniture and office systems, nor mastery of computer tools for planning.

At the time she was hired, Ms. Goodenough was asked to supervise installation of state-of-the-art partitions and furniture to enable the company to improve electrical and telecommunications facilities including intranet, Internet, and VOIP telephone cabling. To date this has not been accomplished; with this evaluation, she is instructed to meet with the appropriate department heads to begin advanced planning. She will be re-evaluated on this matter in 90 days.

Ms. Goodenough must work closely with facilities management and the purchasing department to establish a budget and master contract for re-engineering and updating office spaces; the job description for space and facilities planner requires that the officeholder assist in the development of a master contract for furniture and fixtures. She is also expected to be of counsel to the executive committee in all discussions involving major capital expenditures. It is expected that she make progress in this area in the next 90 days, and she will be re-evaluated at that time.

Ms. Goodenough needs to demonstrate greater capability in working with outside architectural and office design consultants and vendors. She has not shown a commitment to keep up to date on new trends in facilities planning and management and has not accomplished a previous assignment to create a library of catalogs and a directory of online resources available to all departments in preparing for changes to their workspaces.

With this evaluation, she is directed to seek advanced training and courses and attend appropriate trade shows and conventions. She is asked to produce a plan to improve her abilities in time for an interim re-evaluation in 60 days.

Ms. Goodenough needs to improve her understanding of the organization's products, services, and goals. In her first year in her current job, Ms. Goodenough has not provided the expected level of assistance to executive planning committees that is specified in her job description. With this evaluation, she is directed to seek opportunities for greater involvement in long-range planning; she will be reassessed on this matter in 120 days.

At her previous evaluation, Ms. Goodenough was directed to work with the MIS department to obtain and implement computer-based facilities planning software and make it available to all appropriate departments for use in blue-sky planning. This task has not been accomplished; she is directed to immediately begin work on this objective and to report to the executive committee on her progress within 90 days.

UNSATISFACTORY

Mr. Belowpar has failed to fulfill his assigned tasks as a space and facilities planner; the organization has incurred unexpected expenses for outside consultants in redesigning office, storage, and production resources.

With this evaluation, Mr. Belowpar is directed to meet with the contracts administrator and office manager to identify long-range planning needs and set up a plan to make use of in-house resources as well as cost-effective outside architectural and office design consultants and vendors. He is specifically directed to prepare a detailed plan and cost estimate for the installation of state-of-the-art partitions and furniture to bring improved electrical and telecommunications facilities including intranet, Internet, and VOIP telephone cabling. Mr. Belowpar will be re-evaluated in 120 days on this matter.

Mr. Belowpar has also demonstrated a lack of understanding and dedication to company values and the organization's mission statement; he will be re-evaluated in 90 days on his understanding and support of the organization's products, services, and goals.

Mr. Belowpar is instructed to seek advanced education through the training department and from outside consultants to add to his understanding of new trends in facilities planning and management; he is also asked to attend appropriate trade shows and conventions. As specified in the job description, he is also asked to create and maintain a library of catalogs and a directory of online resources available to all departments in preparing for changes to their workspaces. These efforts should commence immediately;

a special re-evaluation on progress toward accomplishment of these goals will be conducted in 60 days.

At the time of his appointment and in a subsequent progress meeting 60 days later, Mr. Belowpar was specifically directed to work with outside vendors and the MIS department to seek computer-based facilities planning software for use in blue-sky planning and to make the software available across the enterprise. The intent was to allow quick and easy preplanning using computer-aided design software before the need for hiring outside consultants for redesign projects. This goal has not been accomplished.

With this evaluation, Mr. Belowpar is directed to meet with the MIS director within 20 days to set a schedule for acquisition and implementation of this software and to create a schedule for user training. He is instructed to deliver a written report to the executive committee on plans for accomplishment of this goal within 45 days and will be re-evaluated on this matter in 90 days.

Telecommunications Manager

Electronic workplace
Personal use of telephone and Internet
Technical interpretation of contracts
Telecommunications
Teleconferencing
Telephone system
Video conferencing
Voice and data system
VOIP (Voice Over Internet Protocol)

MEETS OR EXCEEDS

Ms. Paragon has been a major contributor to the company's success in the past year, leading the transition to a highly productive and cost-efficient electronic workplace.

During her tenure, the company has managed the changeover from an outdated Centrex telephone system and a separate and unconnected office computer network to a completely integrated electronic voice and data system. Every employee, depending on properly safeguarded access codes, can access research, production, sales, shipping, and accounting information from any telephone or workstation in the enterprise.

Working with a task force that included the accounting, purchasing, MIS, sales, marketing, and shipping departments, Ms. Paragon brought to fruition a comprehensive overhaul of enterprisewide telecommunications policies. She helped negotiate a master contract for installation of fiber optic cable in all workspaces, purchase of new LCD screen telephones, and adaptation of existing computer workstations.

Ms. Paragon exhibited a high degree of cooperation with the purchasing department in seeking bids for equipment and services and provided essential technical interpretation of proposed contracts.

In its first year of operation, the system has operated very close to plan, and the capital costs are expected to be balanced by savings within two years. Sales and marketing departments report great satisfaction with the speed with which they can respond to customer inquiries and their ability to place and track orders on a real-time basis.

Ms. Paragon has also helped the company reduce telecommunications expenses by 32 percent in the past 12 months through the use of VOIP (voice over internet protocol) within the workplace and with our suppliers and customers.

In cooperation with the travel planner and meeting coordinator, Ms. Paragon has helped develop plans for voice and video teleconferencing which is expected to significantly reduce the need for certain types of travel in coming years.

Ms. Paragon has shown exemplary commitment to understanding new technologies and trends in telecommunications and applying them, as appropriate, to company operations. She has sought and received advanced certification from several professional associations and has worked with the training department to establish courses for members of her department as well as classes to introduce the entire company to the new telecommunications system.

She has worked with the MIS and the human resources departments to update the employee manual in areas such as guidelines on the use of company telephones or the Internet for personal purposes.

NEEDS IMPROVEMENT

Ms. Goodenough has fallen behind the curve in addressing the company's need to transition to a highly productive and cost-efficient electronic workplace.

During her tenure, the company has only partially succeeded in the changeover from an outdated Centrex telephone system and a separate and unconnected office computer network to a completely integrated electronic voice and data system. Despite expectations that by this time every employee could access research, production, sales, shipping, and accounting information from any telephone or workstation in the enterprise, the new telephone and computer links have not been fully implemented.

As a key member of the telecommunications task force that included the accounting, purchasing, MIS, sales, marketing, and shipping departments, Ms. Goodenough proved ineffective in bringing to fruition a comprehensive overhaul of enterprisewide telecommunications policies. Leadership of the committee was assumed by the MIS director in her stead.

Ms. Goodenough was unable to provide much assistance to the purchasing department in seeking bids for equipment and services; that department was forced to hire an outside consultant to provide essential technical interpretation of proposed contracts.

At the direction of the executive committee, the travel planner and meeting coordinator asked Ms. Goodenough to help develop plans for voice and video teleconferencing to significantly reduce the need for certain types of travel in coming years. That goal has not been accomplished, and with this evaluation, Ms. Goodenough is directed to produce a plan of action within 15 days and offer a reasonable timetable for implementation within 60 days.

At the heart of Ms. Goodenough's inability to fulfill all of her assignments has been a lack of commitment to understanding new technologies and trends in telecommunications. She is directed to seek training and advanced certification from several professional associations and to work with the training department to establish courses for members of her department as well as classes to introduce the entire company to the new telecommunications system.

She is also directed to meet with the MIS and the human resources departments within 15 days to update the employee manual in areas such as guidelines on the use of company telephones or the Internet for personal purposes.

UNSATISFACTORY

Mr. Belowpar has failed to make a meaningful contribution to addressing the company's transition to a highly productive and cost-efficient electronic workplace.

As a key member of the telecommunications task force that included the accounting, purchasing, MIS, sales, marketing, and shipping departments, Mr. Belowpar resisted a comprehensive overhaul of enterprisewide telecommunications policies. Leadership of the committee was instead assumed by the MIS director.

Mr. Belowpar was also unable to provide assistance to the purchasing department in seeking bids for equipment and services; that department was forced to hire an outside consultant to provide essential technical interpretation of proposed contracts.

At the heart of Mr. Belowpar's inability to fulfill all of his assignments has been a lack of commitment to understanding new technologies and trends in telecommunications. He is directed to seek training and advanced certification from professional associations and to work with the training department to establish courses for members of his department as well as classes to introduce the entire company to the new telecommunications system.

He is also directed to meet with the MIS and the human resources departments within 15 days to update the employee manual in areas such as guidelines on the use of company telephones or the Internet for personal purposes.

Research Librarian

Cataloging resources
In-house seminars
Internet
Intranet
Library
Managing multiple projects
Research and development
Search engines
Time management

MEETS OR EXCEEDS

Mr. Paragon has demonstrated a great devotion to assisting staff in all manner of research and development projects. He took a small and underutilized section and greatly expanded available resources.

Working closely and effectively with the MIS department, Mr. Paragon cataloged in-house materials on the computer and made them accessible over the intranet to staff. He also enhanced the use of search engines for internal resources, as well as files and information from the Web in the library. In addition, he has conducted in-house seminars and offered individual training in the advanced use of research tools.

Mr. Paragon has shown great skill in managing multiple and sometimes conflicting tasks and deadlines. He is persistent in following through on long-range and complex projects.

He is a ready and willing guide for employees seeking assistance in beginning new research projects, directing them to in-house resources as well as outside sources of information.

He fully supports the organization's mission statement and demonstrates a strong understanding and knowledge of products, services, and goals. Mr. Paragon attends trade shows, conventions, and sales meetings on a regular basis and has worked closely with the training department in seeking advanced education in his field as a librarian and in support of the needs of other staffers.

NEEDS IMPROVEMENT

Ms. Goodenough has not demonstrated consistency in assisting staff in varying types of research and development projects. When she was first assigned to the library, it was a small and underutilized section, and she has made minimal improvements to available resources.

Ms. Goodenough needs to work much more closely and effectively with the MIS department to catalog in-house materials on the computer and make them accessible to the staff using the in-house intranet.

An important goal, not yet realized, is increased use of search engines for internal resources, as well as files and information from the Web in the library. With this evaluation, she is asked to prepare and conduct in-house seminars and individual training on the advanced use of research tools.

Ms. Goodenough is advised to meet with the training department to seek guidance on the availability of advanced education in her field as a librarian and in support of the needs of other staffers. She has also not taken advantage of trade shows, conventions, and sales meetings to advance her understanding of the organization's operations and needs.

It has been noted on several occasions that Ms. Goodenough has been unable to adequately manage multiple and sometimes conflicting tasks and deadlines. She is advised to seek assistance from the training department as appropriate and to consult with human resources about ways to involve other departments when necessary.

She needs to improve her ability to offer assistance to staffers beginning new research projects, directing them to in-house resources as well as outside sources of information.

UNSATISFACTORY

Mr. Belowpar has failed to offer an adequate level of assistance to staff in various research and development projects. He has not successfully used the facilities made available to him when he was first assigned to his current job and has not made a significant effort to improve and expand available resources; this was a key element of his job description.

Mr. Belowpar is directed to review his available budget and to meet with appropriate department heads to improve the level of services he can provide. He will be re-evaluated on his progress in expanding research facilities in 90 days.

He is also instructed to meet with representatives of the MIS department and to immediately begin a project to catalog in-house materials on the computer and make them accessible over the intranet to staff.

At the same time, Mr. Belowpar is directed to seek training on the advanced use of search engines for internal resources, as well as files and information from the Web in the library, and prepare to offer in-house seminars and individual training for users of the library. He will be re-evaluated on these skills in six months.

Mr. Belowpar has demonstrated on numerous occasions that he has great difficulty managing multiple and sometimes conflicting tasks and deadlines. He is advised to seek assistance and training on task management; courses are available through the training department and consultants. He will be re-evaluated on this matter in 120 days.

Mr. Belowpar has also failed to adequately follow through on long-range and complex projects including a request from the sales department for assistance in developing new customer research methodologies.

In his daily work, he has not shown a sufficient level of understanding of the organization's mission statement, products, services, and goals.

With this evaluation, Mr. Belowpar is directed to review the job description for research librarian with a representative of the human resources department and to seek advanced education in his field as a librarian and in support of the needs of other staffers.

There will be a complete re-evaluation of Mr. Belowpar's job performance in 120 days. It is expected that by that time he will be able to demonstrate significant progress toward meeting the goals of his job.

Meeting Coordinator

Air travel
Board of Directors
Company manual
Company picnic
Conferences
Conventions
Executive Committee
Holiday parties
Meetings
Promotion
Sales conferences
Shareholders meeting
Stockholders
Trade shows
Travel

MEETS OR EXCEEDS

Ms. Paragon has represented the company very well in the high quality of all of the events she has coordinated and managed in the past year, including product introductions, the annual sales conference, trade shows, conventions, and the shareholders meeting.

She has demonstrated exceptional skills in collaborating with nearly every department in the company, providing meeting planning and administrative support. On her own initiative, she produced a company manual which lists policies and procedures for nearly every recurring meeting to assist departments in staying within their budgets while getting the most for their time and effort.

Ms. Paragon has shown the same eagerness to excel in assisting departments preparing for in-house meetings, conferences, and assemblies.

She has instituted a highly effective program to meet regularly with the sales, marketing, promotion, and advertising departments well in advance of major events and product introduction to ensure that every deadline is met.

If out-of-town travel is required, Ms. Paragon has demonstrated great skills and advance planning in coordinating with the corporate travel planner for booking hotel accommodations, air travel, car rental, and other transportation.

Her exceptional attention to detail has resulted in a noticeable improvement in the logistics of conferences under her management. She has shown an extraordinary ability to anticipate all of the requirements for conferences and has worked very well with other departments in preparing for setup, registration, signs, badges, and breakdown.

Well in advance of any meeting, Ms. Paragon exhibits strong skills in working with the advertising, promotion, and marketing departments to assure production of materials required for meetings and arranges for warehousing and timely distribution.

The secretaries for the Board of Directors and Executive Committee have conveyed senior management's appreciation of the skill she shows in setting up their meetings.

The most recent stockholder meeting, the company's largest gathering ever, was considered by the chairman and president to be an unqualified success down to the smallest detail.

Ms. Paragon's department is also responsible for the planning and conduct of annual holiday parties and the summer picnic. Employee surveys commended her selection of a day at an amusement park as a highlight of the summer.

NEEDS IMPROVEMENT

Mr. Goodenough needs to be more consistent in the quality of services and venues for the various events he is called upon to coordinate, including product introductions, the annual sales conference, trade shows, conventions, and the shareholders meeting.

He needs to meet more regularly with staffers in other departments, including sales, marketing, promotion, and advertising, that are responsible for various meetings within the company and at remote sites. Meetings should be well in advance of events in order to assure that all deadlines are met.

In his most recent evaluation, Mr. Goodenough was directed to produce a company manual which lists policies and procedures for anticipated meetings; that document has not been completed and should be a high priority within the next 60 days.

Mr. Goodenough has not demonstrated adequate advance preparation in working with the travel planner when it is necessary to book hotel accommodations, air travel, car rental, and other transportation for out-of-town meetings.

He needs to greatly improve attention to detail for the logistics of conferences, anticipating details of setup, registration, signs, badges, and breakdown.

Well in advance of any event, Mr. Goodenough should initiate meetings with the advertising, promotion, and marketing departments to assure timely production of materials required for meetings.

The secretaries for the Board of Directors and Executive Committee have expressed some concern about the level of quality of services provided at these critical meetings.

In addition, the most recent stockholder meeting, the company's largest gathering ever, did not show evidence of adequate advance planning and did not take into account the fact that other nearby facilities were in use for a much larger convention, resulting in a serious shortage of hotel rooms, taxis, and restaurant reservations. Mr. Goodenough is advised to coordinate future major meetings with the city's convention and visitors' bureau, which maintains an inclusive calendar of events.

Employee surveys indicated a high level of disapproval of the location chosen for this past summer's picnic, objecting to the use of the company cafeteria instead of an amusement park or private beach as has been used in previous years. Mr. Goodenough is directed to poll the staff well in advance of next year's event to seek a consensus for this important employee get-together.

UNSATISFACTORY

Ms. Belowpar has failed to provide an acceptable level of services and venues for the various events she is called upon to coordinate, including product introductions, the annual sales conference, trade shows, conventions, and the shareholders meeting. She has not demonstrated an ability to assist departments in making the most of their budgets and has not negotiated any special deals on behalf of the company in this regard.

She is instructed to meet at least monthly with staffers in other departments, including sales, marketing, promotion, and advertising, that are responsible for various meetings within the company and at remote sites.

Ms. Belowpar has not produced a company manual which lists policies and procedures for anticipated meetings; with this evaluation, she is directed to do so within 30 days.

Travel costs throughout the enterprise have risen well beyond expectations and industry averages. Ms. Belowpar must initiate contact with the travel planner well in advance of out-of-town meetings and events requiring invited guests to come to visit. The goal for such advance planning is to seek ways to reduce costs through use of discounts, bulk purchases, and negotiated contracts.

Ms. Belowpar has failed to devote adequate attention to detail for the logistics of conferences, including setup, registration, signs, badges, and breakdown. Well in advance of any event, Ms. Belowpar is also directed to initiate meetings with the advertising, promotion, and marketing departments to assure timely production of materials required for meetings.

A major concern expressed by the secretaries for the Board of Directors and Executive Committee and senior management has been a generally unsatisfactory level of quality of services provided at these critical meetings.

With this evaluation, Ms. Belowpar is directed to prepare a detailed plan for the next stockholder meeting no later than six months before its scheduled date and to personally present it to the executive committee.

Travel Coordinator

Airline expenses
Business travel
Car rental expenses
Conventions
Corporate meeting planner
Expense reports
Guidelines
Hotel expenses
Insurance for business travel
Online travel profiles
Product introductions
Sales conferences
Spending patterns
Travel expense reports
Travel itineraries
Unusual spending patterns

MEETS OR EXCEEDS

Mr. Paragon has demonstrated exemplary skills in managing expenses incurred for business-related travel. He has successfully held overall costs within budgetary goals and worked with department heads to reduce or eliminate unnecessary or inefficient travel plans.

As directed by senior management, he has negotiated bulk contracts with airlines, car rental companies, and other providers yielding significant discounts. He has worked closely with department heads to inform them of available negotiated rates and other special offerings.

Mr. Paragon exhibits great attention to detail in tracking travel expenses across the entire enterprise; working in conjunction with the MIS department, he developed an automated alert system to notify department heads of unusual or unanticipated spending patterns.

He has suggested ways for departments to get more from their travel expenditures by scheduling trips to include multiple goals on a single itinerary or take advantage of lower-price travel during nonpeak periods.

Mr. Paragon keeps current on travel trends and prices through research, participation in professional associations, and the use of tools offered by outside travel providers.

He has clearly defined the company's business travel guidelines and kept them up to date. As part of this effort, he has worked closely with the accounting and legal departments to assure that employees understand recordkeeping requirements and allowable expenses.

Mr. Paragon meets regularly with the accounting department to update and modify the company's expense report forms as needed.

The travel coordinator has made himself available to employees to discuss security and health concerns for domestic and international destinations.

Working with the benefits and legal departments, Mr. Paragon has improved the company's insurance coverage for employees on business trips and has assured the availability of a 24-hour hotline in case of unforeseen difficulties while out of the office or in emergency situations.

Mr. Paragon has demonstrated exceptional skills in working with the corporate meeting planner to control costs for sales conferences, product introductions, conventions, and other group travel.

Working closely with the MIS department, Mr. Paragon has done an excellent job of creating online travel profiles for all employees who make business trips. The profiles allow one-click submission of requests for airline, hotel, car rental, and other travel services and indicate special preferences and requirements.

Employee feedback supports a very high rating for Mr. Paragon's interpersonal skills and written and verbal communication.

NEEDS IMPROVEMENT

Ms. Goodenough has not yet demonstrated satisfactory skills in managing expenses incurred for business-related travel. Overall costs have risen above budgetary goals, and she needs to work more effectively with department heads to reduce or eliminate unnecessary or inefficient travel plans.

The enterprise's bulk contracts with airlines, car rental companies, and other providers are not yielding significant discounts and in some cases may cost the company more than standard rates. Ms. Goodenough needs to seek new contracts where possible and work more closely with department heads to inform them of available negotiated rates and other special offerings.

Although Ms. Goodenough exhibits great attention to detail in tracking travel expenses across the entire enterprise, she needs to better communicate unusual or unanticipated trends and patterns to department heads before they result in overspending.

She has lacked creativity in suggesting ways for departments to get more from their travel expenditures by making alterations to schedules or itineraries.

Ms. Goodenough has not demonstrated flexibility in dealing with departments forced to exceed their budget for unforeseen but allowable reasons. Although her job involves supervision of travel expenditures, department heads are granted leeway in meeting overall company goals.

She needs to do a better job of keeping current on travel trends and prices through research, participation in professional associations, and the use of tools offered by outside travel providers.

The company's business travel guidelines are not clearly defined and include out-of-date information and requirements. Ms. Goodenough needs to work more effectively with the accounting and legal departments to assure that employees understand recordkeeping requirements and allowable expenses. As part of that effort, she also needs to meet regularly with the accounting department to update and modify the company's expense report forms as needed.

With growing concern about political and health situations in various parts of the world, the travel coordinator needs to do a better job of informing employees about security and medical concerns.

The company's insurance coverage for employees on business trips is inadequate, and employees have also asked for availability of a 24-hour hotline in case of unforeseen difficulties while out of the office or in emergency situations. Executive management has directed Ms. Goodenough to work with the benefits and legal departments to implement these services within 30 days.

Ms. Goodenough needs to make herself available to the corporate meeting planner to help control costs for sales conferences, product introductions, conventions, and other group travel.

Employees have requested the creation of online travel profiles to allow one-click submission of requests for airline, hotel, car rental, and other travel services and indicate special preferences and requirements. This program has not been implemented as of this evaluation and should be a high priority in coming months.

UNSATISFACTORY

Mr. Belowpar has failed to demonstrate the ability to effectively manage expenses incurred for business-related travel. Overall costs have risen above budgetary goals without evidence of an effort to work with department heads to reduce or eliminate unnecessary or inefficient travel plans.

One reason for excessive spending is the lack of cost-effective bulk contracts with airlines, car rental companies, and other providers. Mr. Belowpar needs to seek such contracts where appropriate and to inform department heads and all employees of available negotiated rates and other special offerings.

Mr. Belowpar has failed to exhibit appropriate attention to detail in tracking travel expenses across the entire enterprise and needs to communicate unusual or unanticipated trends and patterns to department heads before they result in overspending.

He has not shown creativity in suggesting ways for departments to get more from their travel expenditures by making alterations to schedules or itineraries.

Mr. Belowpar has not enforced company guidelines in dealing with departments that exceed their budget. Although department heads are granted leeway in meeting overall goals, company guidelines call for approval by senior management for any unusual or excessive travel expense.

He has not made an effort to keep current on travel trends and prices through research, participation in professional associations, and the use of tools offered by outside travel providers.

Mr. Belowpar has made no attempt to update and clarify the company's business travel guidelines; he has been directed to do so within 30 days of this evaluation. In a related area, Mr. Belowpar needs to work more effectively with the accounting and legal departments to assure that employees understand recordkeeping requirements and allowable expenses and to update and modify the company's expense report forms as needed.

Mr. Belowpar has neglected to seek ways to reduce costs for sales conferences, product introductions, conventions, and other group travel. He needs to establish a mechanism to work closely with the corporate meeting planner for these purposes.

Employee feedback indicates dissatisfaction with Mr. Belowpar's interpersonal skills and written and verbal communication. With this evaluation, we are recommending specific guidance and instruction available through the corporate training and human resources departments.

Security Manager

Alarm systems
Background checks
Child care
Fire alarms
Fire inspector
First aid
First responders
Loading docks
Police department
Smoke alarms
Visitors lobby
Warehouse

MEETS OR EXCEEDS

Ms. Paragon has done an excellent job managing the overall security of the enterprise. She has enhanced safety precautions at all access points, including employee entrances, the front visitors lobby, and loading docks.

Working with the warehouse manager, she has upgraded the existing alarm and motion detection system. In conjunction with the MIS department, she has initiated tracking of valuable assets tagged with RF identifiers; security officers are able to see warnings any time a tag is taken out of the warehouse or other exit from the office complex.

Ms. Paragon has greatly enhanced training for members of the security staff to allow them to assist in the delivery of first aid or to provide the first response to medical emergencies.

The security department received top marks from the city fire inspector six months ago in an annual assessment. Members of the department regularly check the operation of fire and smoke alarms, including fire drills conducted in cooperation with local fire departments.

Ms. Paragon has demonstrated a high degree of cooperation with loss prevention specialists from the company's insurance carrier in search of ways to reduce fire and water damage hazards and eliminate pilferage.

Working with the training department, she has set up classes on fire and hazardous chemical preparedness, dealing with suspicious packages and unknown visitors, and working with local police and fire departments.

Classes have been extended to members of the security department as well as receptionists, mailroom personnel, and drivers of company vehicles.

Ms. Paragon has provided valuable services to the human resources staff in assisting with the background checks conducted on security staff, employees in sensitive areas including those working on government research projects, and workers in the on-site child care facility.

NEEDS IMPROVEMENT

Ms. Goodenough needs to greatly improve her ability to manage the overall security of the enterprise. Employees have expressed concern about personal safety and the security of company property; she is directed to present a report to the department of office services within 15 days suggesting security enhancements at all access points, including employee entrances, the front visitors lobby, and loading docks.

At her previous evaluation, Ms. Goodenough was asked to work with the warehouse manager to upgrade the existing alarm and motion detection systems. As of this date, this assignment has not been accomplished; she is directed to meet with the warehouse manager and the director of office services within 30 days to deliver plans to deal with this problem.

Ms. Goodenough needs to improve training for members of the security staff to allow them to assist in the delivery of first aid or to provide the first response to medical emergencies. As of this date, only one member of the security staff has received certification in first aid.

The city fire inspector gave the company an "adequate" rating in his most recent assessment six weeks ago; our insurance carrier demands that all substandard or problematic areas be brought up to code within 90 days. Ms. Goodenough is directed to meet with the legal department within 10 days to advise on the status of remediation.

Ms. Goodenough must also demonstrate a greater degree of cooperation with loss prevention specialists from the company's insurance carrier to search for ways to reduce fire and water damage hazards and eliminate pilferage.

Ms. Goodenough needs to update the catalog of security and safety classes and available professional certificates offered to members of the security department as well as receptionists, mailroom personnel, and drivers of company vehicles. At her most recent evaluation, it was suggested that she work with the training department to offer classes on fire and hazardous chemical preparedness, dealing with suspicious packages and unknown visitors, and working with local police and fire departments.

The human resources staff has requested that the security department assist in making background checks conducted on security staff, employees in sensitive areas including those working on government research projects, and workers in the on-site child care facility. With this evaluation, she is directed to provide this service.

UNSATISFACTORY

Mr. Belowpar has not adequately managed the overall security of the enterprise. There have been several documented instances of unauthorized intruders on company grounds and breaches of security in the warehouse and motor pool in the past three months. Employees have expressed concern about personal safety and the security of company property.

Mr. Belowpar is directed to meet with the department of office services and the purchasing and legal departments within 10 days to begin development of a plan detailing security enhancements at all access points, including employee entrances, the front visitors lobby, and loading docks. It is the expectation of the executive committee that these changes will be made within 45 days.

Mr. Belowpar has neglected the training needs of members of the security staff to allow them to assist in the delivery of first aid or to provide the first response to medical emergencies. As of this date, only one member of the security staff has received certification in first aid.

Mailroom Manager

Accounts receivable
Billing codes
Bulk contracts
Bulk mailing
Courier services
Customer service
Customs regulations
Government correspondence
Legal matters
Mailroom management
Misdeliveries of mail
Overnight mail delivery
Prioritization of mail
Security
Shipping supplies
Suspicious packages
Tracking mail
Unanticipated spending

MEETS OR EXCEEDS

Mr. Paragon has demonstrated a high level of commitment to customer service in his management of the mailroom. According to employee surveys, under his direction pickup and delivery of mail within the enterprise has improved markedly in recent years.

He has worked closely with department heads to find ways to reduce costs of outgoing mail. Under his leadership, the company has negotiated discount contracts with several major overnight and ground service delivery companies; as a result, the level of service has improved while costs have been kept in line with expectations.

Mr. Paragon has successfully negotiated bulk contracts with Federal Express, United Parcel Service, and other services that have resulted in significant savings on package shipments. He has worked closely with department heads to educate them about available mail services and to help them reduce or eliminate unnecessary spending.

Under his direction, the mailroom added computerized tracking services offered by major shippers and the U.S. Postal Service to permit the mailroom to verify addresses before items are shipped, sharply reducing misdeliveries and rejected mail and speeding delivery of postal mail through the use of nine-digit ZIP codes automatically applied to labels.

In conjunction with the MIS department, Mr. Paragon has introduced several advanced technologies including optical character recognition scanners that speed the sorting of mail. Contracts with shippers have resulted in an improved ability to track outgoing packages.

Automated billing codes applied to outgoing mail, a program instituted by Mr. Paragon at the request of the accounting department, has permitted precise tracking of shipping costs and application of those costs against departmental budgets. On his own initiative, Mr. Paragon arranged for the MIS department to compare costs and budgetary amounts on an ongoing basis and to issue notices to department heads when spending reaches unanticipated levels.

Under his direction, the mailroom staff has worked with departments to identify types of mail that are considered of highest priority, including overnight courier packages, accounts receivable, legal matters, and correspondence from local, state, and federal government agencies. These priority items are delivered first, often arriving on desks throughout the enterprise before 9 A.M.

Mr. Paragon has maintained a proactive effort to stock the mailroom with supplies of boxes, shipping material, padding and protective foam, sealing tape, and labels for use by corporate clients. Cost of all supplies is tracked along with postage and is applied to departmental accounts at the time of shipping.

As requested, Mr. Paragon has made himself available to consult with department heads to plan cost-effective bulk mailing of catalogs and direct marketing pieces; managers report that his suggestions have greatly contributed to the effectiveness of their programs and resulted in real cost savings.

The mailroom, under Mr. Paragon's guidance, has offered exceptional service to departments in preparing documentation and shipping labels for international shipments, and dealing with customs and security regulations.

Mr. Paragon exhibited exceptional initiative in coordinating with area police and fire authorities on a plan for proper handling of suspicious packages.

NEEDS IMPROVEMENT

Mr. Goodenough needs to substantially improve the level of commitment to customer service in the mailroom. Employee surveys have consistently reported delays in pickup and delivery and misdirection of mail within the enterprise.

He was asked at his last employee evaluation to work closely with department heads to find ways to reduce costs of outgoing mail, but this has not been accomplished. Under his leadership, the company has not sufficiently benefited from its position as a large customer of several major overnight and ground service delivery companies.

Mr. Goodenough is instructed to review the existing agreements with Federal Express, United Parcel Service, and other services to seek negotiated contracts that should result in significant savings on package shipments.

He must improve his efforts to work with department heads to educate them about available mail services and to help them reduce or eliminate unnecessary spending.

At the direction of senior management, Mr. Goodenough has been instructed to investigate and acquire, as appropriate, computerized tracking services from major shippers and the U.S. Postal Service that permit the mailroom to verify addresses before items are shipped, significantly reducing misdeliveries and rejected mail and speeding delivery of postal mail through the use of nine-digit ZIP codes automatically applied to labels.

The mailroom has not implemented an effective method to track shipping costs and apply them against departmental budgets. With this evaluation, Mr. Goodenough is directed to work with the MIS department to develop such a tracking system and to include a means to compare costs and budgetary amounts and to issue notices to department heads when spending reaches unanticipated levels.

Employee surveys have reported dissatisfaction with the handling of packages and mail considered high priority for the enterprise. These would include overnight courier packages, accounts receivable, legal matters, and correspondence from local, state, and federal government agencies. Mr. Goodenough is directed to develop a program to give special handling to such items and speed their delivery to recipients ahead of regular delivery.

Mr. Goodenough has not kept the mailroom properly stocked with supplies of boxes, shipping material, padding and protective foam, sealing tape, and labels for use by corporate clients. He also needs to work with the accounting department to develop a system to track the use of these materials on outbound packages and apply their cost to the appropriate budget.

There has not been an effective effort to share information with department heads to allow them to plan cost-effective bulk mailing of catalogs and direct marketing pieces. Similarly, there is a lack of expertise in preparing documentation and shipping labels for international shipments and dealing with customs and security regulations.

UNSATISFACTORY

Ms. Belowpar has failed to deliver an acceptable level of customer service in the mailroom. Employee surveys have consistently reported significant and recurring delays in pickup and delivery and misdirection of mail within the enterprise.

Despite a direction to find ways to reduce costs of outgoing mail in her previous evaluation, actual costs have increased by an unacceptable amount. According to a presentation made to the office services department by one shipping vendor not currently used by our company, this enterprise is spending 15 to 25 percent above typical costs for a similar operation.

Ms. Belowpar is instructed to review all existing contracts with shipping companies and to seek bids from other services and present options to the executive committee within 45 days.

Once new contracts are in place, Ms. Belowpar is directed to meet with department heads and staff to inform them of cost-saving alternatives for shipping and to clarify the company's policies about acceptable and inappropriate use of overnight services.

To reduce the incidence of misdirection of outgoing mail, Ms. Belowpar is directed to investigate and acquire, as appropriate, computerized tracking services from major shippers and the U.S. Postal Service that permit the mailroom to verify addresses before items are shipped.

Ms. Belowpar has failed to put into place means to track shipping costs and apply them against departmental budgets on a timely basis. Ms. Belowpar is directed to work with the MIS department to develop such a tracking system and to also compare costs and budgetary amounts and to issue notices to department heads when spending reaches unanticipated levels.

Maintenance Foreman

Bids for equipment
Downtime
Emergency response team
Equipment failure
Extended warranties
Maintenance
Mean time between failure
Mission-critical
Obsolescence
Refurbished equipment
Repair
Scheduled maintenance
Service contracts
Service intervals
Spare parts
Upkeep

MEETS OR EXCEEDS

Mr. Paragon has demonstrated excellent skills as foreman of the maintenance group. Under his leadership, the company has experienced a measurable reduction in downtime as the result of equipment failure and a related increase in productivity. He has demonstrated exceptional skills in working with the manufacturing, shipping, and MIS departments to proactively schedule maintenance on equipment and prepare for failures.

Mr. Paragon has overseen the creation of a stock of repair parts and tools for a wide range of manufacturing and office machinery and has assured that in-house staff has proper training to maintain this equipment. At the same time, he has successfully negotiated contracts with outside companies for repair and upkeep of major pieces of equipment requiring special expertise, tools, and parts.

He has worked closely with equipment manufacturers to assure that his department is aware of all recommended service intervals and part replacement schedules.

Mr. Paragon expanded the company's emergency response team for mission-critical repairs to include seven-day, 24-hour coverage; working with the human resources department, he developed a mechanism to pay overtime or compensatory time to eligible employees. He has also coordinated his efforts with the company's labor relations manager to include emergency availability in contracts with unions as required.

On his own initiative, Mr. Paragon created a task force with the manufacturing and purchasing department to establish criteria to determine when major pieces of equipment reach the point of obsolescence because of advances in technology or are no longer cost-effective to maintain and repair.

Mr. Paragon has been an effective and well-informed member of the committee that solicits and reviews bids for major equipment purchases. He has brought to the meetings his expertise on mean time between failure statistics and cost of repair for new and refurbished devices. Mr. Paragon also makes significant contributions to decisions about the purchase of service contracts and extended warranties.

Working closely with the legal and purchasing departments, he has assisted the company in successfully pursuing refunds, reimbursements, and return of unacceptable equipment.

Mr. Paragon has done an excellent job of keeping current on industry trends. He attends trade shows, sometimes together with other department heads looking for new equipment. He has received advanced certification from professional associations in several technical and mechanical fields.

He is a key member of the company's hazardous materials response team, working in conjunction with the janitorial, security, and government relations departments. Under his leadership, every member of the maintenance department has received training in this area.

NEEDS IMPROVEMENT

Ms. Goodenough needs to greatly improve her skills as foreman of the maintenance group. The company has experienced an unexpected increase in downtime as the result of equipment failure and a related decrease in productivity.

She needs to improve her cooperation with the manufacturing, shipping, and MIS departments to proactively schedule maintenance on equipment and prepare for failures.

The maintenance department has not established an adequate inventory of repair parts and tools for many pieces of manufacturing and office machinery; in consultation with the manufacturing and purchasing departments, she is directed to begin to do so within 30 days of this review. She also needs to make contact with equipment manufacturers to assure that her department is aware of all recommended service intervals and part replacement schedules.

The company does not have in place an appropriate set of negotiated contracts with outside companies for repair and upkeep of major pieces of equipment requiring special expertise, tools, and parts. At her last evaluation, she was asked to begin this process; she is directed to report progress in this area to the executive department within 30 days.

Department heads have noted that one reason for unexpected and costly downtime in the manufacturing department is the lack of seven-day, 24-hour coverage by the maintenance department. With this review, Ms. Goodenough is directed to meet with affected departments and prepare a plan to add such coverage for all mission-critical equipment. The plan will also need the involvement of the human resources department and the labor relations manager to provide for a mechanism to pay overtime or compensatory time to affected employees.

The company lacks objective criteria to determine when major pieces of equipment reach the point of obsolescence because of advances in technology or are no longer cost-effective to maintain and repair. Ms. Goodenough is asked to assemble a task force with the manufacturing and purchasing departments for that purpose and to report progress to the executive committee within 60 days.

The legal and purchasing departments have asked for the involvement of the maintenance foreman in successfully pursuing refunds, reimbursements, and return of unacceptable equipment.

Ms. Goodenough needs to improve her background and training on technologies and maintenance procedures through courses, trade shows, and advanced certification from professional associations.

She needs to become a more active participant on the company's hazardous materials response team, working in conjunction with the janitorial, security, and government relations departments. Other department heads have noted a lack of training among the maintenance staff in this very important area.

UNSATISFACTORY

Mr. Belowpar has failed to address a significant and unexpected increase in downtime as the result of equipment failure. He needs to improve his cooperation with the manufacturing, shipping, and MIS departments to proactively schedule maintenance on equipment and prepare for failures.

In a previous evaluation, Mr. Belowpar stated the increase in equipment failure was due to an inadequate budget line for his department; at that time, he was asked to prepare a report for the executive committee outlining his concerns and making specific recommendations to deal with the situation. No such report was presented.

With this evaluation, Mr. Belowpar is directed to convene a task force of manufacturing, purchasing, inventory, and other departments as appropriate to make recommendations including replacement of obsolete equipment, proactive repair of other devices, and possible increases in service contracts and staffing.

Over the past year, the maintenance department has failed to establish an adequate inventory of repair parts and tools for many pieces of manufacturing and office machinery; in consultation with the manufacturing and purchasing departments, Mr. Belowpar is directed to begin to do so within 30 days of this review. He also needs to make contact with equipment manufacturers to assure that his department is aware of all recommended service intervals and part replacement schedules.

The company does not have in place an appropriate set of negotiated contracts with outside companies for repair and upkeep of major pieces of equipment requiring special expertise, tools, and parts. At his last evaluation, he was asked to begin this process; he is directed to report progress in this area to the executive department within 30 days.

The company lacks seven-day, 24-hour coverage by the maintenance department, a situation which has been the cause of several costly downtimes in the manufacturing department. The executive committee directs Mr. Belowpar to meet with affected departments and prepare a plan to add such coverage for all mission-critical equipment. The plan will also need the involvement of the human resources department and the labor relations manager to provide for a mechanism to pay overtime or compensatory time to affected employees.

Mr. Belowpar has not shown sufficient initiative to improve his background and training on technologies and maintenance procedures through courses, trade shows, and advanced certification from professional associations. He is asked to meet with the training department within 30 days to establish a plan to address these shortcomings.

Although he has attended meetings of the company's hazardous materials response team, Mr. Belowpar has not taken the initiative to add emergency response training for the maintenance staff.

Janitorial Foreman

Alarm codes
Bulk purchases
Cafeteria
Cleanliness of the workplace
Hazardous waste
Janitorial services
Keys
Managerial skills
Outside services
Painting
Personal inspections
Power equipment
Recycling
Restrooms
Security
Suspicious activities
Tracking of supplies
Trash collection

MEETS OR EXCEEDS

Ms. Paragon has greatly improved the janitorial services of the company in her first year on the job. Employee surveys indicate a high degree of satisfaction with the cleanliness of the workplace.

She has done an excellent job of keeping within the departmental budget and has worked closely with the purchasing department to find ways to save money and improve the quality of supplies by negotiating bulk purchases and participating in the review of bids for outside services including window washing, carpet cleaning, and painting.

Ms. Paragon has become well known throughout the company for her weekly personal inspections of the enterprise; she encourages staffers to point out areas requiring special attention or repair.

Employees have expressed general satisfaction with the cleanliness of restrooms and the company cafeteria and the availability of paper, soap, and other supplies at all times.

The janitorial staff, under Ms. Paragon's management, has closely followed company guidelines regarding the collection of trash, including separate handling of sensitive financial documents and hazardous waste. She has also overseen a successful recycling program that has reclaimed a significant amount of plastic, glass, and metal from paper waste.

Working with the MIS department, she has improved the computerized tracking and reordering of necessary supplies. This has also resulted in an easy-to-use report for the purchasing department's use in seeking bulk contracts.

She has shown excellent initiative in collecting information about pieces of equipment throughout the company that are in need of repair or upkeep and providing this information to the maintenance department on a timely basis.

The human resources department reports a high level of approval of Ms. Paragon's managerial skills by her supervised staff. It is recommended that she take advantage of available training and certification courses that could lead to advancement in the company.

Ms. Paragon has demonstrated a strong understanding of company policy and state and federal regulations regarding the use and disposal of hazardous materials used in the manufacturing, technical, clerical, and janitorial processes. She has availed herself of in-house training and has attended several industry conferences on the subject; within the company, she has cooperated with the human resources department in the development of a section on this subject in the employee handbook.

Ms. Paragon has worked closely with vendors to assure proper training of the janitorial staff in the operation of power equipment including floor cleaners, polishers, and industrial vacuum cleaners.

Ms. Paragon has proven herself to be very conscientious in maintaining the security of the work environment. She has worked closely with the security department to assure proper safeguarding of keys, alarm codes, and other security features. She has also made sure that she and her staff are prepared to report suspicious or unusual activities or persons to security.

NEEDS IMPROVEMENT

Mr. Goodenough needs to improve the quality of services provided by the janitorial department. Employee surveys indicate mixed degrees of satisfaction with the cleanliness of the workplace, especially in common areas including restrooms and company lounges.

He has not demonstrated a consistent ability to keep within the departmental budget and needs to work closely with the purchasing department to find ways to save money and improve the quality of supplies by negotiating bulk purchases.

Mr. Goodenough is asked to make himself known to employees and to conduct weekly personal inspections of the enterprise; in doing so, he should encourage staffers to point out areas requiring special attention or repair.

The janitorial staff, under Mr. Goodenough's management, must revisit its procedures in order to follow company guidelines regarding the collection of trash, including separate handling of sensitive financial documents and hazardous waste. He is also directed to develop a recycling program to reclaim plastic, glass, and metal from paper waste.

The purchasing department has recommended that Mr. Goodenough work with the MIS department to implement a program that permits computerized tracking and reordering of necessary supplies.

Members of the janitorial staff under Mr. Goodenough's supervision need to expand their efforts to collect information about pieces of equipment throughout the company that are in need of repair or upkeep and provide this information to the maintenance department on a timely basis.

There has been an unusually high rate of turnover in the janitorial department over the course of the past year, and the human resources department recommends that he take advantage of available training and certification courses that could advance his management and supervisory skills.

Mr. Goodenough needs to improve his knowledge of company policy and state and federal regulations regarding the use and disposal of hazardous materials used in the manufacturing, technical, clerical, and janitorial processes. He is directed to make use of in-house training on this subject as well as to seek certification from professional associations.

Mr. Goodenough has not taken advantage of available training offered to his staff by vendors to assure proper operation of power equipment including floor cleaners, polishers, and industrial vacuum cleaners.

The security department has expressed concern over inconsistent observance of guidelines regarding the proper safeguarding of keys, alarm codes, and other security features. He is also asked to make sure that he and his staff are prepared to report suspicious or unusual activities or persons to security. Because of the mission-critical nature of this problem, with this evaluation he is directed to report to the executive committee within 30 days on progress in training and procedures.

UNSATISFACTORY

During Mr. Belowpar's tenure as foreman, the quality of services provided by the janitorial department has declined to unacceptable levels in some areas. Employee surveys express particular dissatisfaction with the cleanliness of the workplace, especially in restrooms and company lounges.

Despite the low quality of services, he has consistently overspent the departmental budget and needs to work closely with the purchasing department to find ways to save money and improve the quality of supplies by negotiating bulk purchases. He is directed to meet with the purchasing department within 30 days and to produce a plan that will stay within budget.

The janitorial staff, under Mr. Belowpar's management, has failed to follow company guidelines regarding the collection of trash, including separate handling of sensitive financial documents and hazardous waste. Mr. Belowpar is directed to make this a high priority for remediation within the next 30 days, reporting to the department of office services on his progress on a weekly basis until further notice.

The purchasing department has asked Mr. Belowpar to work with the MIS department to implement a program that permits computerized tracking and reordering of necessary supplies, and he is hereby directed to begin that process within 30 days.

Members of the janitorial staff under Mr. Belowpar's supervision have not properly informed the maintenance department about pieces of equipment that are in need of repair or upkeep. He is directed to instruct his staff about this element of their job description and to meet with the director of the maintenance department within 15 days to review these efforts.

Mr. Belowpar has not demonstrated an acceptable level of knowledge of company policy and state and federal regulations regarding the use and disposal of hazardous materials used in the manufacturing, technical, clerical, and janitorial processes. He is directed to make use of in-house training on this subject a high priority within the next 30 days.

Mr. Belowpar is directed to take advantage of available training offered to his staff by vendors to assure proper operation of power equipment including floor cleaners, polishers, and industrial vacuum cleaners.

The security department has expressed serious concern over lack of observance of guidelines regarding the proper safeguarding of keys, alarm codes, and other security features. Because of the mission-critical nature of this problem, with this evaluation he is directed to report to the executive committee within 10 days on progress in training and procedures.

Food Services Director

Cafeteria
Cashless billing
Caterers
Employee surveys
Food service
Food spoilage
Health codes
Menus
Subsidy

MEETS OR EXCEEDS

Mr. Paragon has greatly improved the quality of food served in the company cafeteria during his tenure. Surveys and comment cards have shown a high degree of satisfaction.

Although the cafeteria receives a subsidy from the company that reduces the cost to the employee, Mr. Paragon has done an excellent job of holding prices steady while maintaining superior quality and service. His budget line calls for him to operate the food service department on a break-even basis, including the fixed subsidy from the company, and he has stayed within these parameters.

In cooperation with the MIS department, Mr. Paragon has moved the cafeteria to a "cashless" department, debiting the cost of meals from accounts established by employees through the payroll department. This system has completely eliminated losses due to errors in billing and the potential for theft of cash.

He has worked closely with the purchasing department to negotiate contracts for food, supplies, and major equipment at advantageous prices. He has had great success managing perishable food in cold storage and freezers and thereby reducing waste.

In conjunction with the janitorial and maintenance departments, Mr. Paragon has demonstrated excellent attention to state and local health codes as they apply to the cafeteria, kitchen, and food storage areas.

Upon request from departments and the executive committee, Mr. Paragon has delivered excellent service providing coffee and snacks or meals for in-house meetings and conferences or utilizing contracts with caterers.

Over the course of the past year, the company cafeteria has expanded and varied its menu. Mr. Paragon has taken the initiative to offer items that take into account special diets including vegetarian and low-fat recipes. With advance notice and special arrangement, Mr. Paragon has demonstrated great flexibility in offering medically approved diets or meeting religious requirements, most often through the use of prepared foods from an outside, approved supplier.

Mr. Paragon and his staff have held their suppliers to very high standards for the quality of meat, poultry, fish, fruit, and vegetables used in preparation of meals.

Employee comment cards have also given high praise for special holiday and theme meals. Under his initiative, he has invited employees to share favorite recipes and dishes for "At Home at Work Days."

NEEDS IMPROVEMENT

Mr. Goodenough has not improved the quality of food served in the company cafeteria during his tenure. Surveys of employees and comment cards report general dissatisfaction with the cafeteria.

Although the cafeteria receives a subsidy from the company that reduces the cost to the employee, Mr. Goodenough has been forced to raise prices in the past year because of declining use of the cafeteria.

In his most recent evaluation, Mr. Goodenough was instructed to work with the MIS department to develop a "cashless" system, debiting the cost of meals from accounts established by employees through the payroll department. This has not been accomplished, and with this evaluation, he is directed to prepare a plan within 30 days for such a system and to implement it within six months.

Mr. Goodenough has not been effective in negotiating contracts for food, supplies, and major equipment at advantageous prices; he is directed to meet with the purchasing department within 30 days to request a review of all existing contracts and seek bids for new suppliers.

Health inspectors have issued warnings in several areas requiring remedial work to bring the kitchen and food preparation areas up to code; Mr. Goodenough is instructed to seek whatever training, certification, or special services and equipment that are necessary to keep the cafeteria facility at or above cleanliness standards.

Meals, coffee, and snacks provided by the food service department to meetings and conferences have been reported, on occasion, to be substandard. It is the expectation of the company that the department provide high-quality food at all times, and Mr. Goodenough is directed to investigate preparation for such in-house services.

The cafeteria has not significantly expanded and varied its menu over the past year and has not responded to requests for special diets including vegetarian, low-fat, medically prescribed recipes, or those meeting religious requirements.

One reason for a perceived decline in quality of food may be a failure to hold suppliers to the highest standards for meat, poultry, fish, fruit, and vegetables used in preparation of meals. With this evaluation, Mr. Goodenough is directed to prepare a report on his plans in this area and present it to the executive committee within 30 days.

UNSATISFACTORY

Ms. Belowpar has allowed the quality of food served in the company cafeteria to decline below acceptable levels. Surveys of employees and comment cards give the department very low grades.

The continuing decline in use of the cafeteria has caused a significant increase in prices for menu items; although food services receives a subsidy from the company for the specific purpose of reducing costs to the employee, the department's budget was exceeded in the fourth quarter last year, the first time this has happened since the cafeteria was established. This is unacceptable, and with this evaluation, Ms. Belowpar is directed to produce a report and present it to the office services department head within 30 days addressing plans to increase use of the cafeteria, reduce prices, and stay within the budget line.

As a key component of the effort to reduce prices and increase usage of the cafeteria, Ms. Belowpar is directed to immediately begin the process of negotiating new contracts for food, supplies, and major equipment. She is directed to meet with the purchasing department within 15 days to request a review of all existing contracts and seek bids for new suppliers.

The forced closure of the cafeteria for two days in November because of health code violations is an unacceptable occurrence and cannot be allowed to happen again. Ms. Belowpar is instructed to seek whatever training, certification, or special services and equipment that are necessary to keep the cafeteria facility at or above cleanliness standards.

The cafeteria has failed to expand or improve its menu over the past year. Further, Ms. Belowpar has not responded to requests for special diets including vegetarian, low-fat, medically prescribed recipes, or those meeting religious requirements. With this evaluation, she is directed to develop a plan for the overhaul of menus within 30 days.

CHAPTER 8

MANAGEMENT INFORMATION SERVICES

MIS Manager

Computer Services Technician

Database Analyst

Web Designer/Webmaster

MIS Manager

Computer hardware
Computer software
Computing strategies
Confidentiality of information
Corporate e-mail
Corporate intranet
Information processing
Information technology
Internet use by employees
Virus protection

MEETS OR EXCEEDS

Mr. Paragon has performed ably as manager of the company's overall computing strategies. He has successfully enhanced the company's use of information as a core tool and has consistently demonstrated a dedication to a cost-effective information processing budget.

Mr. Paragon has shown a strong commitment to working with every department in the company in an effort to get the most from the company's major investments in hardware and software. He has more than met the assignment given him by the executive committee to use information technology (IT) to improve the company's productivity; efficiency and profits have increased at higher-than-anticipated rates over the past two years. It is the expressed belief of senior management that IT has played a major role in this success.

Under his capable leadership, the information technologies task force has methodically examined every cost and profit center in the enterprise in search of ways to better collect, process, and analyze information. Mr. Paragon has assisted department heads in working with the experts on their own staffs to find new ways to save costs or produce greater profits.

Mr. Paragon has done an excellent job of fostering and maintaining systems that safeguard the confidentiality of personnel and company proprietary information stored in databases. He has also worked with in-house and outside consultants to assure that the company has backups of all data maintained in a secure location and a robust disaster recovery plan.

Under his management, the department has put into place important protections to improve the security of the corporate e-mail system, guarding against virus and hacker attacks. Mr. Paragon has also worked closely and effectively with the human resources department to keep current the company's policies on personal use of the Internet and e-mail.

The MIS department has extended a high degree of cooperation to the training department to offer courses on the use of computer equipment and software and on company policies. He has also assisted the training department in contracting with outside consultants and colleges. Under his initiative, the training department has also begun a series of on-site and online classes with instructors from hardware and software vendors to the company.

Mr. Paragon has exhibited a commitment to staying current on technologies and products and has received advanced certification from professional associations. He has taken advantage of the company's tuition reimbursement program to expand his areas of expertise.

NEEDS IMPROVEMENT

Ms. Goodenough has not shown a sufficient level of skill as manager of the company's overall computing strategies. She needs to improve her ability to accomplish her basic job assignment to enhance the company's use of information as a core tool.

Ms. Goodenough has not displayed an adequate level of effectiveness in working with departments throughout the company to get the most from the company's major investments in hardware and software. She has fallen short of the assignment given her by the executive committee to use information technology to improve the company's productivity; efficiency and profits have increased at lower-than-anticipated rates in the past 12 months. At least some of that shortfall can fairly be blamed on problems with information technology.

At the time of her previous evaluation, Ms. Goodenough was asked to form an information technologies task force to methodically examine every cost and profit center in the enterprise in search of ways to better collect, process, and analyze information. Although such a committee was established, the executive committee has not received any report from the group or seen any evidence of accomplishments. With this evaluation, Ms. Goodenough is directed to produce a plan of action on this matter within 30 days and provide the report to the executive committee.

Ms. Goodenough must do a better job of fostering and maintaining systems that safeguard the confidentiality of personnel and company proprietary information stored in databases. The legal department and chief compliance officer have each reported potential or actual exposure of confidential information on several occasions in the past six months. Ms. Goodenough is advised that she will be re-evaluated on this matter in 90 days.

A key element of the job description for MIS manager is to assure that the company has backups of all data maintained in a secure location and a robust disaster recovery plan. The recent failure of a data server (see attached report) highlights the fact that not all of the company's essential information is adequately backed up or otherwise available in the event of an emergency. With this report, Ms. Goodenough is directed to work with in-house and outside consultants to produce an effective plan for backup and recovery and to present a report on this matter to the executive committee within 30 days.

Under her management, the department has not put into place an adequate level of protection against virus and hacker attacks on the corporate e-mail system. Further, she has not shown the ability to work closely and effectively with the human resources department to keep current the company's policies on personal use of the Internet and e-mail.

The MIS department must also extend a higher degree of cooperation to the training department to offer courses on the use of computer equipment and software and on company policies. With this evaluation, Ms. Goodenough is directed to assist the training department in contracting with outside consultants and colleges. She should also work with the training department to seek on-site and online classes with instructors from hardware and software vendors to the company. She will be re-evaluated on this matter in 90 days.

Ms. Goodenough has not shown a commitment to staying current on technologies and products. She is asked to seek advanced certification from professional associations where available, and it is suggested she take advantage of the company's tuition reimbursement program to expand her areas of expertise.

UNSATISFACTORY

Mr. Belowpar has failed to show an adequate level of skill as manager of the company's overall computing strategies. He has not demonstrated the ability to accomplish his basic job assignment to enhance the company's use of information as a core tool.

He has fallen short of expectations in working with departments across the company to get the most from the company's major investments in hardware and software. At the time of his appointment to the position of MIS manager, he was charged with using information technology to improve the company's productivity; the executive committee has seen no evidence of success in Mr. Belowpar's efforts in this area.

At his most recent evaluation, Mr. Belowpar was directed to form an information technologies task force to methodically examine every cost and profit center in the enterprise in search of ways to better collect, process, and analyze information. Although such a committee was announced, it has only met once in formal session. With this evaluation, Mr. Belowpar is directed to make this his highest priority for the coming quarter; he is directed to inform the executive committee of the agenda for task force meetings within 15 days and to brief the committee within 45 days by written memo with a plan for action.

Mr. Belowpar has on several occasions in the past year failed to ensure the confidentiality of personnel and company proprietary information stored in databases. Attached is a memo coauthored by the head of the legal department and the chief compliance officer that documents potential or actual exposure of confidential information. Mr. Belowpar is advised that this is an unacceptable situation that must be rectified as soon as possible; he will be re-evaluated on this matter in 30 days.

Another area of great concern is the apparent lack of an adequate system to create and maintain backups of all data in a secure location and the establishment of a robust disaster recovery plan. The recent loss of a week's worth of orders due to a flood in the data center is unacceptable; the costs to the company in reconstructing the orders were significant and damaging to the company's reputation.

With this report, Mr. Belowpar is directed to immediately begin work with in-house and outside consultants to produce an effective plan for backup and recovery and to present a preliminary report on this matter to the executive committee within 10 days and to keep the committee up to date on progress with written memos every 10 days thereafter. He will be re-evaluated on his accomplishment of this essential assignment within 90 days.

Under his management, the MIS department has failed to put into place an adequate level of protection against virus and hacker attacks on the corporate e-mail system. Further, Mr. Belowpar has not responded to several requests from the human resources department to update the employee handbook about the company's policies on personal use of the Internet and e-mail. He is directed to make both of these matters a high priority within the next 45 days; he will be re-evaluated on his management of e-mail policy at the end of that time period.

Computer Services Technician

Computer services
Computer virus
E-mail guidelines
Increasing workload
Internet
Personal use of Internet
Repair computers
Spam
Troubleshooting
Update computers

MEETS OR EXCEEDS

Ms. Paragon has demonstrated excellent skills as an in-house computer services technician. She has greatly improved the uptime and efficiency of desktop computers throughout the enterprise.

Over the past year, Ms. Paragon worked closely with the purchasing department to develop a program to upgrade all of the personal computers now in use for research and development, engineering, and manufacturing purposes; through installation of additional memory and access to shared workgroup storage space, the program has saved the company hundreds of thousands of dollars over the cost of replacing the three-year-old machines.

Despite a steadily increasing workload, she has shown herself to be an effective and capable resource in the company. Working in conjunction with the training department, she has initiated a series of courses on computer troubleshooting that allows many users to diagnose problems; Ms. Paragon's guidelines to users give instructions for self-repair of many basic problems and lay the groundwork for rapid fixes to more serious issues.

Ms. Paragon has also assisted the training department in setting up and running a series of courses on computer technologies and software.

She has kept current on new technologies and software, attending trade shows and conventions and receiving advanced certification from professional organizations. Ms. Paragon has also been pursuing a master's degree program in computer technology, with the support of the training department's tuition reimbursement program.

Ms. Paragon worked with the purchasing department to negotiate a cost-effective site license program with a major software company, allowing a systemwide upgrade to products including word processors, project managers, spreadsheets, and collaborative calendars.

At the direction of the MIS manager, she convened a task force to study available antivirus and antispam programs and implement a new enterprisewide strategy. She provided the human resources department with information to update the employee handbook on issues including the personal use of the Internet and safe computing practices to avoid introduction of viruses and the overloading of the system with spam and other inappropriate e-mail.

Ms. Paragon has demonstrated superior skills in managing the technical side of the corporate intranet and the external Internet; she has shown great cooperation with the sales department and the outside Web site consultant. Working with the purchasing department, she assisted in the negotiation of a contract for ISP broadband service at a significant reduction in cost over the previous leased-line connection.

She has been extremely responsive to requests from the MIS manager as part of the ongoing development of the enterprise's overall corporate computing strategies, assuring that individual PCs and workstations are able to interface with the corporate mainframe and essential databases.

NEEDS IMPROVEMENT

Ms. Goodenough needs to improve her skills as an in-house computer services technician. At times she has seemed to be overwhelmed by a steadily increasing and complex workload.

It is suggested that Ms. Goodenough work closely with the training department to develop a series of courses on computer troubleshooting to allow users to diagnose problems and perform basic fixes. This should help reduce some of the demand on Ms. Goodenough's services.

A large number of the company's desktop computers were purchased more than three years ago, and users have requested replacement with more current machines. Ms. Goodenough is directed to work closely with the purchasing department to investigate the possibility of upgrading many or all of these machines through installation of additional memory and access to shared workgroup storage space. Based on industry surveys, many similar-sized companies have saved hundreds of thousands of dollars by upgrading rather than replacing certain classes of machines.

Ms. Goodenough has not demonstrated a commitment to keeping current on new technologies and software; she should attend trade shows and conventions and seek advanced certification from professional organizations.

Rather than approving individual requests for updated or improved software, Ms. Goodenough should work with the purchasing department to negotiate a cost-effective site license program with a major software company, allowing a systemwide upgrade to products including word processors, project managers, spreadsheets, and collaborative calendars.

The company has suffered downtime and significant costs in dealing with viruses allowed into the network by users and through the volume of spam that has on occasion clogged the enterprise's mail servers. With this evaluation, she is directed to convene a task force to study available antivirus and antispam programs and implement a new enterprisewide strategy. She is also asked to provide the human resources department with information to update the employee handbook on issues including the personal use of the Internet and safe computing practices to avoid introduction of viruses and the overloading of the system with spam and other inappropriate e-mail.

Ms. Goodenough needs to improve her skills in managing the technical side of the corporate intranet and the external Internet; she is directed to work more closely with the sales department and the outside Web site consultant.

UNSATISFACTORY

Mr. Belowpar has failed to demonstrate an adequate level of skill as an in-house computer services technician and has not proven able to keep up with a steadily increasing and complex workload.

With this evaluation, Mr. Belowpar is directed to meet with the training department to develop a series of courses on computer troubleshooting to allow users to diagnose problems and perform basic fixes. This should help reduce some of the demand on Mr. Belowpar's services.

A large number of the company's desktop computers were purchased more than three years ago, and users have requested replacement with more current machines. The executive department has not approved Mr. Belowpar's major capital expenditure request to replace more than 125 machines with new devices; Mr. Belowpar is directed to meet with the purchasing department within 30 days to investigate the possibility of upgrading many or all of these machines through installation of additional memory and access to shared workgroup storage space. He is authorized to engage a consultant to perform a cost-benefit analysis of a systemwide upgrade.

In a related matter, Mr. Belowpar has failed to demonstrate current knowledge on new technologies and software; he should attend trade shows and conventions and seek advanced certification from professional organizations.

Mr. Belowpar has not adequately dealt with several recent system crashes that are blamed on viruses allowed into the network by users. With this evaluation, he is directed to convene a task force within 30 days to study available antivirus and antispam programs and implement a new enterprisewide strategy. He is also directed to provide the human resources department within that same 30-day period with information to update the employee handbook on issues including the personal use of the Internet and safe computing practices to avoid introduction of viruses and the overloading of the system with spam and other inappropriate e-mail.

Database Analyst

Archiving data
Computer processing
Custom programming
Data reports
Data storage
Database analyst
Database retrieval
Disaster recovery
Information archive
Information reports

MEETS OR EXCEEDS

Mr. Paragon has demonstrated great skill as a database analyst and exceptional cooperation with every department of the company. As a modern company, the core of all operations is built around information and the systems that manage it, and Mr. Paragon has shown exceptional initiative in expanding and enhancing enterprisewide and special-purpose systems.

He has shown an ability to work closely and effectively with the MIS department to assure adequate processing power and storage capacity for information systems; at the same time, he regularly meets with departments throughout the company to assess new information collection, distribution, and analysis needs.

Mr. Paragon exhibits a close attention to detail in commissioning custom programming for database retrieval and reports, supervising the work of in-house staff and serving as the liaison to outside consultants.

He does a commendable job of keeping up to date on the company and all of its products and services. He has taken advantage of courses offered by the training department and received advanced certification from professional organizations. This fall, Mr. Paragon is due to take advantage of company-paid tuition for postgraduate courses to advance his skills.

He has ably assisted the training department in setting up general and specialized courses on data input, report generation, and other elements of the use of database systems.

Mr. Paragon has shown exceptional commitment to ensuring that databases are updated and monitored for performance on a regular basis. He has also led the way in developing and implementing a companywide plan to archive information and prepare for disaster recovery.

NEEDS IMPROVEMENT

Ms. Goodenough needs to improve her skills as a database analyst and especially in the area of communications with nontechnical clients in every department. As a modern company, the core of all operations is built around information and the systems that manage it, and Ms. Goodenough must show improvement in expanding and enhancing enterprisewide and special-purpose systems.

She needs to work more closely and effectively with the MIS department to assure adequate processing power and storage capacity for information systems; over the course of the past year, demand for information retrieval has exceeded the capacity of installed systems. She must also meet more regularly with departments throughout the company to assess new information collection, distribution, and analysis needs and coordinate demand with available system capacity.

Ms. Goodenough lacks a close attention to detail in commissioning custom programming for database retrieval and reports. She must devote more time to supervising the work of in-house staff and outside consultants.

She must also devote more effort to ensuring that databases are updated and monitored for performance on a regular basis.

At the time of her previous evaluation, she was asked to convene a task force to explore the development and implementation of a companywide plan to archive information and prepare for disaster recovery. Although a committee was formed, it has not produced recommendations; Ms. Goodenough is directed to make this a high priority in the next three months and will be reevaluated on this matter 90 days from now.

She has not kept up to date on the company and all of its products and services. She is advised to take advantage of courses offered by the training department and to seek advanced certification from professional organizations. With this evaluation, she is directed to meet with the training department to discuss available courses, including company-paid tuition for postgraduate courses to advance her skills.

Ms. Goodenough also needs to assist the training department in setting up general and specialized courses on data input, report generation, and other elements of the use of database systems.

UNSATISFACTORY

Mr. Belowpar has proved unable to exhibit adequate skills as a database analyst and has fallen especially short in the area of communications with nontechnical clients in every department. As a modern company, the core of all operations is built around information and the systems that manage it, and Mr. Belowpar has not adequately expanded and enhanced enterprisewide and special-purpose systems.

He has failed to work closely and effectively with the MIS department to assure adequate processing power and storage capacity for information systems; over the course of the past year, demand for information retrieval has greatly exceeded the capacity of installed systems.

He is directed to meet at least monthly with departments throughout the company to assess new information collection, distribution, and analysis needs and coordinate demand with available system capacity.

Mr. Belowpar has not demonstrated sufficient attention to detail in commissioning custom programming for database retrieval and reports. With this evaluation, he is directed to greatly increase the amount of time spent supervising the work of in-house staff and outside consultants; he will be re-evaluated on this matter within 45 days.

Mr. Belowpar is instructed to devote more effort to ensuring that databases are updated and monitored for performance on a regular basis. With this evaluation, he is asked to report to the MIS director within 15 days to detail his plans for greater supervision.

At the time of his previous evaluation, Mr. Belowpar was directed to convene a task force to explore the development and implementation of a companywide plan to archive information and prepare for disaster recovery. No such committee was formed; Mr. Belowpar is directed to make this his highest priority. The executive committee asks for a progress report within 30 days and a proposal for action within 60 days.

Mr. Belowpar is charged with assisting the training department in setting up general and specialized courses on data input, report generation, and other elements of the use of database systems. He will be re-evaluated on this matter within 60 days.

Web Designer/Webmaster

Consultants
Credit card billing
Customer support department
Electronic access to sales brochures
Emergency debugging
Internet
Internet shopping carts
Links
Live chat
Webmaster

MEETS OR EXCEEDS

Ms. Paragon has ably led the company onto the Internet, making the company's products and services available for sale on the Web, and has helped promote the company's overall operations through the electronic publication of sales, support, and other documentation.

Through her chairmanship of the Internet task force, Ms. Paragon has worked with nearly every department in the enterprise. A series of programming tools, implemented with a high degree of cooperation with the MIS department, has permitted departments to create their own Web pages.

Ms. Paragon and her staff have met regularly with departments to assist them in making the best use of the Internet to support company goals.

The company's customer support department received national recognition at a recent industry trade show for their use of the Internet. They were acknowledged for their efforts to make electronically available sales brochures, instruction manuals, parts and supplies inventory, and a live chat function for quick questions to customer support engineers.

As part of the transition to the Web, Ms. Paragon has made members of her department available 24 hours a day, seven days a week for emergency debugging and repair of problems with the new system. Staffers in Ms. Paragon's department are able to perform much of their after-hours work from their homes or on the road, using portable computers that can tie into the enterprise's servers.

Before the system was put into place, Ms. Paragon met with the sales and marketing departments to determine a reasonable set of expectations and to set a budget for the project. As a result, the cost of the Web presence stayed within the budget, and the company expects to recoup its investment within 18 months through increased sales and decreased costs for support.

Ms. Paragon preceded her effort with six months of intensive training through professional associations and effective consultation with an outside Web design firm. She continues to keep herself up to date on developing technologies.

Working closely with the training department, Ms. Paragon has established a set of classes on Internet strategies and the use of the various software tools for programming Web pages.

As first launched, the company's Web pages used an outside service bureau to handle shopping carts, credit card billing and collection, and secure file serving. Ms. Paragon's task force is currently working to bring these services in-house, reducing costs of operation for the Web pages and adding an equivalent amount of profit to the bottom line.

Ms. Paragon has worked effectively with sales and marketing departments to promote the availability of the Web site in company advertising sales collateral materials. She has encouraged the marketing department to seek cooperative links with noncompetitive partners.

NEEDS IMPROVEMENT

Mr. Goodenough needs to greatly improve the company's offerings on the Internet, making the company's products and services available for sale on the Web and helping promote the company's overall operations through the electronic publication of sales, support, and other documentation.

Mr. Goodenough was asked 12 months ago by the executive committee to chair the Internet task force, working with nearly every department in the enterprise. Although meetings took place, members of the group reported little opportunity to make requests or suggestions for elements of the resulting Web site.

The consultant employed by Mr. Goodenough produced a set of Web pages that seemed to be very generic and not especially appropriate for the products, services, and mission statement of the company.

With this evaluation, Mr. Goodenough and his staff are directed to meet regularly with departments to listen to requests for customization and adaptation of the Web pages; he is asked to report to the executive committee within 30 days with specific responses to departmental requests.

The customer support department has asked that the Web site include electronic access to sales brochures, instruction manuals, parts and supplies, and a live chat function for quick questions to customer support engineers. Mr. Goodenough is directed to make this a high priority for implementation within 60 days of this evaluation.

As part of the transition to the Web, Mr. Goodenough is asked to make members of his department available 24 hours a day, seven days a week for emergency debugging and repair of problems with the new system. This can be accomplished from their homes or on the road, using portable computers that can tie into the enterprise's servers.

Mr. Goodenough has not demonstrated a commitment to educating himself about use of the Internet and current technologies. He is directed to immediately seek additional training and certification from professional associations.

Further, he must work closely with the training department to establish a set of classes on Internet strategies and the use of the various software tools for programming Web pages.

As first launched, the company's Web pages used an outside service bureau to handle shopping carts, credit card billing and collection, and secure file serving. With this evaluation, Mr. Goodenough is directed to make plans to bring these services in-house within 90 days, reducing costs of operation for the Web pages and adding an equivalent amount of profit to the bottom line.

Mr. Goodenough needs to work more effectively with the sales and marketing departments to promote the availability of the Web site in company advertising sales collateral materials. He should also encourage the marketing department to seek cooperative links with noncompetitive partners.

UNSATISFACTORY

Ms. Belowpar has failed to adequately launch the company on the Internet, making the company's products and services available for sale on the Web and helping promote the company's overall operations through the electronic publication of sales, support, and other documentation.

In Ms. Belowpar's year as chairman of the Internet task force, working with nearly every department in the enterprise, the results have been well beneath the expectations of the executive committee.

Members of the task force report Ms. Belowpar gave them little opportunity to make requests or suggestions for elements of the resulting Web site. The consultant engaged by Ms. Belowpar produced a set of Web pages that seemed to be very generic and not especially appropriate for the products, services, and mission statement of the company.

With this evaluation, Ms. Belowpar and her staff are directed to immediately meet with departments to listen to requests for customization and adaptation of the Web pages; she is directed to deliver to the executive committee within 30 days a plan to greatly improve the company's Web presence. This is to be Ms. Belowpar's highest priority in the next 90 days; she will be re-evaluated at that time on these matters.

Among the first tasks expected to be accomplished is addition of electronic access to sales brochures, instruction manuals, parts and supplies, and a live chat function for quick questions to customer support engineers.

Ms. Belowpar has not kept up to date on the use of the Internet and current technologies. She is directed to immediately seek additional training and certification from professional associations.

Further, she is directed to meet with the head of the training department within 15 days to establish a set of classes on Internet strategies and the use of the various software tools for programming Web pages.

CHAPTER 9

SECRETARIAL AND CLERICAL

Office Manager

Administrative/Executive Assistant

Secretary/Personal Assistant

Receptionist

Clerical Assistant

Office Manager

Budgets
Communications needs
Compliance
Employee evaluations
Expense accounts
Hiring and evaluation
Office equipment
Office support staff
Officer services
Sick leave
Special events
Time sheets
Travel reimbursement
Vacation leave

MEETS OR EXCEEDS

Mr. Paragon has demonstrated exceptional skills as office manager, planning and overseeing administrative support and office services for his department and ably cooperating with other elements of the company when they need assistance.

He has shown considerable skill in representing the department in coordinating with the human resources department for the hiring and evaluation of office support staff. Working closely with departmental supervisors, he contributes to the annual employee evaluations of support staff.

Mr. Paragon displays an outstanding commitment to company goals in overseeing the communications needs of the department. On his own initiative, he surveyed members of the department seeking suggestions for improvement in office services; he conveyed that information to managers in the mailroom, telecommunications, and computer services departments that resulted in significant changes in equipment and procedures.

Mr. Paragon consistently demonstrates a high degree of attention to detail in managing fiscal matters for the department. He capably assists supervisors in developing the annual budget for office support staff, equipment, and supplies. Each month he carefully evaluates ledgers from cost centers, including mailroom, telecommunications, research, and training expenses to assure that the department is being properly billed for services and to guard against unanticipated overages in budget lines.

He receives and verifies expense accounts and travel reimbursement forms, obtaining a sign-off from the department head before passing them along to accounting for audit and payment. In performing these tasks, he demonstrates close attention to company guidelines and procedures.

He skillfully manages the departmental calendar, scheduling meetings and other appointments for executives and staff. He also has demonstrated close attention to the management of requests for vacation leave, coordinating with executives when necessary to assure proper coverage of all important tasks. He oversees and processes time sheets for hourly employees and documents sick leave for all employees efficiently and accurately.

On a day-to-day basis, he displays excellent skills in managing the daily administrative operations of the department including establishing work priorities. As needed, he reassigns office staff to meet the needs of special projects.

He demonstrates competence above expectations in working with the meeting planner and the sales, marketing, and public relations departments in the preparation for special events including the annual shareholders meeting, product introductions, and sales conferences. He also ably represents the department on procedural task forces as requested.

Mr. Paragon works effectively with the legal and compliance departments to monitor their observance of employee guidelines and federal, state, and local mandates and laws.

NEEDS IMPROVEMENT

Ms. Goodenough needs to improve her skills as office manager. She is asked to devote attention to her capabilities in planning and overseeing administrative support and office services for her department and displaying greater cooperation with other elements of the company when they need assistance.

She must enhance her ability to represent the department in coordinating with the human resources department for the hiring and evaluation of office support staff.

Ms. Goodenough was asked six months ago by the department head to survey members of the department seeking suggestions for improvement in office services; there is no indication that the resulting information was conveyed to managers in the mailroom, telecommunications, or computer services departments. With this evaluation, she is directed to prepare a report on proposed enhancements and present it to her department head within 15 days; once it has been reviewed, she is asked to meet with appropriate service departments to seek improvements in equipment and procedures.

Ms. Goodenough has not consistently demonstrated a high degree of attention to detail in managing fiscal matters for the department. Among the elements of the job description for office manager are:

- Assisting supervisors in developing the annual budget for office support staff, equipment, and supplies;
- Evaluating monthly ledgers from cost centers, including mailroom, telecommunications, research, and training expenses to assure that the department is being properly billed for services and to guard against unanticipated overages in budget lines;
- Receiving and verifying expense accounts and travel reimbursement forms and obtaining sign-off from a department head before passing them along to accounting for audit and payment.

In performing these fiscal review assignments, Ms. Goodenough has not demonstrated a sufficient degree of attention to detail, company guidelines, and procedures. With this evaluation, she is asked to meet with the training department within 30 days to seek further in-house education and to explore available advanced certification from professional associations.

Ms. Goodenough is asked to improve her management of the departmental calendar in the scheduling of meetings and other appointments for executives and staff. She is also directed to integrate the department's listing of approved vacation leaves into the calendar. She is asked to meet with the training department within 15 days to seek training on the use of the company's shared calendar system.

As office manager, Ms. Goodenough is charged with managing the approval of requests for vacation leave, coordinating with executives when necessary to assure proper coverage of all important tasks. She is asked to meet with the human resources department to review company policy on these matters and to seek further training if necessary.

Ms. Goodenough has not shown adequate skills in managing the daily administrative operations of the department including establishing work priorities. As stated in the job description for office manager, she is expected to take note of major special projects and to reassign office staff if needed. She is also expected to represent the department on procedural task forces as requested.

Ms. Goodenough has not worked effectively with the legal and compliance departments to monitor the department's observance of employee guidelines and federal, state, and local mandates and laws. With this evaluation, she is instructed to meet with those departments within 15 days to discuss this matter.

UNSATISFACTORY

Mr. Belowpar has failed to display adequate skills as office manager. He has not shown an acceptable level of attention to key requirements of his job, including planning and overseeing administrative support and office services for his department. He has also not cooperated well with other elements of the company when they need assistance.

He is directed to meet with the human resources department within 15 days to discuss company procedures regarding the hiring and evaluation of office support staff.

Mr. Belowpar was asked six months ago by the department head to survey members seeking suggestions for improvement in office services; no such survey was conducted. With this evaluation, he is directed to seek input from every member of the department within 21 days and to present a report on requests, together with a reasonable set of proposed enhancements, to his department head within 30 days. He is advised to meet with the office services department for guidance on new technologies and procedures adopted elsewhere in the company.

Mr. Belowpar has failed to demonstrate a high degree of attention to detail in managing fiscal matters for the department. Among problems noted by supervisors are:

- A lack of meaningful assistance in developing the annual budget for office support staff, equipment, and supplies;
- Errors and omissions in evaluating monthly ledgers from cost centers, including mailroom, telecommunications, research, and training expenses. On five occasions in the past 12 months departmental managers were not notified when budget lines were

exceeded. In two of those instances, Mr. Belowpar failed to catch errors in billing of services;

- Inattention to expense accounts and travel reimbursement forms. Mr. Belowpar is expected to verify forms and obtain sign-off from the department head before passing them along to accounting for audit and payment.

In performing these fiscal review assignments, Mr. Belowpar has not demonstrated a sufficient degree of attention to detail, company guidelines, and procedures. With this evaluation, he is directed to meet with the training department within 10 days to seek further in-house education. He will be re-evaluated on this matter in 45 days.

Mr. Belowpar is instructed to improve management of the departmental calendar in the scheduling of meetings and other appointments for executives and staff. He is also directed to integrate the department's listing of approved vacation leaves into the calendar. He is directed to meet with the training department within 15 days to seek training on the use of the company's shared calendar system. Mr. Belowpar will be re-evaluated on this matter within 45 days.

Mr. Belowpar has not adequately managed the approval of requests for vacation leave, resulting in an inadequate level of staffing at various times. He is directed to meet with the human resources department within 10 days to review company policy on these matters.

Mr. Belowpar was instructed six months ago to cooperate with the legal and compliance departments in the monitoring of the department's observance of employee guidelines and federal, state, and local mandates and laws. There is no evidence of an improvement in performance in these matters. With this evaluation, he is directed to meet with those departments within 15 days; he is further directed to report to his direct supervisor within 25 days to discuss his efforts.

Administrative/Executive Assistant

Administrative assistant
Confidential information
Demeanor
Editing correspondence
E-mails
Executive assistant
Intraoffice meetings
PowerPoint presentations
Prioritizing communication
Professional appearance
Scheduling appointments
Telephone calls

MEETS OR EXCEEDS

As executive assistant to the director of marketing, Ms. Paragon has become an important asset to the entire department. She demonstrates excellent attention to detail in planning and scheduling appointments and meetings. She coordinates the complex calendars of more than 25 staffers with great skill.

She manages and prioritizes the large volume of incoming and outgoing communication for the department with considerable efficiency and consistency. In her direct assignments for the director, she answers incoming telephone calls and screens messages very well, delegating some requests to support staff when appropriate. She reviews incoming e-mails, responding on behalf of the director when possible, redirecting some when possible, and prioritizing those to be answered by the director.

Ms. Paragon shows a high degree of discretion and trustworthiness in handling personnel, salary, and other confidential information.

For departmental functions and campaigns, Ms. Paragon demonstrates great proficiency and knowledge in working with the travel planner to arrange air, car, and hotel reservations and other details. She also works well with in-house departments including food service for informal intraoffice meetings.

Ms. Paragon represents the department ably on task forces for annual shareholder meetings and sales conferences.

She presents a professional appearance and demeanor at all times.

She demonstrates strong skills in the use of the computer for preparing or editing correspondence and in performing research tasks as requested by the director. She is also very capable in creating PowerPoint presentations and managing department databases and spreadsheets.

Ms. Paragon has shown a strong commitment to keeping current on all company products and services and has taken courses offered by the training department and received advanced certification from professional organizations.

NEEDS IMPROVEMENT

As executive assistant to the director of marketing, Ms. Goodenough needs to expand her role to provide necessary services to the entire department on behalf of her supervisor.

She has not demonstrated adequate attention to detail in planning and scheduling appointments and meetings. There have been numerous instances of conflicts and overlapping appointments and assignments during events she has set up for the 25 staffers in the department.

Ms. Goodenough has not shown that she can consistently and efficiently manage and prioritize the large volume of incoming and outgoing communication for the department. In her direct assignments for the director, she answers incoming telephone calls and screens messages very well but has not shown good judgment in delegating some requests to support staff when appropriate. Similarly, she needs to greatly improve her skills in reviewing incoming e-mails, responding on behalf of the director when possible, redirecting some when possible, and prioritizing those to be answered by the director.

Ms. Goodenough is directed to meet with the human resources department within 15 days to review company policy regarding the privacy of personnel, salary, and other confidential information.

For departmental functions and campaigns, Ms. Goodenough is asked to improve her ability to work with the travel planner to arrange air, car, and hotel reservations and other details. She is asked to meet with the training department within 30 days to seek advanced education on these matters.

Ms. Goodenough needs to make herself available as a representative of the department on task forces for annual shareholder meetings and sales conferences.

Ms. Goodenough is asked to review company guidelines on the dress code. She has, at times, not presented a professional appearance. She will be re-evaluated on this matter within 30 days.

She needs to greatly improve her skills in the use of the computer for preparing or editing correspondence and in performing research tasks as requested by the director. Specifically, she is asked to request training or certification in creating PowerPoint presentations and managing department databases and spreadsheets; both of these tasks are elements of the job description for an administrative assistant.

Ms. Goodenough has not shown a commitment to keeping current on all company products and services. She is asked to meet with the training department within 30 days to seek assistance on these matters.

UNSATISFACTORY

As executive assistant to the director of marketing, Mr. Belowpar has failed to provide necessary services to the entire department on behalf of his supervisor. He is asked to meet with the human resources department within 15 days to review the job description for an administrative assistant.

He has not proven himself able to devote adequate attention to detail in planning and scheduling appointments and meetings. At the most recent departmental meeting, more than half of the staff was not notified in advance, and six others were scheduled to be out of town at the time of the gathering.

Mr. Belowpar has shown disappointing results in consistently and efficiently managing and prioritizing the large volume of incoming and outgoing communication for the department.

With this evaluation, Mr. Belowpar is directed to meet with the training department to seek assistance in the following tasks:

- Answering incoming telephone calls;
- Taking messages accurately;
- Delegating requests to support staff when appropriate;
- Reviewing incoming e-mails;
- Responding to e-mail on behalf of the director when possible;
- Redirecting e-mail when appropriate; and
- Prioritizing e-mails to be answered by the director.

In several instances, Mr. Belowpar has disclosed confidential information or otherwise mishandled matters that are not to be disclosed. Mr. Belowpar is directed to meet with the human resources department within 10 days to review company policy regarding the privacy of personnel, salary, and other confidential information. He will be re-evaluated on this matter within 21 days.

Mr. Belowpar has, on several occasions, declined to work with the travel planner to arrange air, car, and hotel reservations and other details for departmental functions and campaigns. This is part of his job description; he is asked to meet with the human resources department within 10 days to review assigned tasks. He is expected to be available to members of the department for assistance in making travel arrangements within 30 days.

Mr. Belowpar has also not participated as a representative of the department on task forces for annual shareholder meetings and sales conferences. With this evaluation, he is directed to make himself available for such purposes immediately. He will be re-evaluated on this matter within 45 days.

He needs to greatly improve his skills in the use of the computer for preparing or editing correspondence and in performing research tasks as requested by the director. With this evaluation, he is directed to seek available training offered in-house, through professional associations, and at area colleges under the company's tuition reimbursement program.

Specifically, he is asked to become an expert on creating PowerPoint presentations for departmental meetings and managing department databases and spreadsheets; both of these tasks are elements of the job description for an administrative assistant.

Mr. Belowpar has failed to keep current on all company products and services. He is asked to meet with the training department within 30 days to seek assistance on these matters.

Secretary/Personal Assistant

Attendance record
Calendar
Civil discourse
Enterprise calendar
Medical excuse
Overtime
Punctual
Secretarial services
Sick days
Special projects
Telephone
Training
Weekend work
Writing skills

MEETS OR EXCEEDS

Mr. Paragon demonstrates an exceptional degree of professionalism as a secretary and personal assistant. He is highly organized and makes excellent use of his time in advance planning.

In his first weeks on the job, he made suggestions to the MIS department that resulted in valuable enhancements to the shared enterprisewide calendar. Over the course of the year, he has consistently shown a willingness to take on new assignments and responsibilities.

He has made himself very knowledgeable about the company and its products and services and has gotten to know members of senior management, department heads, and other staffers as appropriate for the conduct of his job. He has enrolled in several courses offered by the training department and has also begun the process of receiving advanced certification from professional management and technical associations.

He demonstrates great attention to detail and accuracy, reorganizing computer folders and coordinating them with paper files to save time and effort on retrieval.

In dealings with the public, Mr. Paragon represents the company well, showing professionalism and sincerity on the telephone, in written correspondence, and at functions with clients.

Mr. Paragon volunteered to be a member of the President's Committee on Civil Discourse, a group that is drafting a company policy to state more clearly our corporate position on political, religious, and other forms of expression and how they relate to employee behavior on and off the job.

Mr. Paragon recorded an exemplary record of attendance over the course of the past year, missing only one day of work because of illness. At the same time, he managed to be at his desk every day during the severe winter storms last January, assisting his department in completion of a major marketing campaign.

He has made himself available for overtime and weekend work in support of his own department as well as other departments as requested for special projects, sales conferences, conventions, stockholder meetings, and other mission-critical events.

NEEDS IMPROVEMENT

Mr. Goodenough has performed all of the core assignments of his job description but has not demonstrated a willingness to take on new responsibilities or to expand the scope of present assignments. Although he has done an exemplary job in maintaining essential corporate files, he has not coordinated his work with other departments or worked closely with the MIS department to allow efficient sharing of information across the enterprise.

He needs to become more knowledgeable about the company and its products and services and to acquaint himself with members of senior management, department heads, and other staffers as appropriate for the conduct of his job. In dealings with the public, Mr. Goodenough has not consistently represented the company well; he needs to improve his professionalism and sincerity on the telephone, in written correspondence, and at functions with clients.

Mr. Goodenough has not taken advantage of courses offered by the training department on computer and secretarial skills and should do so.

Although he has shown himself to be generally dependable and punctual, he chose to take his summer vacation during a period when his supervisor asked him to be at work for completion of the annual budget, resulting in a significant extra load on coworkers. Similarly, he has not made himself available for overtime and weekend work in support of his own department as well as other departments as requested for special projects, sales conferences, conventions, stockholder meetings, and other mission-critical events.

Mr. Goodenough's writing skills are not at the level expected; his supervisor offered the services of a writing coach through the company's training and employee development department soon after he began his employment in February and again in June, but as of this date, no such training has taken place. With this evaluation, he is directed to meet with the training department within 30 days to set a schedule for such training.

UNSATISFACTORY

Ms. Belowpar has not demonstrated that she can be depended upon to complete assignments on time and with acceptable accuracy and detail. At times, she seems overwhelmed by basic tasks but has never asked for assistance or for additional training.

In May, she was asked to attend a two-day training course entitled "Enhancing Organizational Efficiency" conducted by an independent contractor at an off-site location; according to the report of the trainer, Ms. Belowpar missed the first hour of the opening session and was uncooperative in role-playing games and other exercises.

Her attendance record exceeded allowable sick days and personal days in three of the four quarters over the last year. Although it is company policy not to require documentation from a doctor for short absences claimed as necessary for medical reasons, her supervisor points out that all but one of the 16 days she was absent in the past year occurred on a Monday or Friday, resulting in extended weekends. Several coworkers complained to supervisors about her attendance record because of the added burden it placed on them.

Ms. Belowpar has failed to demonstrate a willingness to take on new responsibilities or to expand the scope of present assignments. She has not coordinated her work with other departments or worked closely with the MIS department to allow efficient sharing of information across the enterprise.

She has not shown a commitment to becoming knowledgeable about the company and its products and services or to acquaint herself with members of senior management, department heads, and other staffers as appropriate for the conduct of her job.

In her previous evaluation, Ms. Belowpar was instructed to take advantage of courses offered by the training department on computer and secretarial skills and has failed to do so; she is directed to meet with the training department within 15 days to set up a schedule for such classes.

Receptionist

Assist special projects
Electronic message system
Entrance lobby
ID cards
Knowledge of company's products and services
Overtime and weekend work
Package inspection
Scheduling appointments
Security task force
Security threats
Visitors
Voice mail

MEETS OR EXCEEDS

Mr. Paragon represents the company very well as lead receptionist. To most visitors, he is the point of first contact with the company when they visit or call the main telephone number without seeking a specific individual or department. He has consistently demonstrated a high degree of knowledge about the company and its products and services; at the same time, he has shown great discretion and attention to security issues when appropriate.

He consistently greets visitors in a professional and friendly manner, answering basic questions about products and services when appropriate and directing them to particular departments when necessary. He has worked closely with the MIS department to enhance and refine the electronic message system for the company, merging voice mail systems with manual entries resulting from telephone calls handled by the receptionist directly and inquiries from visitors to the reception desk.

Upon request, he has shown great flexibility and accuracy in managing a scheduling book for job interviews, product presentations, and other events and services.

He always presents a good appearance in dress and grooming; he has done an excellent job of working with the maintenance and janitorial staff to assure that the entrance lobby is neat and attractive and stocked with company brochures.

Mr. Paragon has shown great flexibility in making himself available for overtime and weekend work when requested, helping out at special events including sales conferences, conventions, and other company functions. In exceptional situations, he has also been available to assist secretarial and other support staff in production of documents, preparation of mass mailings, and handling excessive incoming or outgoing correspondence.

He has demonstrated excellent computer skills and has taken advantage of several advanced courses offered by the training department. He has shown himself to be very well organized and able to handle multiple tasks.

Working with the office services department, he has taken on added responsibility as liaison with the telephone company and the vendor for the intraoffice telephone and voice mail system.

He has been an active participant in the companywide security task force and has accepted responsibility as one of the keepers of the gates to the enterprise. He pays close attention to employee ID cards and verifies the identity of visitors with great care. Mr. Paragon has been trained on company procedures aimed at handling unknown visitors and possible threats. He works closely with the mailroom and the security department to divert incoming packages for inspection.

NEEDS IMPROVEMENT

Ms. Goodenough needs to improve her skills as lead receptionist. To most visitors, she is the point of first contact with the company when they visit or call the main telephone number without seeking a specific individual or department. She has not demonstrated a high degree of knowledge about the company and its products and services; she is directed to meet with the training department within 30 days to seek assistance in this area.

On occasion, employees have noted proprietary interoffice memos and other private information in plain sight on her desk; she needs to closely follow company guidelines regarding sensitive information and security issues.

According to reports received by some department heads, she does not always greet visitors in a professional and friendly manner. She needs to improve her ability to answer basic questions about products and services when appropriate and direct them to particular departments when necessary.

She has not demonstrated flexibility and accuracy in managing a scheduling book for job interviews; this was a specific need identified by department heads to assist in setting up product presentations and other events and services.

While she presents a good appearance in dress and grooming, she has allowed the entrance lobby to become sloppy and disorganized; with this evaluation, she is directed to meet with the maintenance and janitorial staff to assure that the entrance lobby is neat and attractive and stocked with company brochures.

Ms. Goodenough has not made herself available for overtime and weekend work when requested; working occasional extra hours is a component of the job description. She is directed to meet with human services to review her schedule and availability for special projects.

She has not advanced her abilities with computer systems and should take advantage of advanced courses offered by the training department. In exceptional situations, the receptionist is expected to be available to assist secretarial and other support staff in production of documents, preparation of mass mailings, and handling excessive incoming or outgoing correspondence.

As the point of first contact for visitors, Ms. Goodenough must become an active participant in the companywide security task force. She is directed to meet with the head of security within 15 days to review procedures including checking employee ID cards, verifying the identity of service providers, and handling unknown visitors and possible threats.

UNSATISFACTORY

Mr. Belowpar is not performing at an acceptable level as lead receptionist. To most visitors, he is the point of first contact with the company when they visit or call the main telephone number without seeking a specific individual or department. He has failed to educate himself about the company and its products and services; he is directed to meet with the training department within 15 days to seek assistance in this area.

He has not maintained appropriate safeguards for proprietary interoffice memos and other private information on his desk; he needs to closely follow company guidelines regarding sensitive information and security issues.

According to reports received by some department heads, he does not always greet visitors in a professional and friendly manner. He must improve his ability to answer basic questions about products and services when appropriate and direct them to particular departments when necessary.

Mr. Belowpar has failed to set up and manage a scheduling book for job interviews, despite specific requests for this assistance from departments preparing for product presentations and other events and services. With this evaluation, he is directed to accomplish this task within 60 days.

On occasion, he has dressed in an inappropriate manner; he is instructed to meet with the human resources department within 5 days to review company guidelines on dress codes including the display of political, religious, and personal slogans and advertising on the job.

With this evaluation, he is also directed to meet with the maintenance and janitorial staff to assure that the entrance lobby is neat and attractive and stocked with company brochures.

Mr. Belowpar has not shown advanced abilities with computer systems, and as a result, he has not been able to assist secretarial and other support staff in production of documents, preparation of mass mailings, and handling excessive incoming or outgoing correspondence. With this evaluation, he is directed to meet with the training department within 15 days to enroll in appropriate courses on computer and secretarial skills.

The security department has expressed concern about Mr. Belowpar's training and ability to assist them in safeguarding the main entrance to the building. He is directed to meet with the head of security within 5 days to review procedures including checking employee ID cards, verifying the identity of service providers, and handling unknown visitors and possible threats.

Clerical Assistant

Advance planning
Attendance records
Calendar
Civil discourse
Clerical tasks
Communications skills
New responsibilities
Organizational skills
Telephone manners
Writing skills

MEETS OR EXCEEDS

Ms. Paragon is highly organized and makes excellent use of her time in making advance plans. In her first weeks on the job, she made suggestions to the MIS department that resulted in enhancements to the shared enterprisewide calendar. Over the course of the year, she has consistently shown a willingness to take on new assignments and responsibilities.

She has demonstrated great attention to detail and accuracy, reorganizing computer folders and coordinating them with paper files to save time and effort on retrieval.

Ms. Paragon represents the company well, showing professionalism and sincerity in all of her dealings on the telephone, in written correspondence, and at functions with clients.

Ms. Paragon volunteered to be a member of the Chairman's Committee on Civil Discourse, a group that is drafting a company policy to state more clearly our corporate position on political, religious, and other forms of expression and how they relate to employee behavior on and off the job.

She has shown excellent verbal and writing skills and has taken advantage of available courses offered by the training department. Ms. Paragon plans to enroll in courses at the community college this fall and has been given approval to seek reimbursement for tuition costs provided she receives a grade of B or greater.

Ms. Paragon recorded an exemplary record of attendance over the course of the past year, missing only one day of work because of illness. At the same time, she managed to be at her desk every day during the severe winter storms last January, assisting her department in completion of a major marketing campaign.

NEEDS IMPROVEMENT

Mr. Goodenough has completed all of the core assignments in his job description but has not demonstrated a willingness to take on new responsibilities or to expand the scope of present assignments. Although he has done an exemplary job in maintaining essential corporate files, he has not coordinated his work with other departments or worked closely with the MIS department to allow efficient sharing of information across the enterprise. He has not taken advantage of in-service training on new computer applications.

Mr. Goodenough has not shown an ability to make good use of his time in making advance plans. At times, he appears overwhelmed and has not demonstrated sufficient attention to detail and accuracy in working with computer folders and coordinating them with paper files. With this evaluation, he is directed to meet with the training department to seek courses that will be of assistance in these matters.

He is generally dependable and punctual, although he chose to take his summer vacation during a period when his supervisor had asked him to be at work for completion of the annual budget, resulting in a significant extra load on coworkers. With this evaluation, he is directed to review company policy about scheduling of vacation time and to meet with his supervisor within 15 days to discuss his understanding of these matters.

Mr. Goodenough's writing skills are merely adequate. His supervisor offered the services of a writing coach through the company's training department at the start of Mr. Goodenough's employment in February and again in June, but as of this date, no such training has taken place. Mr. Goodenough is also encouraged to consider enrollment in a writing course at the community college this fall; as stated in the company handbook, tuition costs for approved courses will be fully reimbursed provided the employee receives a grade of B or greater.

He needs to improve his ability to work well with others in his department and elsewhere in the company and to show greater professionalism and sincerity in all of his dealings on the telephone, in written correspondence, and at functions with clients. He is directed to meet with the training department within 15 days to seek available courses in this area.

UNSATISFACTORY

Mr. Belowpar has failed to demonstrate a sincere effort to learn to work better with other individuals. He has been the source of several complaints—unsubstantiated by this reviewer—about verbal confrontations with coworkers. With this review, he is directed to meet within 10 days with a designated counseling team made up of representatives of the human resources and training departments to seek in-house training on these matters.

His attendance record exceeded allowed sick days and personal days in three of the four quarters over the last year. Although it is company policy not to require documentation from a doctor for short absences claimed as necessary for medical reasons, Mr. Belowpar's supervisor points out that all but one of the 16 days he was absent in the past year occurred on a Monday or Friday, resulting in extended weekends. Several coworkers complained to supervisors about his attendance record because of the added burden it placed on them.

CHAPTER 10

LEGAL AND GOVERNMENTAL AFFAIRS

In-house Legal Counsel

Paralegal/Legal Assistant

Contract Administrator

Chief Compliance Officer

Director of Government Contracting

In-house Legal Counsel

Codes of conduct
Contracts
Copyrights
Corporate ethics
Disability
Employee discrimination
Employment contracts
Government compliance
Intellectual property
Legal counsel
Mergers and acquisitions
Occupational safety
Patents
Real estate leases
SEC filings
Trademarks
Workers' compensation

MEETS OR EXCEEDS

Mr. Paragon has performed with the highest degree of skill and professionalism as the company's in-house legal counsel. He has demonstrated great success in working with nearly every department on a variety of contractual, government compliance, employment law, and intellectual property management issues.

Over the course of the past year, Mr. Paragon served with distinction as the company's principal liaison with outside mergers and acquisitions counsel in negotiations that led to the purchase of Interglobal Transnational Services in July. He worked closely with the executive committee and the board of directors, advising them on technical details of the deal.

Mr. Paragon displayed a high degree of cooperation with the tax specialist, assisting in review of filings to the SEC and other regulatory agencies.

He has shown a dedication to understanding the company and all of its products and services. In doing so, he has been of great assistance in defending the company's intellectual property assets including patents, trademarks, and copyrights.

At the heart of his job is participation in negotiation and review of all major contracts including real estate purchases and leases, vehicle and building deals, and master contracts for supplies and raw materials. He has demonstrated great competence in drafting and keeping current the contracts used by the sales department in dealings with customers.

The human resources department has reported great satisfaction with Mr. Paragon's counsel, including assistance with employment contracts, terminations, and proper practices under various government mandates including equal opportunity, disability, and occupational safety. He worked effectively with outside counsel in approving the contractual elements of the master work agreement with the technical union.

Mr. Paragon showed great skill and compassion in dealing with two recent workers' compensation cases that were based on workplace injuries. He also worked effectively with outside counsel in defending the company against a spurious employee discrimination lawsuit that was dismissed for lack of merit.

Mr. Paragon has made important contributions to the human resources department in the drafting and updating of the employee guidebook, especially in the areas of codes of conduct.

On his own initiative, Mr. Paragon has offered advice to the executive committee on corporate ethics as they relate to various laws and regulations including accounting practices under the Sarbanes-Oxley Act.

He has also demonstrated a commitment to excellence in assisting the company's insurance department in reviewing policies and coverage and assuring that federal, state, and local mandates are followed.

Mr. Paragon has taken full advantage of available courses offered by the training department, has obtained advanced certification from several professional associations, and is taking part in postgraduate classes to enhance his background on legal, taxation, and technical areas.

NEEDS IMPROVEMENT

Mr. Goodenough needs to improve his skills and professionalism as the company's in-house legal counsel. He has demonstrated inconsistency in dealing with some departments on a variety of contractual, government compliance, employment law, and intellectual property management issues.

Over the course of the past year, Mr. Goodenough has devoted much of his attention to working with outside mergers and acquisitions counsel in negotiations that led to the purchase of Interglobal Transnational Services in July. Although this task was a high priority and was successfully accomplished, many other assignments were left unfinished or delegated to paralegal staff who were at times working in areas with which they were not familiar.

Mr. Goodenough has not displayed a high degree of understanding of tax matters, especially in his necessary review of filings to the SEC and other regulatory agencies. With this evaluation, he is directed to seek additional training and professional certification in this area.

He has shown a less-than-adequate understanding of the company and all of its products and services. This has hindered him from being of assistance to outside counsel in defending the company's intellectual property assets including patents, trademarks, and copyrights.

At the heart of his job is participation in negotiation and review of all major contracts including real estate purchases and leases, vehicle and building deals, and master contracts for supplies and raw materials. The sales department has reported several instances of confusion and lost business due to contract provisions inserted into purchase agreements drafted by Mr. Goodenough. He is directed to meet with the executive committee within 15 days to discuss this matter and to present a plan to seek additional training and certification on business contracts.

The human resources department has repeatedly requested his assistance and counsel in reviewing employment contracts, terminations, and proper practices under various government mandates including equal opportunity, disability, and occupational safety. According to the head of that department, he has been unavailable to them for these purposes. With this evaluation, Mr. Goodenough is directed to meet with the human resources director within 10 days to review the backlog of requests and to come up with a plan to deal with them and future requests for assistance in a timely manner.

Mr. Goodenough has not responded to requests from the human resources department for assistance in the updating of the codes of conduct section of the employee guidebook. He is directed to work with human resources on this matter within 30 days.

Although it is an element of the job description for in-house legal counsel, Mr. Goodenough has delegated to paralegal staff the review of the contractual elements of the master work agreement with the technical union. The executive committee asks that Mr. Goodenough personally review all such contracts in the future.

At the start of the fiscal year, the executive committee asked Mr. Goodenough to take on the additional role of chief ethics officer, offering counsel to the company on accounting and other practices with particular attention to the provisions of the Sarbanes-Oxley Act. As of this date, he has not done so; the executive committee directs that he report to them on these matters at their next regularly scheduled meeting.

Mr. Goodenough has not demonstrated a depth of understanding of insurance matters and has not been able to offer significant assistance to the company's insurance department in reviewing policies and coverage and assuring that federal, state, and local mandates are followed. He is directed to make this a high priority in the next 90 days, seeking training and professional certification in these areas.

UNSATISFACTORY

Ms. Belowpar has failed to demonstrate adequate skills and professionalism as the company's in-house legal counsel. She has demonstrated inconsistency and a high degree of inaccuracies and errors in dealing with some departments on a variety of contractual, government compliance, employment law, and intellectual property management issues.

She has not displayed sufficient understanding of tax matters, especially in the necessary review of filings to the SEC and other regulatory agencies. With this evaluation, she is directed to seek additional training and professional certification in this area.

She has failed to show an acceptable understanding of the company and all of its products and services. As a result, she was unable to be of assistance to outside counsel in defending the company's intellectual property assets including patents, trademarks, and copyrights.

At the heart of her job is participation in negotiation and review of all major contracts including real estate purchases and leases, vehicle and building deals, and master contracts for supplies and raw materials. There have been numerous cases of errors and faulty language in sales, purchase, and real estate contracts drafted by Ms. Belowpar or submitted to her for review. She is directed to meet with the executive committee within 15 days to discuss this matter and to present a plan to seek additional training and certification on business contracts.

The insurance department has repeatedly requested her review of pending policies protecting the company from the costs of negligence, errors, and omissions claims. According to the head of that department, Ms. Belowpar has refused involvement in this matter, claiming that it is outside of her job description. With this evaluation, Ms. Belowpar is directed to meet with the human resources director within 10 days to review the job description which clearly includes insurance matters as one of her responsibilities and to come up with a plan to respond to all such pending and future requests for assistance in a timely manner.

Paralegal/Legal Assistant

Accounting software
Americans with Disabilities Act
Annual reports
Board of directors
Closings
Computerized scheduling program
Contracts
Corporate counsel
Database
Discrimination law
Employment law
Internet research
Legal assistant
LEXIS/NEXIS
Paralegal
Prioritizing correspondence
Sales contracts
Sexual harassment
Track deadlines

MEETS OR EXCEEDS

Mr. Paragon is an exceptional employee, performing at the highest levels of professionalism as a paralegal in the office of the corporate counsel. Under the supervision of the company's in-house legal department, Mr. Paragon has accepted responsibility for a wide range of duties and executed tasks in an accurate and timely manner.

Working within the legally defined parameters of his job, Mr. Paragon helps the legal department file required local, state, and federal documents; on his own initiative, he introduced a computerized scheduling program that helps track deadlines and manage projects.

He has demonstrated excellent research skills, using the Internet, LexisNexis, and other electronic tools as well as traditional sources of information. As a legal assistant, he has produced excellent briefings for the board of directors and the executive committee. He has also done an exemplary job in preparing documents for real estate closings, employee contracts, and purchase agreements.

As assigned by a company in-house lawyer, Mr. Paragon has done an exceptional job serving as the first point of review for all incoming legal documents, prioritizing correspondence and filings.

Mr. Paragon has worked diligently to keep himself up to date on current laws and regulations as they affect the company and has become very knowledgeable about existing employment, purchase, and sales contracts. In many instances, Mr. Paragon has been delegated to produce the first draft for major contracts and has done so with great skill.

Under his supervision, the legal department's clerical staff has improved its filing system to make it easily accessible through searches of an electronic database.

Mr. Paragon participates in a companywide task force that informs department heads and staff about important laws dealing with discrimination, sexual harassment, and compliance with the Americans with Disabilities Act. He also does an excellent job serving as liaison between the legal and the accounting departments to assure that the company is in full compliance with tax and fiscal responsibility codes and statutes.

Mr. Paragon has demonstrated excellent attention to detail and legal requirements in the preparation and filing of annual reports. Under the supervision of the head of the legal department, he has performed exemplary work as advisor to the secretary of the board of directors, helping to craft and record corporate resolutions and minutes.

Mr. Paragon's computer skills and knowledge are above expectations, and he has helped to introduce new software programs to the entire department. Working with the MIS department, he has initiated modifications in database and accounting software to the benefit of the company.

NEEDS IMPROVEMENT

Ms. Goodenough has demonstrated generally acceptable performance as a paralegal in the office of the corporate counsel. Under the supervision of the company's in-house legal department, Ms. Goodenough has been slow to expand the areas of responsibility she is willing to accept.

Ms. Goodenough needs to expand her ability to assist the legal department in filing required local, state, and federal documents. In her most recent evaluation, she was asked to work with the MIS department to develop and introduce a computerized scheduling program that helps track deadlines and manage projects; that project has not been accomplished.

She is directed to produce a realistic schedule for its implementation within 60 days.

She has not shown strong research skills using the Internet, LexisNexis, and other electronic tools as well as traditional sources of information. She is requested to ask the corporate training department for assistance on courses and available professional certification.

As a legal assistant, she has yet to accept full responsibility for briefings for the board of directors and the executive committee.

She has also lagged behind expectations in preparing documents for real estate closings, employee contracts, and purchase agreements.

Ms. Goodenough needs to devote more effort to keeping up to date on current laws and regulations as they affect the company and become very knowledgeable about existing employment, purchase, and sales contracts. It is recommended that she investigate membership in professional organizations that offer advanced training; the company's training department is also able to arrange for specialized in-house instruction.

The legal department has been reluctant to give Ms. Goodenough the responsibility to produce the first draft for major contracts because of her lack of background and training in these areas.

Ms. Goodenough has been asked to make herself aware of the details of discrimination, sexual harassment, and compliance with the Americans with Disabilities Act and participate in meetings with department heads and staff to brief them; as of this evaluation, this assignment has not been accomplished. Ms. Goodenough is directed to make this a high priority over the course of the next 90 days.

Ms. Goodenough is lacking sufficient computer skills and knowledge; as the department moves more and more toward a completely electronic research and filing system, this shortcoming needs to be addressed. She is asked to seek specialized instruction available through the company's training department.

UNSATISFACTORY

Mr. Belowpar has failed to deliver an acceptable level of performance as a paralegal in the office of the corporate counsel.

In addition to a number of gaps in his training and background, Mr. Belowpar has on occasion gone outside of the legally acceptable boundaries for a paralegal. Under state laws and bar association regulations, a legal assistant may not offer legal advice or seek to represent the company in court without the supervision or involvement of a member of the bar.

Mr. Belowpar needs more training to enable him to assist the legal department in filing required local, state, and federal documents.

Another area of concern is a demonstrated weakness in research skills using the Internet, LexisNexis, and other electronic tools. With this evaluation, Mr. Belowpar is directed to ask the corporate training department for assistance on courses and available professional certification.

Despite it being an important component of his job description, Mr. Belowpar has not functioned as advisor to the secretary of the board of directors, helping to craft and record corporate resolutions and minutes. Instead, a member of the legal staff has had to perform this function.

In general, Mr. Belowpar has failed to educate himself in order to keep current on laws and regulations and existing employment, purchase, and sales contracts. He is directed to investigate membership in professional organizations that offer advanced training; the company's training department is also able to arrange for specialized in-house instruction.

Mr. Belowpar was asked to become a company resource on discrimination and sexual harassment laws and compliance with the Americans with Disabilities Act and to convene meetings with department heads and staff to brief them. Despite several requests from the head of the legal department, this assignment has not been accomplished. Mr. Belowpar is directed to make this a high priority over the course of the next 30 days.

Mr. Belowpar has failed to improve his computer skills and knowledge to the level where he can fully utilize the department's research and filing tools. He is directed to seek specialized instruction available through the company's training department.

Contract Administrator

Agreements
Compliance officer
Contract law
Contracts
Database of contracts
Negotiation of contracts
Request for bids

MEETS OR EXCEEDS

Ms. Paragon has performed with great skill as contract administrator; she has brought a new sense of order and uniformity to the company's requests for bids and the review of contracts.

She has shown great cooperation in dealing with requests from nearly every department for assistance in the negotiation or renewal of agreements for provision of materials and services. Ms. Paragon has demonstrated a deep understanding of contract law in the drafting of contracts that follow company guidelines including compliance with all relevant federal, state, and local regulations and laws. When appropriate, she works closely and effectively with the in-house legal department for review of nonstandard provisions in contracts.

Ms. Paragon received a written commendation from the executive committee for her work in setting up and maintaining a central electronic register to track all current contracts and agreements. She has worked closely with department heads to ensure that proper attention is paid to the system's calendar of due dates for signature, inspections, certifications, payments, and expiration.

She has demonstrated a high degree of competence in assisting the establishment of departmental committees to research potential bidders. Under her guidance, the committees construct requests for bids that are intended to result in participation only by qualified companies, ensure the quality demanded, and result in the most competitive price.

Ms. Paragon has also shown excellent cooperation with the compliance officer, assuring that the bidding process is fair and open to all interested parties. In certain circumstances, the requests for bids may also include special preferences to meet the requirements of federal grants or programs.

On her own initiative, Ms. Paragon set up a database of information on publications, online Web sites, and established contacts for use by departments in publicizing and soliciting bids.

She has assured that the section on contract procedures in the employee handbook is kept up to date, working closely with the human resources department. Ms. Paragon has also made presentations to departments and has assisted the training department in establishing and keeping current courses in this area.

NEEDS IMPROVEMENT

Ms. Goodenough needs to improve her skills as contract administrator. At the time of her hiring, she was asked to regularize the company's requests for bids and the review of contracts; there has been little apparent progress.

Ms. Goodenough is asked to expand her knowledge of contract law in order to allow her to assist departments in the drafting of contracts that follow company guidelines including compliance with all relevant federal, state, and local regulations and laws. She is directed to seek additional education through the training department. Further, she is instructed to work more closely and effectively with the in-house legal department in the review of nonstandard provisions in contracts.

In her previous evaluation, Ms. Goodenough was asked to set up and maintain a central electronic register to track all current contracts and agreements. No such database has been established; with this evaluation, Ms. Goodenough is directed to make completion of this assignment her highest priority for the next 60 days. She will be re-evaluated on this matter in 60 days.

Ms. Goodenough needs to improve her cooperation with the compliance officer, assuring that the bidding process is fair and open to all interested parties. She is also directed to work closely with the human resources department to assure that the section on contract procedures in the employee handbook is kept up to date.

Ms. Goodenough is asked to set up an enterprisewide task force to encourage the establishment of departmental committees to research potential bidders. With this evaluation, she is directed to meet with the task force within 45 days and establish a plan to assist departments in the authoring of requests for bids that are intended to result in participation only by qualified companies, ensure the quality demanded, and result in the most competitive price. She will be re-evaluated on this matter in 90 days.

UNSATISFACTORY

Mr. Belowpar has failed to demonstrate an acceptable level of skill as contract administrator. He has not accomplished the primary assignment of the job description: regularizing the company's requests for bids and the review of contracts.

Mr. Belowpar does not display adequate knowledge of contract law. This is an essential skill for this job. He is directed to seek additional education through the training department, professional organizations, and area colleges. He will be re-evaluated on progress in this area within 90 days.

At the time of his hiring, Mr. Belowpar was asked to set up and maintain a central electronic register to track all current contracts and agreements. No such database has been established; with this evaluation, Mr. Belowpar is directed to establish this database within 60 days. He will be re-evaluated on this matter at that time.

Mr. Belowpar has not shown adequate cooperation with the compliance officer. It is company policy that the bidding process be fair and open to all interested parties; with this evaluation, he is directed to immediately address this issue.

Chief Compliance Officer

Antidiscrimination laws
Confidentiality
Conflict of interest
Corporate citizenship
Environmental regulations
Equal opportunity employer
Ethical standards
Federal mandates
Government compliance
Investor fraud
Occupational safety
Outside auditing firms
Personnel matters
Settlement of claims
State mandates

MEETS OR EXCEEDS

Mr. Paragon has performed admirably as the chief compliance officer, leading our efforts to implement policies, procedures, and standards mandated by federal, state, and local laws and regulations. He has demonstrated a steadfast commitment to ensuring that equal opportunity, antidiscrimination, occupational safety, environmental, investor fraud, and other legal and ethical standards are fully supported throughout the enterprise.

He has shown exceptional skills in monitoring all proceedings that are identified as within the purview of the compliance officer. He has offered well-informed advice to the in-house legal department and outside counsel on settlement of claims and compliance agreements.

Mr. Paragon has greatly enhanced the company's efforts to promote its commitment to being an equal opportunity employer and a good corporate citizen; he has worked closely with the human resources and public relations departments in support of this effort.

Mr. Paragon has demonstrated a high degree of professionalism in leading a companywide task force that informs every department of government requirements and any initiatives of the executive committee. Within the guidelines set forth by the employee handbook, he works closely and effectively with the human resources and legal departments to enforce standards with disciplinary measures including warnings, suspensions, and dismissal.

Required to follow the law in reporting any violation within a timely manner, Mr. Paragon also has the full support of the executive committee and the board of directors in proactive efforts. He is empowered to launch investigations with the in-house legal department, the outside auditing firm, or consultants he may choose to engage on his own. He maintains safeguards of state and federal whistleblower laws, ensuring that employees are able to report serious violations without fear of repercussion.

His job is considered key to the fulfillment of the company's mission statement. As a concomitant benefit, his efforts help reduce the enterprise's exposure to fraud, loss, and liability. A letter of commendation from the head of the insurance department, attached to this evaluation, attests to Mr. Paragon's supportive efforts in helping reduce the cost of liability coverage through implementation of a federally sponsored assessment and training program.

Mr. Paragon has carefully kept away from any conflicts of interest as a compliance officer; he has demonstrated a commitment to ensuring that the company follows mandates and its mission statement without attention to profits. At the same time, he has worked closely with the training department to assist department heads in adjusting their own operations to be in compliance and meet budgetary goals.

He has shown excellent written and verbal communications skills and the ability to maintain professional relations with all levels of management and staff. Mr. Paragon has also consistently maintained the highest degree of confidentiality in dealing with personnel matters and company proprietary information.

He has worked closely with the training department to establish courses presented to every employee and assisted the department in regularly updating the company handbook.

NEEDS IMPROVEMENT

Ms. Goodenough has not demonstrated adequate skills and background as the chief compliance officer. She is charged with leading our efforts to implement policies, procedures, and standards mandated by federal, state, and local laws and regulations. She has been very direct in stating a commitment to ensuring that equal opportunity, antidiscrimination, occupational safety, environmental, investor fraud, and other legal and ethical standards are fully supported throughout the enterprise. However, the results are very limited in scope.

Ms. Goodenough has to improve her ability to monitor all proceedings that are identified as within the purview of the compliance officer. She must boost the level of cooperation with the in-house legal department and outside counsel in offering well-informed advice on settlement of claims and compliance agreements.

The job description for chief compliance officer calls on Ms. Goodenough to work closely with the human resources and public relations departments to promote the company's commitment to being an equal opportunity employer and a good corporate citizen. There has been little effort in this area; with this evaluation, Ms. Goodenough is asked to meet with the involved departments within 15 days to plan a strategy to accomplish this important goal. Ms. Goodenough will be re-evaluated on this matter in 90 days.

Ms. Goodenough has not shown sufficient leadership as chair of a companywide task force on compliance issues. That committee is charged with informing every department of government requirements and any initiatives of the executive committee. She needs to improve her ability to work closely and effectively with the human resources and legal departments to enforce standards with disciplinary measures including warnings, suspensions, and dismissal.

Required to follow the law in reporting any violation within a timely manner, Ms. Goodenough also has the full support of the executive committee and the board of directors in proactive efforts. She is asked to demonstrate her use of this power in coming months.

Her job is considered key to the fulfillment of the company's mission statement. As a concomitant benefit, her efforts can be aimed at helping to reduce the enterprise's exposure to fraud, loss, and liability.

Ms. Goodenough needs to strengthen her understanding of the need to keep away from any conflicts of interest as a compliance officer; at the heart of this component of the job description is ensuring that the company follow mandates and its mission statement without attention to profits. At the same time, she should work closely with the training department to assist department heads in adjusting their own operations to be in compliance and meet budgetary goals. With this evaluation, Ms. Goodenough is directed to meet with the human resources department to review the job description.

She has not consistently shown adequate written and verbal communications skills. Ms. Goodenough also needs to improve the level of professional relations she maintains with all levels of the company, up to and including the board of directors. Further, she has not demonstrated a consistent ability to maintain the highest degree of confidentiality in dealing with personnel matters and company proprietary information. With this evaluation, she is directed to seek the assistance of the training department within 15 days for in-house courses and special assistance from consultants and colleges; she will be re-evaluated on these matters in 90 days.

UNSATISFACTORY

Mr. Belowpar has failed to demonstrate adequate skills and background as the chief compliance officer. He is charged with leading our efforts to implement policies, procedures, and standards mandated by federal, state, and local laws and regulations, but results have been very limited in scope and sometimes counterproductive to the company's commitment to ensuring that equal opportunity, antidiscrimination, occupational safety, environmental, investor fraud, and other legal and ethical standards are fully supported throughout the enterprise.

Mr. Belowpar must show a greatly enhanced ability to monitor all proceedings that are identified as within the purview of the compliance officer. He has not shown an adequate level of cooperation with the in-house legal department and outside counsel in offering well-informed advice on settlement of claims and compliance agreements.

The job description for chief compliance officer calls on Mr. Belowpar to work closely with the human resources and public relations departments to promote the company's commitment to being an equal opportunity employer and a good corporate citizen. We have seen no evidence of a serious attempt to do so. With this evaluation, Mr. Belowpar is asked to meet with the involved departments within 15 days to plan a strategy to accomplish this important goal. Mr. Belowpar will be re-evaluated on this matter in 90 days.

Mr. Belowpar has not been a significant contributor to the company-wide task force on compliance issues. This committee was established as the focal point of all of the company's proactive compliance issues. He is directed to produce a report outlining his plans to make use of this task force and deliver it to the executive committee within 14 days.

Mr. Belowpar has also failed to show an ability to work closely and effectively with the human resources and legal departments to enforce standards with disciplinary measures including warnings, suspensions, and dismissal.

Mr. Belowpar needs to avoid any real or implied conflicts of interest as a compliance officer; in some of his efforts, he has seemed to focus on helping the company avoid having to spend money to meet government mandates. He is directed to review the job description, which clearly states that the compliance officer is charged with ensuring the company follows mandates and its mission statement without attention to profits.

At the same time, Mr. Belowpar is directed to work closely with the training department to assist department heads in adjusting their own operations to be in compliance and meet budgetary goals. He will be re-evaluated on this matter within 90 days.

Mr. Belowpar has not demonstrated an acceptable level of written and verbal communications skills and has been inconsistent in establishing and maintaining cordial and professional relations with all levels of the company, up to and including the board of directors. With this evaluation, he is directed to seek the assistance of the training department within 15 days for in-house courses and special assistance from consultants and colleges; he will be re-evaluated on these matters in 90 days.

Director of Government Contracting

Background screening of employees
Centralized Contractor Registration (CCR)
Commerce Business Daily
Compliance with federal regulations
Data Universal Numbering System (DUNS) number
Federal procurement
Federal Supply Classification (FSC)
Government contracts
Management skills
Minority preference
North American Industry Classification System (NAICS)

MEETS OR EXCEEDS

Ms. Paragon has demonstrated exceptional skill in negotiating and monitoring procurement contracts, grants, and cooperative agreements with the federal government. In both dollars and percentage of overall bookings, Ms. Paragon and her department have boosted the company's dealings with the federal government by more than 25 percent in the past 12 months.

She has worked closely and effectively with the legal department to assure the company's compliance with federal regulations and participate in the review of contracts. Ms. Paragon has also worked closely with the purchasing department to ensure compliance with elements of the contracts that may require dealing with minority or other specially identified groups.

Ms. Paragon has also demonstrated excellent skills in dealing with the human resources department to provide them with information on necessary background screening.

She has provided the legal and manufacturing departments with current information on Federal Supply Classification (FSC) and North American Industry Classification System (NAICS) codes for products or services offered by the company.

In cooperation with the accounting department, she has assured that the company's Data Universal Numbering System (DUNS) number is properly listed with the federal government's Centralized Contractor Registration (CCR) system. Her close attention to these details has resulted in an exemplary record of on-time payment by government agencies; this represents a significant improvement over the accounts receivable record in previous years.

Ms. Paragon has demonstrated a strong commitment to keeping current on requests for bids for government contracts and has passed along numerous opportunities to the sales and marketing departments. She subscribes to all appropriate federal government publications including the *Commerce Business Daily* as well as Web sites.

On her own initiative, she has assigned a staff member to produce a weekly summary of available government contracts related to the products and services of the company; the resulting publication is distributed by e-mail to department heads.

Ms. Paragon has received top ratings from her own staff on management skills. She has enhanced her abilities by completing appropriate courses offered by the training department and professional organizations.

NEEDS IMPROVEMENT

Mr. Goodenough needs to improve his skills in negotiating and monitoring procurement contracts, grants, and cooperative agreements with the federal government. Over the past 12 months, the company's contracts with the federal government have significantly declined in both dollars and percentage of bookings.

He must work more closely with the legal department to assure the company's compliance with federal regulations and participate in the review of contracts. The company has failed to receive renewal on several major contracts in the past 90 days because of technical or procedural errors or omissions.

Mr. Goodenough must also enhance his skills to be better able to assist the purchasing department in complying with elements of federal contracts that may require dealing with minority or other specially identified groups.

The human resources department has requested Mr. Goodenough to provide more information, in a timely manner, on necessary background screening required for certain contracts. With this evaluation, he is directed to meet with the human resources department within 15 days to present a report on screening requirements.

The legal and manufacturing departments have reported rejection of several bids because of incomplete or incorrect information related to Federal Supply Classification (FSC) and North American Industry Classification System (NAICS) codes for products or services offered by the company. Mr. Goodenough is directed to update all such listings and to report to the affected departments within 15 days to advise them of his efforts.

In his most recent evaluation, Mr. Goodenough was instructed to improve his communication with the accounting department to assure that the company's Data Universal Numbering System (DUNS) number is properly listed with the federal government's Centralized Contractor Registration (CCR) system. According to the head of the accounting department, this continues to be an area of concern, resulting in delayed payments to the company by government agencies.

Mr. Goodenough must improve his attention to changes in the federal bidding process and listings of current opportunities and needs to do a better job of passing along opportunities to the sales and marketing departments. He has not demonstrated a commitment to keeping current and should examine his department's subscriptions to all appropriate federal government publications including *Commerce Business Daily* as well as Web sites.

With this evaluation, Mr. Goodenough is directed to produce a weekly summary of available government contracts related to the products and services of the company and to distribute that report by e-mail to department heads. The executive committee asks that this publication begin within 30 days.

Mr. Goodenough has received less than excellent ratings on management skills from his own staff. He is directed to enroll in appropriate courses offered by the training department and professional organizations within the next 60 days.

UNSATISFACTORY

Ms. Belowpar has failed to demonstrate adequate skills in negotiating and monitoring procurement contracts, grants, and cooperative agreements with the federal government. Over the past 12 months, the company's contracts with the federal government have significantly declined in both dollars and percentage of bookings.

Ms. Belowpar is directed to immediately meet with the training department to seek courses and professional certification aimed at improving skills that are essential to the fulfillment of the job description for the director of government contracting. With this evaluation, she is directed to report to the head of human resources within 30 days to detail progress in obtaining necessary advanced training.

Among areas of significant concern are contracts lost because of failure to fully comply with federal regulations or because of technical or procedural errors on responses to requests for bids. She is directed to meet with the legal department within 15 days to begin a review of procedures and training.

Ms. Belowpar must better assist the purchasing department in complying with elements of federal contracts that may require dealing with minority or other specially identified groups. The human resources department has requested Ms. Belowpar to provide more information, in a timely manner, on necessary background screening required for certain contracts. With this evaluation, she is directed to meet with the purchasing and human resources departments within 15 days to present a report on minority hiring and screening requirements.

Ms. Belowpar has failed to keep current on changes in the federal bidding process and listings of current opportunities and must demonstrate greater skills in passing along opportunities to the sales and marketing departments.

Ms. Belowpar has received several unacceptable ratings on management skills from her own staff. She is directed to meet with the human resources department within 15 days to review the ratings which will remain confidential as to source, and to seek appropriate courses offered by the training department and professional organizations within the next 30 days.

CHAPTER 11

HEALTH CARE
AND
MEDICAL SERVICES

In-house Registered and Occupational Health Nurse

Medical Receptionist

Home Health Care Provider

In-house Registered and Occupational Health Nurse

Acute illness
Automated external defibrillators
Carpal tunnel injuries
Emergency care
First aid
Flu vaccination
Health insurance
Heart attack
Injuries
Insulin shock
Occupational health nurse
OSHA
Registered nurse
Repetitive stress syndrome

MEETS OR EXCEEDS

Mr. Paragon has provided excellent service as an in-house registered and occupational health nurse. He administers excellent emergency care and first aid and works closely and effectively with area doctors, hospitals, and ambulance services as needed.

Most of his work involves treatment of minor illnesses and injuries; he has demonstrated excellent skills in caring for employees and has fulfilled every requirement of insurance, OSHA, and other mandates in doing so. On at least five occasions in the past year, Mr. Paragon has been the first responder to an employee suffering an acute illness or serious injury, and in each of these cases, medical review has resulted in commendation of his skills.

He maintains an appropriate dispensary of nonprescription medicines for ordinary headaches, stomach distress, and other minor problems. Working under the supervision of a physician at a nearby hospital, he also has available drugs to deal with acute problems including heart attacks, insulin shock, inhalation of hazardous substances, and drug overdose. On his own initiative, he has advised all employees of his availability to work with their own doctors to administer and monitor use of prescription drugs.

According to employee surveys, staffers greatly value Mr. Paragon's availability for confidential consultation on health concerns; at the same time, he has demonstrated his understanding of company policy and statutory requirements related to health conditions that make an employee unfit to be at work.

Mr. Paragon initiated an annual flu vaccination program three years ago, and it is the considered opinion of the human resources department that this has resulted in a decrease in absences due to illness during the influenza season.

Working in conjunction with the travel planner, Mr. Paragon has made himself available to employees scheduled for international travel on company business to advise them on health concerns and necessary inoculations.

Mr. Paragon has demonstrated a high level of professionalism in serving as liaison to the benefits manager and the human resources department in analyzing medical insurance coverage and in pursuing payment of claims by employees.

As an occupational health nurse, Mr. Paragon has provided excellent service to the research and development and manufacturing departments to assist in evaluation of health concerns related to new projects. He also consults with employees about strategies to avoid job-related injuries such as repetitive stress syndrome, carpal tunnel injuries, and back strains.

Working with the benefits manager, Mr. Paragon assists new and existing employees in the selection of primary care physicians and specialists.

In conjunction with the security and training departments, Mr. Paragon led the way in the effort to install automated external defibrillators in each major company facility and arranged for instruction for security officers and any staffer who sought training.

NEEDS IMPROVEMENT

Mr. Goodenough needs to improve his abilities to provide service as an in-house registered and occupational health nurse. He administers adequate first aid but needs to greatly improve his skills in emergency care and his ability to work closely and effectively with area doctors, hospitals, and ambulance services as needed.

According to the legal department, Mr. Goodenough has not demonstrated full understanding of required accident forms, medical treatment records, and other requirements or mandates of the company's insurance carrier and state and local occupational safety and health agencies.

He maintains an appropriate dispensary of nonprescription medicines for ordinary headaches, stomach distress, and other minor problems. Reports from emergency room physicians have indicated that incoming patients could have benefited from administration of certain drugs to deal with acute problems including heart attacks, insulin shock, inhalation of hazardous substances, and drug overdose. With this evaluation, he is directed to meet with the training department within 30 days to seek advanced training and certification in emergency medical treatment.

Mr. Goodenough was instructed at his most recent evaluation to investigate setting up an annual flu vaccination program; as of this date, no such plan has been presented. Six months ago, Mr. Goodenough was asked by the chairman of the board to work with the security department to install automated external defibrillators in each major company facility and arrange for instruction for security officers and any staffer who sought training. He is directed to make both of these tasks high priority assignments and prepare a report to the executive committee within 30 days.

The corporate travel planner has requested that Mr. Goodenough make himself available to employees scheduled for international travel on company business to advise them on health concerns and necessary inoculations. He is directed to do so within 30 days.

Mr. Goodenough has not exhibited a commitment to working with the benefits manager and the human resources department in analyzing medical insurance coverage and in pursuing payment of claims by employees.

UNSATISFACTORY

Ms. Belowpar has failed to deliver an adequate level of emergency care as an in-house registered and occupational health nurse. While she has shown herself to be able to administer adequate first aid, she has demonstrated that she lacks adequate skills in situations demanding emergency care.

Reports from emergency room physicians have indicated that incoming patients could have benefited from administration of certain drugs to deal with acute problems including heart attacks, insulin shock, inhalation of hazardous substances, and drug overdose. She is directed to meet with the training department within 5 days to seek temporary emergency medical coverage for the company while she seeks advanced training and certification in emergency medical treatment.

Ms. Belowpar has not followed through on two high-priority assignments that were made part of her job description at her previous evaluation: an annual flu vaccination program and the installation of automated external defibrillators (AEDs) in each major company facility. With this evaluation, she is directed to draw up a plan for implementation of both programs within 5 days and to include a schedule for installation of AEDs within 30 days. Further, she is directed to meet with the training department to initiate courses in use of the AEDs as soon as they are installed.

Medical Receptionist

Appointments
Copayments
Critical care facility
Insurance files
Medical records
Office visits
Privacy laws
Triage
Voice mail

MEETS OR EXCEEDS

Ms. Paragon has demonstrated excellent skills at managing the continually varying demands of being the first point of contact in a medical office. At the heart of her job is understanding the concept of triage as it applies to incoming patients; she has received training and kept up to date on medical conditions to quickly decide whether a client should go to the emergency room (or whether an ambulance should be sent for that purpose), receive an immediate appointment, be scheduled for tests, or be given a lower priority appointment.

She has shown great skill in answering the telephone and managing voice mail. Ms. Paragon worked productively with a consultant to design and implement a computerized scheduling system for doctors, physician's assistants, nurses, and lab technicians in the office.

Working at the front desk, Ms. Paragon manages the waiting room with a high degree of professional command as well as appropriate compassion; she is in constant communication with the medical staff about upcoming appointments and is able to contact patients and reschedule office visits or make alternate arrangements when necessary.

She has clearly shown recognition for the importance of maintaining an orderly and well-organized waiting room; she has made use of her training as necessary to isolate contagious patients and to upgrade seriously ill clients so that they are immediately treated or transferred to a critical care facility.

The medical receptionist is also responsible for establishing and maintaining the billing and insurance files for patients and coordinating them with medical records. Ms. Paragon has sought and received advanced training from a medical management consultant and major insurance companies to assist her in the performance of her duties. She also works closely and productively with the medical billing office and with subcontractors including laboratories, radiology facilities, and hospitals to collect full payment, copayment, or insurance data as necessary.

She has shown strong understanding of recent strengthening of laws regarding the confidentiality of medical records. She has demonstrated a high degree of discretion in handling telephone calls and dealing directly with patients.

Ms. Paragon also devotes a sharp focus to calls from the office to patients, notifying them of the availability of lab test reports and scheduling necessary follow-up appointments.

NEEDS IMPROVEMENT

Ms. Goodenough has not yet fully demonstrated adequate skills in managing the continually varying demands of being the first point of contact in a medical office. At times she has appeared to be completely overwhelmed by the number of visitors and the complexity of determining medical priority for new cases.

She is asked to seek additional available training to understand the concept of triage as it applies to incoming patients. Key to her job is the ability to quickly decide whether a client should go to the emergency room (or whether an ambulance should be sent for that purpose), receive an immediate appointment, be scheduled for tests, or be given a lower priority appointment. The medical receptionist should under no circumstances dispense medical advice.

Ms. Goodenough is asked to review the office guide to procedures as well as publications of the American Medical Association on these matters; nurse practitioners on staff are also available to her for quick confidential consultation about medical conditions.

Ms. Goodenough needs to improve her skills in answering the telephone and managing voice mail. She needs to better comprehend the necessary questions to ask callers in order to make proper use of the office's computer-based scheduling system for doctors, physician's assistants, nurses, and lab technicians in the office. Again, it is always proper to consult a nurse practitioner for advice on priorities.

Ms. Goodenough is asked to better manage the waiting room, staying in constant communication with the medical staff about upcoming appointments and contacting patients, rescheduling office visits, or making alternate arrangements when necessary.

The receptionist needs to balance a high degree of professional command as well as appropriate compassion; Ms. Goodenough is asked to seek training on the need to isolate contagious patients and to prioritize seriously ill clients so that they are immediately treated or transferred to a critical care facility.

The medical receptionist is also responsible for establishing and maintaining the billing and insurance files for patients and coordinating them with medical records. Ms. Goodenough has not yet shown an acceptable level of performance in this area.

Ms. Goodenough also needs to work more closely and productively with the medical billing office and with subcontractors including laboratories, radiology facilities, and hospitals to collect full payment, copayment, or insurance data as necessary.

With this evaluation, she is asked to immediately schedule advanced training from a medical management consultant regularly employed by this office and to make contact with major insurance companies for assistance in the performance of her duties. The office manager will support her in granting paid leave and travel expenses when necessary for these purposes. Ms. Goodenough will be re-evaluated on management and billing practices within 45 days.

Finally, it is essential that Ms. Goodenough exactly follow federal laws regarding the confidentiality of medical records. It is unacceptable to place patient records on the counter in view of visitors, and all telephone conversations must be conducted out of the hearing of waiting room patients. She will be re-evaluated on her understanding and compliance with federal regulations within 30 days.

UNSATISFACTORY

Mr. Belowpar has failed to demonstrate an acceptable level of skill in managing the continually varying demands of being the first point of contact in a medical office. He is often overwhelmed by the number of visitors and the complexity of determining medical priority for new cases.

With this appraisal, he is directed to immediately seek available training on the concept of triage as it applies to incoming patients. He is expected to demonstrate the ability to make timely decisions about whether a client should go to the emergency room (or whether an ambulance should be sent for that purpose), receive an immediate appointment, be scheduled for tests, or be given a lower priority appointment. Under no circumstances is the medical receptionist to dispense medical advice.

The office manager is available to organize in-house and specialized consultation and training in these matters. Mr. Belowpar is also asked to review the office guide to procedures as well as publications of the American Medical Association on these matters; nurse practitioners on staff are also available to him for quick confidential consultation about medical conditions. Mr. Belowpar is asked to report to the office manager within 10 days with a plan of action to deal with this deficiency in training and will be re-evaluated on this matter in 45 days.

Mr. Belowpar has not shown acceptable skills in answering the telephone and managing voice mail. The office manual spells out in great detail the necessary questions to ask callers in order to make proper use of the office's computer-based scheduling system for doctors, physician's assistants, nurses, and lab technicians in the office. Again, it is always proper to consult a nurse practitioner for advice on priorities. He will be re-evaluated on this matter within 15 days.

It is the mission statement of this office, with the exception of serious emergencies, that patients should not be asked to wait more than twenty minutes past their scheduled appointment time to be seen. Mr. Belowpar is asked to better manage the waiting room, staying in constant communication with the medical staff about upcoming appointments and contacting patients to reschedule office visits or make alternate arrangements when necessary.

Mr. Belowpar is also directed to seek training on the need to isolate contagious patients and to prioritize seriously ill clients so that they are immediately treated or transferred to a critical care facility.

The medical receptionist is also responsible for establishing and maintaining the billing and insurance files for patients and coordinating them with medical records. Mr. Belowpar has failed to demonstrate acceptable performance in this area.

Mr. Belowpar has not shown himself able to work closely and productively with the medical billing office and with subcontractors including laboratories, radiology facilities, and hospitals to collect full payment, copayment, or insurance data as necessary.

With this evaluation, he is asked to immediately schedule advanced training from a medical management consultant regularly employed by this office and to make contact with major insurance companies for assistance in the performance of his duties. The office manager will support him in granting paid leave and travel expenses when necessary for these purposes.

This is to be Mr. Belowpar's number one priority; he is asked to advise the office manager on his plans within 10 days and will be re-evaluated on management and billing practices within 30 days. Failure to do so will be considered grounds for initiation of a dismissal process.

Finally, it is essential that Mr. Belowpar exactly follow federal laws regarding the confidentiality of medical records. The office has received a number of complaints from patients about telephone conversations regarding medical conditions being conducted within the hearing of waiting room patients. Further, it is unacceptable to place patient records on the counter in view of visitors. These practices are unfair to clients and place the office in danger of violation of confidentiality laws. Mr. Belowpar will be re-evaluated on his understanding and compliance with federal regulations within 10 days.

Home Health Care Provider

Emergencies
Equipment suppliers
Medical services
Occupational therapists
Proper procedures
Substitute providers
Supervising nurse

MEETS OR EXCEEDS

Mr. Paragon has shown exceptional skills as a home health care provider, regularly receiving the highest possible marks on client surveys.

He keeps in regular contact with the supervising nurse and head of medical services to discuss any changes in conditions and needs of patients and is very willing to adapt his practices as required. He has on a number of occasions asked for and received additional specialized training on atypical medical services.

Mr. Paragon demonstrates great patience and compassion in providing assistance to patients in scheduling medical appointments and necessary tests and works closely with pharmacists and the medical staff in advising on the proper use of prescribed drugs and other procedures. He works well with other providers including physical and occupational therapists, nutritionists, and equipment suppliers.

He has also demonstrated his understanding of the requirement that he not exceed his authority or training by offering medical advice; he instead serves quite ably as a liaison between the client and the appropriate medical office.

According to client surveys, Mr. Paragon makes every effort to maintain his schedule; if there are unanticipated emergencies or delays, he reschedules appointments promptly or makes arrangements for a substitute provider. The office receives regular commendations on his professionalism and courteous attitude.

NEEDS IMPROVEMENT

Ms. Goodenough has not yet demonstrated fully acceptable skills as a home health care provider; client surveys show several areas of concern that must be dealt with immediately.

It is essential that Ms. Goodenough keeps in regular contact with the supervising nurse and head of medical services to discuss any changes in conditions and needs of patients; significant conditions should be called into the office from the patient's home to determine if changes in home health care need to be made or if an office or hospital visit is required.

With this evaluation, Ms. Goodenough is directed to request and undertake additional specialized training on atypical medical services. These courses are available through the supervising medical staff. She will be re-evaluated on these matters within 30 days.

Ms. Goodenough has demonstrated an uneven level of patience and compassion in providing assistance to patients in scheduling medical appointments and necessary tests. She is instructed to work more closely with pharmacists and the medical staff in advising on the proper use of prescribed drugs and other procedures. Although this department recognizes that not all patients are willing or able to be fully cooperative, the home health care provider must rise above personalities at all times. Ms. Goodenough will be re-evaluated on her attitudes, based on fresh surveys of clients, within 30 days.

It is also essential that Ms. Goodenough demonstrate her understanding of the requirement that she not exceed her authority or training by offering medical advice; with this evaluation, she is directed to meet with the medical office manager to discuss proper procedures in serving as a liaison between the client and appropriate doctors and medical specialists.

According to client surveys, Ms. Goodenough regularly falls behind on her schedule, leaving patients concerned about their treatments or unattended; office policy dictates that if there are unanticipated emergencies or delays that the home health care provider is required to contact patients or the supervising office to reschedule appointments promptly or make arrangements for a substitute provider. Ms. Goodenough will be re-evaluated on her scheduling practices within 30 days.

UNSATISFACTORY

Mr. Belowpar has failed to demonstrate acceptable skills as a home health care provider; client surveys show numerous instances of serious violations of office procedure that must be dealt with immediately.

It is essential that Mr. Belowpar keeps in regular contact with the supervising nurse and head of medical services to discuss any changes in conditions and needs of patients; he is specifically instructed not to dispense medical advice on his own.

Specified procedures state that significant changes in condition be called into the office from the patient's home to determine if changes in home health care need to be made or if an office or hospital visit is required.

With this evaluation, Mr. Belowpar is directed to undertake additional specialized training on atypical medical services. These courses are available through the supervising medical staff.

He will be placed on paid leave during this period and not be sent to visit clients until satisfactory completion of training. Mr. Belowpar will be re-evaluated on progress in his training once a week until it is determined that he has become sufficiently aware of the requirements of his job. Failure to accomplish these goals within 45 days will be considered grounds for dismissal.

Mr. Belowpar has not shown an acceptable level of patience and compassion in providing assistance to patients in scheduling medical appointments and necessary tests. He has failed to consult with pharmacists and the medical staff in advising on the proper use of prescribed drugs and other procedures. Although this department recognizes that not all patients are willing or able to be fully cooperative, the home health care provider must rise above personalities at all times.

Mr. Belowpar will be re-evaluated on his attitudes, based on fresh surveys of clients, within 30 days. If improvements are not noted in this area, a dismissal process will commence at that time.

According to client surveys, Mr. Belowpar has consistently failed to keep to his appointment schedule, leaving patients concerned about their treatments or unattended; office policy dictates that if there are unanticipated emergencies or delays that the home health care provider is required to contact patients or the supervising office to reschedule appointments promptly or make arrangements for a substitute provider.

Mr. Belowpar is instructed to make this matter a high priority for improvement; he will be re-evaluated on his scheduling practices within 10 days, and failure to do so will result in commencement of dismissal procedures.

CHAPTER 12

ACADEMIC

Career Counselor

Registrar and Records Manager

Director of International Programs

Career Counselor

AmeriCorps
Career counseling
Employment counseling
Job bank
Job fair
Military recruiters
Outreach to employers
Peace Corps
Professional certification programs
Relocation information
VISTA

MEETS OR EXCEEDS

Mr. Paragon has demonstrated exemplary skills as a career counselor, working in close coordination with students, various academic departments, and in outreach to employers, government agencies, and other educational institutions.

At the request of the dean of students, he organized and managed the institution's first job fair five years ago and has built a model that has generated interest from a number of colleges. Over that period of time, the number of businesses and public institutions that participate and recruit from among our students has grown from about 50 to more than 200.

Mr. Paragon has shown a deep understanding of the programs and degrees the college offers, and he has been very effective in connecting these offerings to the needs of recruiters.

On his own initiative, Mr. Paragon established a working group to create a Job Bank computer database that helps students and employers find matches between needs and wants. He worked closely with the MIS department in the development of the database and has helped set up classes for students and faculty in its use.

Mr. Paragon has also effectively worked to strengthen the college's offerings to graduating students who are not immediately going into the workplace. He has established and maintained links with area graduate schools and professional certification programs, government job initiatives such as AmeriCorps, VISTA, and the Peace Corps, community agencies, and military recruiters.

At the time of his hiring, Mr. Paragon was advised that his appointment was provisional, pending the completion of a master's degree in guidance and counseling. It is noted that he accomplished that requirement six months ahead of schedule and has undertaken advanced studies in education and training offered by the university. He has also attained membership in several national associations and has attended appropriate conferences for professional development.

Mr. Paragon has added an innovative program for follow-up counseling for graduates, encouraging former students to post resumes for advancement beyond entry-level jobs. At the same time, he showed great initiative in involving some of the college's more successful recent graduates in offering seminars to upperclass students preparing to seek their first full-time jobs.

At the request of the dean of students, Mr. Paragon has created a very popular and effective series of seminars, "Real World 101," that offer graduating students advice on such things as how to dress for success, proper conduct at a job interview, and tips on following up on employment leads.

Under his management, the office of career counseling has established a library of employment guides, relocation information, and a listing of Web-based employment sites. His department has also offered a regular schedule of classes on how to use online job search sites.

NEEDS IMPROVEMENT

Ms. Goodenough needs to improve her skills as a career counselor. Her office has been disconnected in many ways from the activities of other departments as they prepare students for graduation.

She needs to work more closely to coordinate her efforts with students, various academic departments, employers, government agencies, and other educational institutions. In a number of instances, she has seemed to place too much emphasis on job categories where employment opportunities are few; in other cases, she has not devoted sufficient attention to employers who have substantial opportunities that could be filled by current students.

At the time of her hiring, she was asked to vastly improve the institution's annual job fair, boosting participation by both students and employers. This has not been accomplished; the number of businesses and public institutions that participate and recruit from among our students has decreased sharply over the past three years and has been largely ineffective as a resource for graduating seniors. With this evaluation, she is directed to make the job fair her top priority for the coming academic year; she will be re-evaluated on this matter on June 15.

Ms. Goodenough has not devoted sufficient attention to a full understanding of the programs and degrees offered by the college, and this has resulted in a disconnect between the needs of students and recruiting institutions.

The current system of job postings does not make adequate use of computer facilities, relying instead upon a bulletin board and newsletter. Ms. Goodenough is asked to establish a working group—including the MIS department, representatives of academic departments, and the student association—to create a Job Bank computer database to help students and employers match needs and wants.

Ms. Goodenough is directed to make the creation of the Job Bank a top priority for the coming year. She is also asked to work with appropriate departments to set up classes for students and faculty in its use.

During the course of the past two years, Ms. Goodenough has not devoted an adequate amount of attention to the college's offerings to graduating students who are not immediately going into the workplace. She is asked to establish and maintain links with area graduate schools and professional certification programs, government job initiatives such as AmeriCorps, VISTA, and the Peace Corps, community agencies, and military recruiters.

At the time of her hiring, Ms. Goodenough was advised that her appointment was provisional, pending the completion of a master's degree in guidance and counseling. As of the date of this appraisal, although she has taken some of the required courses, she has not received that advanced degree. She is directed to advise the dean of students, within 60 days, of her plans for completion of that necessary credential; her appointment will continue to be provisional and subject to cancellation.

Ms. Goodenough is also advised to seek advanced studies in education and training offered by the university and to attain membership in national professional counseling associations.

Six months ago, Ms. Goodenough was asked to develop a new program offering follow-up counseling for graduates, encouraging former students to post resumes for advancement beyond entry-level jobs. This has not been put into place as of this date; with this evaluation, she is directed to provide the dean of students with a written plan and schedule for this program within 30 days.

At the request of the dean of students, Ms. Goodenough created a series of seminars, "Real World 101," that offer graduating students advice on such things as how to dress for success, proper conduct at a job interview, and tips on following up on employment leads. Based on feedback from students, the seminars have not delivered meaningful information and guidance. Ms. Goodenough is directed to establish a conference group including members of the student body, academic departments, and human resources representatives from area employers to enhance offerings under this program. She will be re-evaluated on this matter in 120 days.

Student surveys have noted that the office of career counseling has a very limited library of employment guides, relocation information, and listings of Web-based employment sites. Ms. Goodenough is directed to make improvements in this area a top priority for the coming semester.

UNSATISFACTORY

Mr. Belowpar has failed to demonstrate an adequate level of skill as a career counselor. According to surveys of graduating seniors, the offerings of the career counselor are in many ways unrelated to their college backgrounds and employment needs.

He has not shown an ability to closely coordinate his efforts with students, various academic departments, employers, government agencies, and other educational institutions. Students have reported a number of instances in which he placed emphasis on job categories where employment opportunities are few; several major area employers have noted a lack of attention to substantial opportunities that could be filled by current students.

At the time of his hiring, he was asked to make the establishment of a job fair his highest priority; this institution is one of the few in the region without such an offering. Although a small job fair was conducted 15 months after his hiring, it was judged by the dean of students and participants to be an inadequate effort. With this evaluation, Mr. Belowpar is instructed to develop a plan and schedule within 60 days and present it to the dean of students for approval. He will be re-evaluated on job performance at that time.

Mr. Belowpar has not shown that he has a full understanding of the programs and degrees offered by the college. He is directed to review the course catalog and to meet with representatives of each of the major schools within the university to better acquaint himself with the academic offerings and career objectives of students. He will be re-evaluated on this matter in 90 days.

At the time of his hiring, Mr. Belowpar was instructed to work with the MIS department to computerize the Job Bank. This has not been accomplished; students and employers continue to ask for use of a bulletin board and newsletter. He is directed to create an online database of resumes and job availabilities within the next 90 days; the MIS department has been asked to make available appropriate personnel to assist on the technical side of this very important assignment. He is also asked to work with appropriate departments to set up classes for students and faculty in its use.

Despite a request in his most recent evaluation, Mr. Belowpar has not demonstrated sufficient attention to the college's offerings to graduating students who are not immediately going into the workplace. He is directed to study similar programs at other educational institutions, specifically those that maintain links with area graduate schools and professional certification programs, government job initiatives such as AmeriCorps, VISTA, and the Peace Corps, community agencies, and military recruiters.

At the time of his hiring, Mr. Belowpar was advised that his appointment was provisional, pending the completion of a master's degree in guidance and counseling. As of the date of this appraisal, he has not begun courses toward that advanced degree. He is directed to advise the dean of students, within 60 days, of his plans for completion of that necessary credential on an expedited schedule; his appointment will continue to be provisional and subject to cancellation.

Mr. Belowpar has also not availed himself of advanced studies in education and training offered by the university nor has he attained membership in national professional counseling associations. He is directed to do so.

Student surveys have noted that the office of career counseling does not offer a library of employment guides, relocation information, and listings of Web-based employment sites. Mr. Belowpar is directed to make improvements in this area a top priority for the coming semester. He will be re-evaluated on this matter in 60 days.

Registrar and Records Manager

Accessibility to records
Computerization of paper records
Delinquent accounts
Online registration
Recordkeeping
Registrar
Secure database

MEETS OR EXCEEDS

Ms. Paragon has greatly improved the operations and efficiency of the office of the registrar in her first two years as director.

At the time of her hiring, the department was in the process of completing a conversion from paper and microfiche records to a secure computer database; she demonstrated great skill in managing this changeover for current records as well as initiating a process to convert older files to database entries on a less time-critical basis.

Ms. Paragon has done an excellent job of establishing coordination between the academic record database at the registrar's office and the financial information maintained by the bursar; in doing so, she has assisted the bursar in efficient processing of new students and in identifying delinquent accounts.

Under her administration, the registrar has maintained and enhanced accessibility to records by students and appropriate academic and administrative departments while also safeguarding the confidentiality of information included in the records.

In the past year, the college has completed the process of requiring students to register for classes from an online Web site. Ms. Paragon and her staff performed exceptionally well, under short deadlines, in the establishment of this computer-based service and in its implementation. On her own initiative, Ms. Paragon conducted a survey among students to determine how well the process worked and has already made changes in the program for the coming semester.

Ms. Paragon and her staff have shown a high degree of cooperation in working with other departments in coordinating records to allow supervision of progress toward degree requirements. At the request of the dean of students, Ms. Paragon instituted an automated process to alert students and college departments of any situation where grade point averages have fallen below required levels for matriculation or maintenance of scholarships.

Ms. Paragon has sought and received advanced training in management skills and computer operations and has been an active participant in professional organizations related to her job.

NEEDS IMPROVEMENT

Ms. Goodenough has not made sufficient progress toward improving the operations and efficiency of the office of the registrar in her first two years as director.

At the time of her hiring, the department was about to begin the process of converting from paper and microfiche records to a secure computer database; the work was not completed on schedule. There continue to be problems with retrieval of some current records. The conversion of older files to database entries has not yet begun because of ongoing problems. With this evaluation, Ms. Goodenough is directed to make completion of this task her highest priority; she will be re-evaluated on this matter within 90 days.

Ms. Goodenough has not adequately coordinated the academic record database at the registrar's office with the financial information maintained by the bursar; the board of trustees identified this as a critical task to assist the bursar in efficient processing of new students and identifying delinquent accounts. She is asked to produce, within 60 days, a plan and schedule for accomplishment of this assignment and present it to the board.

Under her administration, the registrar has not demonstrated improvement in access to records by students and appropriate academic and administrative departments; this is related to problems with the computerization of files. At the same time, there has not been adequate attention paid to safeguarding the confidentiality of information included in the records.

Another problem area involves the management of computer-based class registration; this was identified as a high priority task at the time of Ms. Goodenough's most recent evaluation. As of this date, the online registration program continues to be inadequate, resulting in delays and complaints from students and academic departments of errors in scheduling and overbooking of classes. With this evaluation, she is directed to meet with the MIS department and to engage appropriate outside consultants to fix problems and refine the process before the next registration period.

Ms. Goodenough has not engaged in interdepartmental meetings to permit more timely supervision of progress toward degree requirements. In addition, Ms. Goodenough was requested by the dean of students to institute an automated process to alert students and college departments of any situation where grade point averages have fallen below required levels for matriculation or maintenance of scholarships. This has not been accomplished; with this evaluation, she is directed to provide the dean of students with a plan to implement such a program within 90 days.

Ms. Goodenough has not taken advantage of available advanced training in management skills and computer operations and has not been an active participant in professional organizations related to her job. It is recommended she do so in the coming year.

UNSATISFACTORY

Mr. Belowpar has failed to improve the operations and efficiency of the office of the registrar in his first year as director. In some areas, efficiency has declined with repercussions throughout the university.

At the time of his hiring, Mr. Belowpar was directed to accelerate the process of converting from paper and microfiche records to a secure computer database; this task has not been completed. Some records have been computerized while others have not, resulting in an increase in workload for many departments. The second stage of the process, conversion of older files to database entries, has not yet begun because of these problems.

The board of trustees has asked Mr. Belowpar to meet with them at their next scheduled gathering to explain the nature of any outstanding problems and to present a detailed timeline for full completion of this mission-critical assignment. The board's report will become a key element of Mr. Belowpar's re-evaluation in 90 days.

Despite a directive included in his previous evaluation, Mr. Belowpar has not coordinated the academic record database at the registrar's office with the financial information maintained by the bursar. Once again, this is related to the failure to complete the computerization of records. He is asked to produce, within 60 days, a plan and schedule for accomplishment of this assignment and present it to the board of trustees.

Mr. Belowpar has also failed to address concerns about the accessibility and security of records. Students have both the right to see the information in their files and the expectation that the data is protected against inappropriate access by unauthorized persons. With this evaluation, he is directed to make this task a high priority for completion within the coming semester; he will be re-evaluated on this matter in 120 days.

The university continues to experience significant problems with the management of computer-based class registration; this was identified as a high priority task at the time of Mr. Belowpar's previous evaluation. The existing online registration program is inadequate for the demands of a large institution. The board of trustees has directed that Mr. Belowpar meet with the MIS department and engage appropriate outside consultants to make significant improvements in this area before the next registration period.

At the time of his hiring, Mr. Belowpar was instructed to establish an interdepartmental task force to facilitate more timely supervision of progress toward degree requirements. As part of this assignment, he was also directed by the dean of students to institute an automated process to alert students and college departments of any situation where grade point averages have fallen below required levels for matriculation or maintenance of scholarships. Neither of these important tasks has been accomplished; with this evaluation, he is directed to provide the dean of students with a plan to implement such a program within 90 days. Completion of this critical assignment is expected no later than 180 days from this date.

It is noted that Mr. Belowpar has not taken advantage of available advanced training in management skills and computer operations and has not been an active participant in professional organizations related to his job. It is the opinion of this evaluator that Mr. Belowpar would benefit greatly from such further education.

Director of International Programs

Foreign employees
Housing allowances
Immigration policies
International programs
Study-abroad programs
Visa policies

MEETS OR EXCEEDS

Mr. Paragon has performed with great distinction as the university's director of international programs. He has greatly improved the recognition the institution receives for its overseas offerings and in doing so has enhanced its reputation among existing and prospective students.

Since his hiring, Mr. Paragon has added four new highly regarded and popular programs in Rome, London, Paris, and Sydney; he has expanded on existing fine arts and governmental studies curricula in Florence, Madrid, and Glasgow.

He has shown a depth of understanding of the university and has demonstrated great skill in seeking international studies that complement those offerings. He meets regularly with a task force of representatives from academic departments to assure that international course offerings are consistent with degree requirements of the university.

Mr. Paragon has shown exceptional skill in overseeing foreign employees of the university as well as domestic staff on temporary assignment; under his management, effective liaison with the human resources department was established to manage these sometimes complex situations.

He has devoted a great deal of time to establishing good relationships with foreign colleges and service providers. In locations where the university does not have its own facility, Mr. Paragon has worked well in cooperative exchanges with other domestic universities, permitting students to enroll in their programs and receive credit here.

As directed, he has kept up to date on federal policies on immigration and study-abroad and exchange programs. On his own initiative, he established and maintains a database of information for students and their parents interested in international studies.

Mr. Paragon has developed and maintained a well-regarded training course for students headed to international programs; classes are devoted to the logistics of travel, sensitivity to local customs and culture, and safety and security.

NEEDS IMPROVEMENT

In his first two years on the job, Mr. Goodenough has not significantly improved the university's international programs.

At the time of his hiring, he was asked to improve the recognition the institution receives for its overseas offerings and enhance its reputation among existing and prospective students. Specifically, he was directed to seek new programs in foreign cities; as of this date, he has added only one new international alliance.

Mr. Goodenough has failed to demonstrate a great depth of understanding of the university and has not shown sufficient skill in seeking international studies that complement those offerings. With this evaluation, he is directed to establish a task force of representatives from academic departments and to conduct regular meetings to assure that international course offerings are consistent with degree requirements of the university.

Another area of concern involves oversight of foreign employees of the university as well as domestic staff on temporary assignment; Mr. Goodenough has not demonstrated sufficient understanding of the complexities of visas, taxes, and housing allowances. With this evaluation, he is directed to establish a task force that includes the human resources and legal departments to manage these sometimes complex situations.

Mr. Goodenough has also not shown that he can keep up to date on federal policies on immigration and study-abroad and exchange programs. He is directed to improve his understanding of these matters and to establish and maintain a database of information for students and their parents interested in international studies.

UNSATISFACTORY

Under Ms. Belowpar's administration, the quality of the university's international programs has been reduced.

At the time of her hiring, Ms. Belowpar was asked to improve the recognition the institution receives for its overseas offerings and enhance its reputation among existing and prospective students. However, we have instead seen a 32 percent decrease in enrollment in the past two years and the closing of programs in Rome, Florence, and Sydney.

It is apparent that Ms. Belowpar has not devoted the effort to understand the full breadth and mission of the university and as a result has not successfully developed international studies that complement those offerings. She is directed to develop a plan, within 30 days, to establish an advisory committee consisting of representatives from academic departments to assure that international course offerings are consistent with degree requirements of the university.

Under her administration, Ms. Belowpar has run into repeated difficulties handling the complexities of visas, taxes, and housing allowances for foreign employees of the university as well as domestic staff on temporary assignment. This was identified as an area of concern at her previous evaluation; she is now directed to meet with designated representatives of the human resources and legal departments within 30 days to identify specific shortcomings in policies and operations. She will be re-evaluated on this matter in 60 days.

THESAURUS OF NOUNS AND ADJECTIVES

ability—aptitude, skill, capability, capacity, facility, talent, gift, knack

acceptance—approval, agreement, tolerance, acknowledgment, favorable reception, acquiescence, concurrence

access—right of entry, admission, right to use, admittance, entrée, contact

accountability—answerability, responsibility, liability

accounting—secretarial, office, bookkeeping

accuracy—correctness, accurateness, exactness, precision, truth, truthfulness

achievements—accomplishments, successes, feats, triumphs

acknowledgment—recognition, acceptance, admission, appreciation, tribute

actions—events, proceedings, measures, procedures, dealings

administrative support—managerial, directorial, organizational, clerical, secretarial, executive

advancement—progression, progress, development, improvement, expansion, innovation, increase

advice—recommendation, counsel, suggestion, guidance, opinion

advocate—supporter, backer, promoter, believer, activist, campaigner, sponsor

agency—organization, group, society, outfit, bureau

algorithm—formula, computer analysis

allegiance—loyalty, commitment, adherence, faithfulness, duty

allocation—share, portion, part, allotment, allowance

alternate—exchange, swap, interchange, rotate

alternative—option, choice, substitute

ambition—goal, aim, objective, aspiration, dream, hope, desire, purpose

analysis—examination, study, investigation, scrutiny, breakdown

answer—reply, response, retort

appearance—look, form, style, façade

application (1)—software program, program

application (2)—request, claim, submission, use, function, purpose, relevance

appointments—actions, travels, schedule, activities, arrangements, engagements, whereabouts

appraisal—assessment, evaluation, judgment, review, consideration

appropriate—suitable, fitting, apt, proper, right, correct

aptitude—ability, skill, talent, gift, capacity, fitness, propensity

assignment—task, job, prospect, duty, obligation, mission, transfer

attendance—turnout, audience, presence

attention—notice, concentration, thought, awareness, consideration, mind, interest

attitude—approach, outlook, manner, stance, position, feelings, thoughts, mind-set

audit—review, check, inspection, examination, assessment, appraisal, inventory, check

authority—power, right, ability, influence, weight

background—setting, milieu, environment, surroundings, conditions

beliefs—attitude, viewpoint, idea, thinking, way of life, values

bottom line—base, foundation

budget—financial plan, financial statement, resources, account

calm—tranquil, peaceful, quiet, still, composed, serene, relaxed

capability—ability, means, potential, capacity, competence, facility, aptitude, qualifications

capital expenditures—purchases, spending, assets, resources, funds, wealth, money, principal, investment, center

career goals—vocation, job, occupation, profession, calling, livelihood, line of business

cause—reason, grounds, source, root, origin, basis, foundation

chain of command—organization chart, superiors, sequence, series, string, succession, procession

challenge—confrontation, test

change—modification, alteration, adjustment

channels—markets, sales conduits

character—nature, quality, temperament, personality, disposition, spirit, moral fiber, makeup

circumstances—situations, conditions, state of affairs, status, position, circumstance

clarity—clearness, lucidity, simplicity, intelligibility, transparency

classes—lessons, course, program, curriculum

cleanliness—hygiene, sanitation, purity, spotlessness

collaborative—joint, two-way, mutual, shared

collected—joint, two-way, mutual, shared

command—authority, control, rule, domination, power, sway, grasp

comments—commentary, explanation, remarks, observations, notes, clarification, interpretation

commitment—promise, pledge, vow, obligation, assurance, binder, dedication, loyalty

committee—group, board, team, commission, working group, agency

common sense—intelligence, brains, intellect, wisdom, sagacity, logic, good judgment

compassion—sympathy, empathy, concern, kindness, consideration, care

competence—capability, ability, skill, fitness, aptitude, proficiency, competency, know-how

compliance—observance, conformity, obedience, acquiescence, agreement, falling in line, fulfillment

computer maintenance—preservation, safeguarding, protection

computer tools—software, applications, processor, CPU, mainframe, workstation, PC, laptop

concept—idea, notion, thought, perception, impression, conception, theory, model

concern—anxiety, worry, apprehension, fear, alarm, distress, unease, disquiet

conclusion—end, close, termination, wrapping-up, winding-up, finale

confidence—self-assurance, self-confidence, assurance, self-belief, self-reliance, buoyancy, coolness

confidential matters—secret, private, classified, off-the-record

conflict—disagreement, clash, divergence, difference, argument, variance, quarrel, inconsistency

confrontation—argument, disagreement, quarrel, altercation, war of words, conflict

conscientious—careful, thorough, meticulous, painstaking, reliable, diligent, hardworking, assiduous

consensus—agreement, accord, harmony, compromise, consent

consequences—penalty, cost, disruption

consistent—reliable, steady, dependable, constant, unswerving, unfailing, regular

constraint—restraint, restriction, limitation, constriction, limit, check, control

consultant—advisor, mentor, guide, counselor, expert, specialist, professional, authority

contacts—associates, acquaintances, links, friends

contingency—unforeseen events, emergency, incident, possibility, eventuality

contract—agreement, letter of agreement, pact, convention, deal, bond, indenture

contribution—payment, donation, gift, input, role, involvement

convention (1)—meeting, gathering, conference, reunion, get-together, caucus

convention (2)—rule, principle, agreed-upon rule

cooperation—collaboration, assistance, help, support, teamwork, mutual aid

coordination—harmonization, organization, management, synchronization, bringing together, dexterity, skill, adroitness

core principles—central, critical, nucleus, middle, foundation, mission statement

corporate mission—core mission, assignment, task, job, work, charge, undertaking, duty, operation

cost accounting—bookkeeping, expenditure review, expense tracking, profit and loss statement

cost of services—price, charge, rate, fee, price tag, asking price, outlay, expenditure

costs—expenses, outlay, expenditure, overhead

counseling—therapy, psychotherapy, analysis, counsel

course—route, path, way, track, itinerary, line, lessons, classes

courtesy—good manners, politeness, civility, courteousness, consideration

creative—original, imaginative, inspired, artistic, inventive, resourceful, ingenious, innovative

creativity—creativeness, originality, imagination, inspiration, ingenuity, inventiveness, resourcefulness, vision

credibility—trustworthiness, reliability, integrity, authority, standing, sincerity

credible—believable, convincing, plausible, likely, probable, realistic, trustworthy, reliable

credit—praise, recognition, thanks, acclaim, glory, acknowledgment, tribute

crisis—disaster, catastrophe, emergency, calamity, predicament

criteria—decisive factor, principle, standard, norm

customer loyalty—faithfulness, devotion, allegiance, fidelity, steadfastness

customer service—assistance, help, support

data—information, statistics, facts, figures, numbers, records

databases—files, records, information

deadlines—time limits, goals, aims, targets, cutoff date

deal—contracts, agreements, arrangements

decision—results, choices, conclusions, judgments, assessments, evaluations

decisive—critical, clear-thinking, resolute, firm, steadfast

decisiveness—certainty, determination, resolve

decorum—good manners, politeness, propriety, manners, courtesy, correctness

dedication—devotion, commitment, allegiance, loyalty

delay—postponement, deferment, deferral

delegated tasks—handed over, farmed out, relinquished

delegation—allocation, sharing

deliberative—calculated, planned, purposeful

delivery—release, liberation, rescue, relief, escape, freedom, deliverance

demands—stress, strain, anxiety, difficulty, load, burden, hassle, requirements

demeanor—manner, conduct, behavior, character, deportment, performance, appearance, bearing

demonstration—expression, display, show, exhibition, revelation, manifestation, protest

dependable—reliable, trustworthy, loyal, faithful, steady, responsible, steadfast, worthy

details—particulars, facts, information, minutiae, niceties, fine points

development—growth, expansion, progress, advance, increase, maturity, enlargement, improvement

diplomacy—mediation, negotiation, peacekeeping, tact, skill, subtlety, discretion, political skills

discipline—regulation, order, control, authority, punishment, restraint, obedience

discount—reduction, money off, markdown, price cut, concession

discretion—carefulness, judgment, prudence, caution, good judgment, maturity, diplomacy, tact

disposition—nature, character, temperament, temper, outlook

dispute—argument, disagreement, quarrel, difference of opinion, heated discussion, clash, row

distributor—reseller, selling agent

diversity—variety, assortment, multiplicity, range, miscellany, mixture

documentation—instructions, reports, certification, verification, credentials, documents, citations, records

education—teaching, learning, schooling, tutoring, instruction, edification, culture

effectiveness—efficiency, efficacy, success, use, usefulness, helpfulness, value

efficiency—competence, good organization, effectiveness

effort—attempt, try, endeavor, work, exertion

e-mail—electronic mail, correspondence, electronic message, message, communication, news item, piece of mail

emotion—feeling, sentiment, sensation, passion

energy—power, force, vigor, liveliness, get-up-and-go

enterprise—venture, project, endeavor, activity

enthusiasm—eagerness, interest, keenness, fervor, passion, gusto, zeal, zest

equanimity—composure, calmness, levelheadedness, equability, self-control, poise

equitable—evenhanded, fair, reasonable, impartial, just, unbiased

ethics—principles, morals, beliefs, moral values, moral code

evaluation—assessment, estimate, appraisal, valuation, estimation

example—instance, case, case in point, illustration, model, pattern, exemplar, paradigm

expectations—prospect, outlook, potential, opportunity, hope

expenditure—spending, expenses, costs, outlay, outflow, disbursements, payments, overhead

expenses—operating cost, fixed cost, operating expense, everyday expenditures

expert—specialist, authority, professional, guru, connoisseur, skilled, practiced, proficient

expertise—know-how, skill, knowledge, proficiency, capability

facilities—amenities, services, conveniences

fairness—justice, equality, evenhandedness

financial—monetary, fiscal, economic, accounting

fire—passion, ardor, excitement, enthusiasm, vigor

flexibility—adaptability, compliance, conformity, elasticity, give, plasticity

forecast—prediction, estimate, guess, calculation, conjecture

formal—official, proper, prescribed, recognized, strict, ceremonial, reserved

formula—method, recipe, prescription, procedure, principle, rule, blueprint

forthrightness—frankness, candor, directness, candidness, outspokenness, bluntness, honesty

fundamentals—basics, rudiments, essentials, ground rules, brass tacks, nitty-gritty

goal—objective, aim, ambition, purpose, target, object, aspiration

grace—elegance, refinement, loveliness, polish, style, poise, charm, beauty

grammar—syntax, sentence structure, language rules

groupware—collaborative software, workgroup software, networked computer applications

guest register—list, record, sign-in book, appointment book, catalog, roll, index, chronicle, schedule

guidance—leadership, direction, supervision, management, control, regulation, help, assistance

guidelines—rule, strategy, plan, guiding principle, course of action, procedure

high-quality—high-class, first-class, first-rate, choice, luxury, premium, super, expert

history—account, narration, record

honesty—sincerity, truthfulness, integrity, frankness, candor, openness

humor—good attitude, pleasantness, wit, comedy

ideas—thoughts, dreams, opinion, judgment, belief

image—representation, account, demonstration

impression—sense, connotation, impact, effect, influence

incentives—inducement, enticement, motivation, encouragement, inspiration, impetus

independence—autonomy, self-sufficiency, self-reliance

independent—self-determining, autonomous, self-directed

industry—business, trade,

influence—power, authority, control, command

informal—relaxed, unceremonious, comfortable, stressless, hassle-free

information—data, facts, details, specifics, essentials

ingenious—clever, smart, knowledgeable, well-informed

ingenuity—cleverness, skill, cunning, resourcefulness, inventiveness

initiative—scheme, plan, method, proposal, strategy

innovation—originality, inventiveness, creativity, improvement, enhancement

innovative—groundbreaking, revolutionary, inventive, novel, pioneering

input—effort, contribution

insight—knowledge, experience, familiarity, appreciation

instructions—orders, guidelines, commands, rules, strategies, course of action, procedure

insurance—indemnity, protection, security

Internet—Web, online

inventory—supply, stock, stockpile, reserve

issues—problem, crises, trouble, difficulty, setback

job description—assignment, definition of duties, job requirements

judgment—opinion, ruling, decision, assessment, evaluation, appraisal

knowledge—experience, education, wisdom, learning

labor disruptions—strike, labor unrest, work action, job action, slowdown

language—verbal communication, speech, discourse, spoken language, words, expression, vocabulary, terms, terminology, lingo

laws—rules, regulations, directives, dictates, decrees

leader—manager, director, person in charge, supervisor

leads—prospects, possibilities

legislators—lawmakers, policymakers, officials

letters—mail, correspondence, communication, messages

level—stage, plane, point, echelon, rank, intensity, height

logic—reason, judgment, common sense, rationale, foundation, basis

logical—rational, reasonable, sound, commonsense

loyalty—faithfulness, devotion, allegiance, fidelity, steadfastness

maintenance—upkeep, repairs, preservation

managerial skills—decision-making, administrative, executive, supervisory

manner—way, method, means, technique, approach, style

market research—investigation, study, exploration, inquiry

market strategies—plans, policies, tactics, methods

marketplace—industry, sales area, sales arena

materials—resources, equipment, supplies, tools, goods, provisions

maturity—wisdom, understanding, knowledge, insight, perception

maximization—making the most of, exploiting, taking full advantage of, capitalizing on

measurements—capacity, ability, capability, aptitude

media—press, newspapers, television and radio, reporters, journalists

mediation—arbitration, negotiation, adjudication

mediator—go-between, intermediary, arbitrator, negotiator, moderator, referee

meeting facilities—amenities, services, convention center, conference room

meetings—conferences, gatherings, get-togethers, discussions, talks, consultations

memos—memorandum, communication, notes, messages, letters, interoffice communication

methodology—method, tactic, approach, technique, system, procedure

mission statement—guidelines, charge, assignment

missteps—mistakes, errors, blunders, slipups, gaffes

motivation—incentive, inspiration, impetus, stimulus

negotiation—bargain, agreement, contract, deal, settlement

negotiator—mediator, go-between, intermediary, arbitrator, referee

objections—opposition, resistance, antagonism, hostility, disagreement

objectives—purpose, intention, intent, goal, target, aim

objectivity—impartiality, neutrality, fairness, independence, lack of prejudice, open-mindedness, evenhandedness, lack of bias

observation—scrutiny, study, inquiry, search, analysis

online—Internet, Web, network

openness—frankness, sincerity, candidness, directness, honesty, forthrightness

opportunity—chance, occasion, prospect, possibility

options—alternatives, choices, opportunities

orator—speaker, spokesman, spokeswoman, spokesperson

orderly—arranged, neat, tidy, methodical, systematic, organized, well-thought-out

organization (1)—business, company, concern, establishment, outfit, institution, agency, enterprise, venture

organization (2)—orderliness, order, method, regulation, neatness, tidiness

orientation (1)—course, route, path

orientation (2)—preparation, lessons, classes, program, classes, curriculum

originality—innovation, inventiveness, creativity, inspiration, ingenuity, vision

output—production, productivity, yield, manufacture, amount produced

payroll services—bookkeeping, payroll processing

performance—presentation, accomplishment, act, deed

personality—character, behavior, traits, personal qualities

personnel—employees, staff, workers, workforce, human resources

pilferage—theft, shrinkage, loss

planning—preparation, forecasting, research, exploration

plans—policy, tactic, strategy, approach

poise—bearing, deportment, manner

police—law enforcement

policies—rules, guidelines, procedures, guiding principles

polish—refinement, sophistication, finesse, civility

polished—refined, cultured, sophisticated

politeness—good manners, courtesy, civility, graciousness

popularity—recognition, esteem, high regard, admiration

positions—opinions, views, thinking

positive—encouraging, constructive, helpful, affirmative, upbeat

potential—promise, capability, aptitude, possibilities

preparation—training, homework, research, grounding

presence—charisma, aura, authority, appeal

presentation—talk, lecture, seminar, address, speech

presentation aids—audiovisual aids, props, slides, charts, PowerPoint presentations

pressure—stress, strain, demands, load, burden

prevention—avoidance, deterrence, anticipation

pricing—valuation, evaluation, worth, charge

principles—values, beliefs, philosophies, ideology

priorities—main concerns

priority—preference, primacy, superiority

privacy—protection of records, seclusion, isolation, solitude, time alone, space to yourself, retreat

problems—evils, troubles, harms, tribulations

problem-solving—analytic, analytical, diagnostic, investigative, troubleshooting

procedure—process, method, system, means

process—procedure, method, manner

productivity—output, efficiency, yield, amount produced

professional—expert, specialist, authority

proficiency—skill, ability, expertise, talent, aptitude, know-how

program (1)—plan, arrangement, strategy, design

program (2)—software, software application

progress—development, advancement, improvement, steps forward, movement

projects—ventures, undertakings, tasks, assignments, jobs

promotion—advancement, upgrade, elevation, new responsibilities

proposals—suggestions, ideas, plans, propositions

punctual—on time, prompt, precise

quality—excellence, superiority, distinction

questions—inquiries, queries

rapport—relationship, affiliation, bond, liaison, affinity, involvement, association, attachment

reaction—response, reply, answer

realistic—practical, pragmatic, sensible, matter-of-fact

reason—good sense, intelligence, logic, wisdom, rationale

reasonableness—sensibleness, rationality, judiciousness

reasoning—way of thinking, analysis, reckoning, estimation

recognition—credit, acknowledgment, acceptance, appreciation

records—accounts, reports, proceedings, actions, documentation, details

recruiting—enlisting, hiring, signing up, enrolling, taking on

reduction—decrease, lessening, diminution, cutback

referee—arbitrator, mediator, go-between, peacemaker

refined—polished, sophisticated, gracious, cultured

regulation—rule, directive, law, guideline, principle, instruction

regulators—lawmakers, supervisory body, watchdog

reinforcement—strengthening, fortification, support, buoy

relationships—interactions, interface, dealings, relations

reliability—dependability, steadfastness, constancy, trustworthiness

reliable—dependable, consistent, steadfast, unfailing, trustworthy

remarks—comments, observations, insights

remote offices—satellite offices, home workers, branch offices, foreign branches

renegotiate—rework, adjust, reconfigure

reorganization—restructuring, reformation, redeployment, overhaul

reports—account, documentation, statement, details

representation—account, relationship

representative—spokesperson, agent, delegate, ambassador

requirements—necessities, supplies, materials, obligations, requisites, fundamentals, essentials, basics

research—investigation, study, examination, inquiry

resource—assets, capital, property

resourceful—ingenious, imaginative, inventive, capable

resourcefulness—ingenuity, imagination, inventiveness

respect—high opinion, esteem, admiration, high regard

response—reaction, feedback, result

responsibility—accountability, answerability, liability, blame

responsible—accountable, in charge, in control, in command, liable

restructuring—reorganization, reformation, reform, overhaul

results—consequences, outcome, product, conclusion, effect

retention—custody, preservation, maintenance, safekeeping, guardianship, supervision

rewards—prize, results, payoff

risk—jeopardy, peril, hazard, threat

role model—example, exemplar, model, paradigm, standard, prototype, archetype

safety—protection, security, precautions

salary—pay, remuneration, income, wages, earnings

sales—deals, transactions, contracts, commerce

sales pitch—proposal, offer, proposition

schedule—calendar, agenda, timetable, program, plan

scope—range, extent, reach

security—safety, safety measures, protection, precautions

self-assurance—confidence, self-confidence

self-confidence—self-assurance, confidence

self-motivated—independent, self-directed, motivated, self-sufficient, autonomous

seminars—class, tutorial, colloquium, roundtable

shipping companies—delivery companies, freight companies, forwarders

sincerity—genuineness, authenticity, earnestness

situations—circumstances, conditions, jobs

skills—abilities, talents, aptitudes, gifts, capabilities

societies—associations, organizations, groups, clubs, guilds, alliances

solutions—answers, responses

speaker—presenter, spokesman, spokeswoman, spokesperson, lecturer

specifications—terms, components, conditions, requisites, needs

speech—language, verbal communication, dialogue, discourse

spokesperson—representative, agent

spreadsheets—worksheet, database, table

staffing—employment, recruitment

standards—values, ideals, point of measurement

statistics—date, facts, figures, information, records

status—condition, stage, level, category, form, rank

steadfast—unwavering, unfaltering, resolute, committed

stockroom—storeroom, warehouse, depot, storage area

strategy—tactic, method, approach, plan

stress—pressure, strain, tension

suggestions—ideas, proposals, propositions, submissions, tenders, pitches

superior—better, greater, higher, finer, advanced, improved, enhanced

superiors—supervisors, bosses, managers

supervision—oversight, administration, management

supervisors—managers, administrators, controllers, overseers, superiors

supplies—provisions, materials, goods, commodities

support—backing, aid, help

tact—diplomacy, discretion, prudence

targets—aims, goals, objectives, purpose

task forces—committees, teams, groups, commissions

tasks—jobs, duties, mission, assignments, responsibilities

team—group, work group, committee, interagency group, intraoffice committee

team player—cooperative worker

teamwork—cooperation, collaboration, joint effort, group effort

technology—tools, devices, equipment, machines

teleconference—telephone conference, audioconference, videoconference

telephone directory—telephone book

temperament—disposition, nature, personality, character

tensions—worries, anxieties, stresses

theory—premise, supposition, hypothesis, conjecture, assumption, speculation, educated guess

thoughts—opinions, beliefs, views, attitudes

time management—efficiency, prioritization, self-direction

tolerances—accuracy, precision

tools—devices, systems, mechanisms

tracking—following, measuring

trade shows—conventions, demonstrations

training—education, instruction, tutoring, lessons, preparation

travel costs—travel expenses, per diems

travel providers—travel agencies, charter companies, airlines, hotel, car rental companies

travel risks—security, safety

trends—tendencies, directions

troubleshooting—problem-solving

trustworthiness—dependability, steadfastness, reliability

understandable—clear, logical, comprehensible, lucid

understanding—empathy, sympathy, compassion, consideration

upgrade—improvement, advancement, stepped-up, enhancement

values—principles, standards, ideals

variances—discrepancies, inconsistencies, differences, disparities

versatility—adaptability, flexibility

vision—foresight, visualization, planning

vocabulary—language, words, terms, terminology, expressions

warehouse—stockroom, depot, storage area

Web-based conferences—teleconference, videoconference, audioconference

workgroups—teams, committees, task forces

workload—assignments, tasks, job description

THESAURUS OF VERBS AND ADVERBS

---

ably—capably, competently

accept—assent, agree, accede, concur, consent, recognize, subscribe

acclimate—become accustomed to, adapt to, adjust to

accomplish—achieve, get things done, attain, reach

achieve—attain, complete, realize, accomplish, reach

adapt—become accustomed, familiarize himself/herself, get a feel for, get used to, acclimatize, find his/her feet, settle in, adjust

adjust—regulate, alter, fiddle with, correct, fine-tune, change, amend

administer—manage, direct, run, order, control, oversee, govern

allow—permit, agree to, consent to, tolerate, allocate, let

analyze—examine, study, investigate, scrutinize, evaluate, consider, question, explore

anticipate—expect, foresee, be prepared for, look forward to, await, wait for, predict, be hopeful for, think likely

apply—be relevant, relate, be appropriate, be valid, pertain, affect, concern, submit an application

appreciate—be grateful for, be thankful for, be glad about, be pleased about, value, welcome, understand, realize

articulate—speak about, express, put into words, convey, verbalize, communicate

ask—inquire, request, solicit, pose, put, raise, invite

assist—help, aid, help out, lend a hand, give a hand, support, back

avoid—keep away from, stay away from, shun, steer clear of, let alone, pass up, evade, circumvent

beat—hit, strike, bang, hammer, thump, thrash, pound, punch

build—construct, put up, erect, make, put together, manufacture, assemble, fabricate

capable—able, competent, accomplished, talented, proficient, skilled, gifted

close—shut, lock, seal, close up, secure, slam

communicate—converse, talk, exchange in a few words, be in touch, correspond, talk

complete—finish, finalize, conclude, end, put the last touches on

conduct—carry out, do, perform, accomplish, effect, achieve

conform to—be conventional, be traditional, do the accepted thing, obey the rules, play the game, kowtow, match

consider—think, believe, deem, regard as, think about, mull over, reflect on

consult—ask, check with, discuss, talk to, sound out, confer with, seek advice from, offer advice to

contribute—add, give, donate, make a payment, supply, put in, have a say

control—manage, organize, be in charge of, run, have power over, direct, be in command of

convert—change, exchange, alter, adapt, translate, switch

convey—express, communicate, suggest, put across, put into words, get across, pass on, transmit

cooperate—help, assist, lend a hand, oblige, work together, collaborate, combine forces

coordinate—organize, direct, manage, synchronize, harmonize, match up, bring together, match

cope—manage, handle, deal with, survive, get by, muddle through

create—make, generate, produce, fashion, form, craft, build, construct

cultivate—develop, nurture, promote, tend

deal—trade, do business, exchange, buy, sell, transact business

decide—make a decision, come to a decision, make up his/her mind, choose, settle on, fix on

delegate—hand over, farm out, pass on, give, allot, entrust, assign

deliver—bring, transport, carry, distribute, send, convey

demonstrate—show, reveal, display, make obvious, exhibit, express, lay bare

develop—expand, build up, enlarge, extend, increase, widen, grow

devote—dedicate, give over, offer, apply, assign, allocate, allot, give

display—show, exhibit, put on show, present, put on view, demonstrate, flaunt

effectively—efficiently, successfully, well, in effect, in fact, in actual fact, in point of fact

encourage—give confidence, hearten, cheer, support, egg on, persuade, push, promote

enhance—improve, augment, add to, develop, increase, boost

establish—set up, found, institute, start, create, begin, launch, ascertain

exceed—go beyond, surpass, go above, go over, beat, top

excel at—do extremely well, shine, stand out, outshine, surpass, outclass, outrival

exhibit—show, display, show signs of, reveal, demonstrate, show evidence of, put on display

expedite—speed up, accelerate, hurry up, advance, further, rush

facilitate—make easy, ease, make possible, smooth the progress of, help, aid, assist

follow—go after, go behind, pursue, chase, trail, track, tag on, tag along

foster—promote, further, advance, cultivate, forward, encourage, look after

give—provide, offer, present, furnish, bestow, grant, award, confer

handle—control, deal with, run, cope with, conduct, carry out, see to, manage, operate, supervise, process

help—assist, aid, lend a hand, help out, facilitate, rally around, be of assistance

identify—recognize, spot, make out, see, name, classify, categorize, discover

influence—manipulate, persuade, control, sway, pressure, power

inform—tell, notify, let someone know, update, report, bring up to date, put in the picture, enlighten

inspire—motivate, stir, encourage, instigate, enthuse, move, arouse, rouse

judge—estimate, guess, consider, say, assess, think, arbitrate, adjudicate, mediate, referee, umpire

keep—stay, remain, maintain, continue, go on, carry on

lead—guide, show the way, direct, escort, pilot, go in front, go ahead, front

maintain—uphold, preserve, keep, continue, keep up, sustain, retain

make—create, build, construct, formulate, compose, put together

manage—run, direct, administer, supervise, handle, deal with, control, cope

meet—get together, convene, assemble, gather, congregate, rally, meet up

monitor—check, watch, observe, keep an eye on, supervise, scrutinize, examine, screen

motivate—inspire, stimulate, prompt, encourage, egg on, induce, cause

negotiate—talk, discuss, settle, agree, parlay, bargain, consult, confer

offer—present, tender, proffer, bid, propose, suggest, recommend, put forward

outsource—subcontract, contract out, farm out

oversee—supervise, manage, run, direct, watch over, administer, keep an eye on

perform—carry out, execute, achieve, make, act on, complete, present

possess—have, own, hold, take, acquire, seize

prepare—get ready, arrange, organize, plan, set up, practice, put in order, train

present—portray, represent, impart, offer, acquaint with, put forward, expound, submit, state, communicate

prioritize—manage by priority, put in priority order, assign importance, manage by importance

produce—create, make, manufacture, construct, fabricate, bring into being, turn out, generate

project—forecast, predict, see into the future, plan ahead, envisage, foresee, foretell

promote—endorse, encourage, help, support, sponsor, uphold, prop up, advance

protect—defend, shield, shelter, guard, look after, care for, keep, save from harm

provide—give, offer, supply, make available, present, afford, grant, endow with

recognize—familiar with, know, distinguish, make out, identify, acquainted with, aware of, on familiar terms with

reduce—decrease, lessen, diminish, cut, trim down, condense, shrink, ease

represent—stand for, symbolize, correspond to, signify, be, characterize, embody, be a symbol of

respect—value, revere, think a lot of, esteem, defer to, have a high opinion of, look up to, admire, regard, appreciate, recognize, acknowledge, accept

respond—react, act in response, take action, counter, reply, answer, retort

seek—look for, search for, try to find, hunt for, seek out, ask for, inquire about, request, get, obtain

select—choose, pick, decide on, opt for, go for

set—put, place, locate, position, situate, deposit, lay down, rest

share—allocate, split, go halves, contribute, divide, carve, carve up, distribute

show—demonstrate, illustrate, explain, give an example of, prove

solve—resolve, crack, answer, get to the bottom of, unravel, decipher, work out

speak—talk, converse, tell, chat, verbalize, articulate, have a word, address

strive for—struggle, endeavor, go all-out, do your best, do your utmost, make every effort, try hard, attempt

supervise—oversee, manage, administer, control, run, direct, take charge of, organize

support—provide for, keep, sustain, take care of, look after, care for, confirm, verify, collaborate, prove, strengthen, substantiate, authenticate

take—get, obtain, receive, acquire, seize, catch, capture, win

think—sense, assume, suppose, consider, feel, reflect, imagine, believe

understand—appreciate, know, recognize, comprehend, realize, be aware of, value, identify with

use—employ, make use of, utilize, exercise, bring into play, exploit, draw on

utilize—use, make use of, exploit, make the most of, employ, operate, develop, consume

welcome—appreciate, accept, embrace, approve of, jump at

work—act, do, perform, bring about, succeed, be successful, come off, operate, control, drive, run

About the Authors

Corey Sandler is author of more than 150 books on business, travel, and technology. He has worked for more than three decades in communications as a reporter and columnist for newspapers and a wire service, as director of public information for an agency of the New York State government, and as editor-in-chief of two national business publications. For the past decade, he has been an author and editor of nonfiction books on a variety of topics including business, computers, travel, and sports through his company Word Association, Inc.

Current titles include *Performance Appraisal Phrase Book* (Adams Media), *1001 Letters for All Occasions* (Adams Media), *Fix Your Own PC* (Wiley Books), and the *Econoguide Travel Book* series (Globe Pequot Press). *Watching Baseball: Discovering the Game Within the Game*, coauthored with Boston Red Sox broadcaster and former major leaguer Jerry Remy, was a *Boston Globe* #1 bestseller.

A former Gannett Newspapers reporter and columnist, he also worked as an Associated Press correspondent covering business and political beats. He became the first executive editor of *PC Magazine* in 1982 at the start of that magazine's meteoric rise. He also was the founding editor of IDG's *Digital News*. He has degrees in psychology and journalism.

Sandler has appeared on NBC's *Today Show*, CNN, ABC, National Public Radio's *Fresh Air*, and dozens of local radio and television shows and has been the subject of many newspaper and magazine articles.

Janice Keefe is coauthor of *Performance Appraisal Phrase Book* (Adams Media) and *1001 Letters for All Occasions* (Adams Media). She is a former manager for an agency of the New York State government and is a researcher for Word Association, Inc.

You can send e-mail to the authors at *info@econoguide.com*.